CISTERCIAN STUDIES SERIES: NUMBER ONE HUNDRED FIFTY-NINE

THE SPIRITUALLY BENEFICIAL TALES OF PAUL, BISHOP OF MONEMBASIA, AND OF OTHER AUTHORS

Seal of Paul of Monembasia.
Photograph courtesy of The Corinth Excavation
used with permission.
Rendition by John Wortley.

CISTERCIAN STUDIES SERIES: NUMBER ONE HUNDRED FIFTY-NINE

THE SPIRITUALLY BENEFICIAL TALES OF PAUL, BISHOP OF MONEMBASIA

AND OF OTHER AUTHORS

Introduction, translation and commentary

by

John Wortley

Cistercian Publications
Kalamazoo, Michigan—Spencer, Massachusetts

The work of Cistercian Publications is made possible in part by support from Western Michigan University to the Institute of Cistercian Studies for Sylvia

MCMXC

TABLE OF CONTENTS

ACKNOWLEDGEMENTS

The author wishes to express his sincere gratitude for the support he has received and which has made the production of this volume possible. The University of Manitoba, the French Government and Le Centre National de la Recherche Scientifique have each made generous subventions, while the Social Sciences and Humanities Research Coucil of Canada has provided sustained support. On a personal level the author has received and continues to receive the counsel and guidance of the Director of the Section grècque at the Institut de Recherche et d'Histoire des Textes in Paris, Père Joseph Paramelle (now retired), also of his assistants, especially M. Bernard Flusin and Mme. M.-Th. Bavavéas, to mention only three members of the Institut who have so generously contributed of their time and learning to this work. To these and also to his wife for her invaluable cooperation, he expresses his most sincere thanks.

J. W.

University of Manitoba

TABLE OF ABBREVIATIONS

Anal. Boll.	*Analecta Bollandiana*
BHG	*Bibliotheca Hagiographica Graeca*, third edition, by François Halkin. 3 volumes, Brussels 1957; and *Novum Auctarium Bibliothecae Hagiographicae Graecae*, ed. François Halkin. Brussels 1984
CS	*Cistercian Studies Series*. Kalamazoo
CSCO	*Corpus Scriptorum Christianorum Orientalium*
DACL	*Dictionnaire d'Archéologie chrétienne et de Liturgie*
DOP	*Dumbarton Oaks Papers*
DS	*Dictionnaire de Spiritualité*
HE	*Historia Ecclesiastica*. See Bibliography: Evagrius
HME	*Historia Monachorum in Ægypto*, (History of the Monks in Egypt): ed. A.-J. Festugière, Brussels 1961 and 1971; translated by Norman Russell, *The Lives of the Desert Fathers*. Kalamazoo - London 1981
PG	*Patrologia Graeca*, ed. J.-P. Migne
PJ	Pelagius and John: See *Apophthegmata Patrum, Collectio systematica, SPD.*

PL	*Patrologia Latina*, ed. J.-P. Migne
PO	*Patrologia Orientalis*
SLNPNF	*A Select Library of Nicene and Post-Nicene Fathers*, ed. Henry Wace and Philip Schaff, 14 vols, 1890–1900 (also known as 'Wace and Schaff')
SPD	*Les Sentences des Pères du Désert*. See Bibliography: *Apophthegmata Patrum, Collectio systematica*
Synax. CP.	*Synaxarium Ecclesiae Constantinopolitanae*. ed. Hippolyte Delehaye. Brussels 1902.

FOREWORD

THIS BOOK IS a second step along the way to familiarising readers with a literary tradition which, until very recently, has remained virtually unknown except to a very small group of scholars, mainly byzantinists: that of the 'spiritually beneficial tale' in its later, longer form (the *récit tardif.*) The first step (upon which this one is based) appeared in 1987: a critical edition (and in many cases the first edition) of sixteen tales, some of which are the work of a known author while the rest are anonymous. The greek text was preceded by an introduction and accompanied by a translation into French; there were no notes.[1] It was a book which had only one object: to make available a complete and critical edition of all the tales which might reasonably be attributed to or (in two cases) were somehow associated with a certain Paul, bishop of Monembasia. It was not that none of those tales had ever before been edited. In fact, quite a few of them had appeared in a diversity of publications.[2]

1. John Wortley, *Les récits édifiants de Paul, évêque de Monembasie et d'autres auteurs* (Paris: C.N.R.S., 1987) in the series Sources d'histoire médiévale published by the Institut de Recherche et d'Histoire des Textes.

2. For a full listing of all the then known manuscripts and editions of the tales, see Athanasio Kominis, 'Paolo di Monembasia', *Byzantion* 29/30 (1959–1960) 231–248.

But some of them (and some of the more interesting) had never before appeared in print; and of those that had, a new edition was much to be desired for two reasons. In the first place, most of the published tales had appeared in journals and books which were exceedingly difficult to locate: so difficult that the present writer never has succeeded in finding some of them even after diligent searching in the specialised libraries of Paris. In the second place, the former editors rarely had access to more than a fraction of the manuscripts which, thanks to microfilm, are available to us today. All too often they worked either from a single manuscript, or from manuscripts which were fairly recent. This last consideration would not perhaps be so grave a matter for certain other kinds of mediaeval literature, but so far as the tales are concerned, the general rule seems to be that the later the manuscript, the more distorted and 'developed' away from its original form the text has been. In the light of these considerations, it seemed better simply to ignore the existing editions and start again from scratch. The object of the exercise was to use the best available manuscripts of the tales and, with their aid, to try to reconstruct not only the text of each tale as nearly as possible to the original, but also to try to recapture the original shape of the collection in the case of Paul's tales.

In the introduction to the french edition it was observed that, although the simple publication of the texts was a necessary first step, it was no more than a first step. The tales in question present many problems beyond that of establishing the text, some of which are quite serious. It was willingly acknowledged that questions of how Paul worked, where his material came from and what his models were would eventually have to be considered. It was also foreseen that the answers to these questions would be discovered not merely by studying the tales alone, but by studying them within the context of the entire tradition to which they belong, the tradition of the *diêgêseis psychôpheleis* ('spiritually beneficial tales', the Bollandists' *narrationes animae utiles*).

The object of the present book is therefore twofold. First, it will render both the Introduction to the former work (somewhat expanded) and the texts of the tales themselves accessible to English readers (those wishing to consult the Greek text will still need to refer to the Paris edition; the line-numbers of the Greek text have been retained to facilitate cross-reference). Also, seven tales not previously available in translation have now been added to the sixteen presented in the earlier volume. Secondly, it is the aim of this book to explain (by way of notes to the text) some of the difficulties arising in the tales, and by longer notes introducing some of the more interesting tales, to link them all (whether the work of Paul or not) to the wider tradition of tale-writing to which he belonged. The reader will quickly discover that medieval Greek literature was not quite so arid and lacking in human interest as it is sometimes portrayed.

INTRODUCTION

PAUL OF MONEMBASIA, THE MAN AND HIS WORK.

Two questions must be dealt with before purely textual problems of Paul's tales can be examined. Who was Paul of Monembasia, and just how much of his work has survived? Normally one would separate these questions from each other and deal with them one at a time, but we cannot do this, as the two questions are tightly bound up in each other. We know almost nothing of Paul apart from his work, and we only know it as his work because it bears his name. So, although we are jumping ahead a little, let us start by giving an hypothetical answer to the question of what Paul wrote. It will emerge below that in all probability there are no more than fourteen tales which might possibly be attributed to Paul; and of these, we are very much less sure about the last four than about the former ten. To facilitate reference to the tales, here is the list of the fourteen. The first arabic numbers indicate their order in the present edition. These are followed by two numbers assigned to the tales by Halkin in *Bibliotheca Hagiographica Graeca* [*BHG*], first the roman numeral identifying the tale within the collection, then what is usually referred to as the *BHG* number, identifying its position in the entire catalogue.

	BHG		
1 I	1449	The three women who were discovered in the time of the Emperor Constantine	W701[1]
2 IV	1449c	The man who was called to account three days before his death	W702
3 VII	1449f	The man who made his confession to an holy elder on Mount Olympus	W703
4 XIIa	1449m	The woman who came to confess to Abba Neophytus	W704
5 XIV	1075d	The poor man who prayed at the church of the all-holy Mother of God at Chalcoprateia	W705
6 VIII	1449g	The priest suspended by his bishop	W706
7 XVII	1449nb	The priest who fell into fornication	W707
8 III	1449b	The three monks taken prisoner in Africa	W708
9 VI	1449e	The child who had a vision at his baptism	W709
10 IX	1449h	The monk in the cave	W710
11 XIII	873n	The man who confessed to the icon of our Lord Jesus Christ	W711
12 II	1449a	The woman found on an island with her son	W712
13 XIb	1449k	The woman who died and came back to life again	W713
14 XVI	1175	Blessed Martha the abbess	W714

Where the manuscripts of these stories name an author (which is by no means always the case), they always agree in attributing them to Paul, bishop of Monembasia.[2] That there was such a person is reasonably certain; his existence is attested in the *Synodikon of Monembasia*.[3] Moreover, the context in which he is mentioned suggests that this is a person of the tenth century. At that time, Monembasia, in the south of the Peloponnese, was a place of no particular importance.[4] It was then, and, until the coming of the Franks at the time of the Crusades, remained an obscure fortress, distinguished from time to time by the exploits of pirates, but otherwise forgotten. Nor was its bishop a person of any consequence; the see of Monembasia occupied the ninety-eighth place in the list of precedence of a hundred byzantine bishoprics.[5]

Archaeology has provided further indication that there was a Bishop Paul of Monembasia. Excavations at Corinth turned up a lead seal in sufficiently good condition for its inscriptions to be read with ease: *Lord, help your servant / Paul by the mercy of God Bishop of Monembasia.* The seal is dated in the tenth century, probably the second half of that century according to Laurent.[6]

This dating fits in very well with other evidence, this time from an hagiographical source: the *Life of Saint Paul the Lesser of Latros*. This document was in all probability written about the year 969 by a monk who was younger than the saint in question, but who had known him.[7] It deserves more respect than the general run of *vitae*; Delehaye held it in high regard, whilst Krumbacher said that it gave an interesting glimpse of tenth-century monastic life.[8] It is not difficult to agree with these assessments, for the author is clearly a writer of integrity with a wealth of detail at his disposal concerning a variety of persons known and referred to elsewhere.

Among these persons is a certain Paul, bishop of Monembasia. Paul is mentioned only once, but it is a mention of considerable importance. It comes towards the end of the *vita*; the saint is on his deathbed at Latros in southwest Asia Minor. At the moment the saint died, far away in Constantinople (says the hagiographer,) a monk named Photeinos—who was living there—heard angels in the air, singing in a most unusual way. He immediately took himself off to Paul, the bishop of Monembasia, who happened to be at the capital. 'Quick' Photeinos cried to him, 'get your thurible and start offering incense.' ('Yes' the writer adds, a little scandalised; 'he spoke to the bishop like *that*!') The bishop naturally wanted to know what this was all about. 'I have just seen Paul of Latros being carried to heaven by angels' was Photeinos' reply.[9]

This is not the sort of tale which inspires much confidence at first reading. It is a fairly common *topos* in hagiographical literature[10] and in fact a very similar example follows immediately in this text. Were it not that the writer of *this* document is a person not much given to hagiographical commonplaces, it might be set aside. But he is a serious writer, not likely to have added anything for which he had no authority. So we can assume that, whatever else may be said of this story, he had some authority for it. And that, in all probability, directly or indirectly, this authority would have been the aforementioned Photeinos himself.

Moreover, on closer examination, this tale has features not normally found in a mere *topos*. More precisely, it contains two specific data which could easily be controlled. These are, first, that the name of the then bishop of Monembasia was Paul; and secondly, that this same Paul was present at the Queen of Cities on 15 December 955, the day on which Saint Paul the Lesser of Latros 'emigrated to the Lord'. This date can therefore be established as a *terminus ante quem* for the commencement of Paul's episcopate at Monembasia—which agrees well with the evidence both of the *Synodikon* and of the Corinth seal.

It also agrees well with the evidence of the writings. The first of Paul's stories (*BHG* 1449, W701) begins: 'In the reign of the Emperor Constantine [VII], son of Leo [VI] and of Zoê [Carbonopsina], son-in-law of Romanus [I, Lecapenus] the elder . . . .' It would appear that the reign of Constantine was already a thing of the past, and that his son Romanus II was ruling (or had ruled); how else would his grandfather have been referred to as 'the elder'? We might not therefore greatly err in taking 959, the year of the death of

Constantine VII, as a *terminus post quem* for the composition of Paul's tales. Given that bishops are not usually very young men and that life was short for many, the 60s and 70s of the tenth century might well have been Paul's period of literary activity.

There may, however, be more to be learned of Paul from the brief mention of him in the *vita*. That the bishop of Monembasia should have been at the capital in December 955, or at any other time of any other year, presents no difficulties. His pastoral responsibilities doubtless required that he be there at certain times, and it is possible that the diocese of Monembasia was a sufficiently easy yoke to permit him to protract his periods of residence at the capital to some considerable length, much as a Canadian might 'winter', say, in Los Angeles.[11] The stories themselves clearly indicate that their writer had greater familiarity with the city and with its prominent citizens than any casual or occasional visitor might have gained. In fact, the reader gets the impression that he might have been more at home in Byzantium than in his remote, storm-battered metropolis.[12]

Paul's presence in Constantinople is, then, easily explained; but not so Photeinos' reactions to his visionary experience. Whether he actually saw a vision, dreamt it, or made it all up is immaterial. The relevant point is that as soon as he heard the angels singing 'in an unusual way' (or 'singing an unwonted hymn'), announcing the death of Paul of Latros, he rushed off to tell it to the bishop of Monembasia. Is this not at least a little odd? Paul of Latros was clearly one of the great luminaries of contemporary monachism. Ought his passing not first to have been announced to the patriarch, or to one of the dignitaries of the Great Church, or at least to the leading monks of the city? And yet the man to whom Photeinos first relates this extraordinary piece of news is a very minor rural bishop! What is to be made of this?

Obviously monk and bishop must have been known to each other, for nobody would go announcing a death to a complete stranger. And they must have known each other fairly well, given the familiarity with which the monk spoke to the bishop. Thirdly, they must both have known, or have known very well *of*, Paul of Latros, or the monk would not have known of whom the angels were singing nor the bishop of whom the monk spoke. He is unlikely to have taken the trouble to announce to a rural bishop the death of a person with whom that bishop was unacquainted in some way or other. In other words, monk, bishop, and saint must all have been acquainted with each other to some extent. Could it be that they were linked by a bond more substantial than that of mere acquaintance?

Photeinos and the saint were, of course, both monks. So was the writer of the *vita*; like the saint, he was a monk of Latros. And he writes of Photeinos as though he, too, were a Latronite; as 'one of us'. It does not take much imagination to guess what this Photeinos was doing at the capital. Large and important monasteries have always found it prudent to maintain representatives to watch over their interests before the powers of this world. Photeinos may well have been the *antiprosôpos* of Latros to the imperial and patriarchal thrones.[13] This would not in the least diminish his membership of the Latronite community; he would merely be a member 'on detachment'. The vision he was vouchsafed was in a sense a guarantee of his membership; it brought him, ahead of all other persons outside the monastic community, the news which that community already shared, *i.e.* that their father-in-God Paul was no longer in this world. Why would he have divulged this privileged imformation to a minor Peloponnesian bishop? Might it conceivably have been because Paul was something else as well as a bishop? That he too was of that same community, a Latronite monk 'on detachment'?

That Bishop Paul was a monk is almost certain. His stories contain more monks than any other kind of people, both individuals and whole communities (of which he mentions no less than five in the first ten stories.) Two of the stories (3 and 10) are completely monastic in character whilst others (1, 7 and 8) contain important monastic elements. The opening of the second story, in fact, seems to imply that when he was living in Monembasia Paul himself led a monastic existence, for he kept the new monk Peter with him rather than send him to a monastery. The entire collection of stories breathes the spirit of the cloister, and it is very easy to believe that to the cloister Paul belonged. The question is, which cloister? Could it have been Latros? There is no conclusive evidence that it was, but then on the other hand, there is absolutely no reason why it should not have been. Monks had been known to become bishops as early as the fourth century[14] and there is at least one known case of a Latronite monk being mitred in the tenth. This was Gabriel, who had already had a distinguished monastic career to his credit before being consecrated bishop of Magnesia towards the end of the tenth century.[15] Is it possible that a monk named Paul had preceded him on the path from the cloister to the cathedral?

So far, the only reason for suspecting that Paul might have been a Latronite is his association with Photeinos. If indeed he were, then there would have been no more likely place for him to stay whilst in the capital than at the house of his community's representative there.[16] If this were the case, his association with Photeinos would be a little closer than simply that of monk with monk.

Yet if Paul were a Latronite, would it not be more than likely that there would be at least some mention of Latros in the stories he wrote? Not only is there not the slightest such mention, but there *is*, on the contrary, a very definite mention of that other great centre of anatolic monachism: Bythinian Olympus. It is named once in the title of the third story and again in the text of the seventh. But appearances can be deceiving, as a detailed examination of the seventh story reveals. It is yet another tale of 'A priest who fell into fornication', a favourite theme of Paul and his contemporaries. The priest—a Constantinopolitan in this case—continues to exercise his priesthood in spite of his sin. He goes to Olympus in search of relief through confession, but the holy elder to whom he bares his soul can offer no relief; the sin is unpardonable. The penitent is reduced to despair and begins his homeward journey with a heavy heart. 'On the way back' writes Paul, 'he encountered Abba Peter'—this is almost the only time the venerable title *abba* is used (see Tale No. 4.) But only when this remark is examined in the context of the rest of Paul's writing is the full extent of its unusual quality revealed. One of the striking features of Paul's stories is the way in which the quality, background and origin of each and every person mentioned is detailed, together with any other pertinent data the writer has to hand.[17] But of this Abba Peter the reader is told nothing more than his name, and, a little later (line 24) he is described as 'the wondrous Peter' [*ho thaumastos Petros*]. The writer seems to assume that all the world knew whom he meant; and if by 'all the world' is meant 'all those with Latronite connections', he might well have been right. For the great luminary of Latros in the generation previous to that of Paul the Lesser had indeed been a Peter, and a very significant Peter. It was he who founded the Karyes monastery at Latros of which he was father-superior for many years, 'shining there no less brightly than a star', says his hagiographer. It was he who had trained Paul the Lesser in the monastic life. The *vita* mentioned above tells how the future saint's brother handed him over while still very young to 'the great and wonder-working [*thaumastourgos*] father Peter'.[18] He might also have trained Paul of Monembasia, which would give added point to Photeinos' haste to tell Paul of the death of his brother-in-religion. There is no evidence of this, but the fact that both saint and bishop had names beginning with the letter π means that it is not impossible. Eastern monks even today maintain the ancient practice of taking at profession a name which has the same initial letter as that of the spiritual father by whom each was trained.[19] This appears to have been what Paul the Lesser had done, and on the one occasion in the stories when Paul tonsures a monk (No. 2, lines 1–4) he does indeed give him a name beginning with π: Peter, in fact. Was this the name of his own spiritual father? That is a question to which there is as yet no answer, which probably indicates that this enquiry must halt here.

Let us then sum up. Leaving aside all speculation, this is what can be said with some confidence: that there was a Paul who was already bishop at Monembasia by December 955; that there are stories written after 959 allegedly by a Paul, bishop of Monembasia; and that these stories clearly demonstrate that they are the work of a monk. More than that, they suggest that their writer may have been a man who was living in the world, but whose heart was still very much in the cloister. We might also, with justice, suspect that he was a Latronite, and that he might even have been the spiritual child of Peter of Karyes.

THE TEXTS

Until now the works of Paul have been rather loosely referred to as stories or as tales. In fact the manuscripts are much more precise: they call them 'spiritually beneficial tales' [*diêgêseis psychôpheleis*] As we have already indicated, the tales of Paul do not stand alone. They are part and parcel of a long-standing tradition of hundreds of such tales. Some of the earliest examples of christian tales—forty in all—are to be found in *Historia monachorum in Aegypto* [*HME*], already in existence by the year 400 AD. There are another forty tales in *Historia Lausiaca* written by Palladius around 419. Then among the *Apophthegmata Patrum* there are approximately one hundred twenty tales in the *collectio systematica* (beginning of the sixth century?) and another fifty in the *collectio alphabetica* which, for the most part, probably dates from the middle of the sixth century.[20] Roughly contemporary with those two collections are the fourteen Tales of Daniel of Scêtê. The collection of sayings and stories which John Moschos put together at the beginning of the seventh century under the name of *The Spiritual Meadow* (*Pratum Spirituale*) contained at least one hundred twenty-five tales, and possibly considerably more, but until a definitive edition of the work appears, we cannot say.[21] Towards the end of the seventh century, Anastasios the Sinaïte produced his series of stories, which may number over seventy in all and which, unlike the stories in the former collections, are not interspersed with sayings.[22] After Anastasios, *i.e.* from about 700 AD, a great silence seems to have descended on tale-creating, as indeed it did on most forms of literary endeavour in what has even been called those 'Byzantine dark ages'. But, in due course, in or just before the tenth century, the flame rekindled; Paul of Monembasia and his anonymous contemporaries revived the art of tale-making, albeit in a slightly different form (the *récit tardif*, see below) and this must be reckoned as yet another aspect of the so-called 'tenth-century renaissance'.

It is very difficult indeed to say how many beneficial tales there are altogether in the christian tradition, in part because no-one has yet been able to produce a satisfactory definition of the *genre* of the tale. On the one hand, it has obvious and very close ties with the *apophthegm*. Indeed, it is tempting to suspect that the earliest tales originated as stories to lead into or launch a saying, much in the same way that certain of the dominical parables 'launch' a *logion* of Jesus in the synoptic gospels. The evidence of this is the obvious cases of 'paired' tales and apophthegmata which can still be found in the older collections; and the cases of tales which seem to imply an apophthegm which is no longer attached to the written text. Yet there are also tales, just as there are episodes in the gospels, which are plainly biographical—a fact which is clearly reflected in the title of the first great collections of desert stories published in the west: the *Vitae patrum*, 'Lives of the fathers'.[23] This inevitably prompts the question: where do tales end and hagiography begin? The question is further complicated by the fact that hagiographers freely borrowed from the tales-tradition to add substance to the *vitae* of otherwise rather insubstantial heroes, while it is scarcely to be doubted that anecdotes from this and that saint's life became detached and entered the tales-tradition. But it is not easy to know which way the process went in any given case. The pseudo-Amphilochian *Vita Sancti Basilii magni*[24] provides a good illustration: is it a hotch-potch of pre-existent tales, or an original composition which subsequently disintegrated into separate tales?

The Bollandists, who first clearly distinguished a separate *genre* of the beneficial tales (*narratio animae utilis*), have also from time to time attempted to do define it. Hippolyte Delehaye said the tales were 'nouvelles destinées à mettre en lumière une doctrine religieuse' [tales designed to shed light on some religious teaching],[25] a particularly apt definition given the double meaning of the epithet *religieux* ('religious' in the English sense, but also 'monastic'). Quoting this definition, François Halkin went further:

> Sans attache nette avec aucun pays ni aucune époque déterminée [les récits] laissent dans un anonymat sans relief les personnages fictifs dont ils rapportent les exploits [without any clear connection to any precise place or time, tales leave the fictitious characters whose deeds they record floating in a featureless landscape].[26]

Elsewhere the same scholar said that the tales are

> . . . des sortes de paraboles développées dont les héros ne sont pas toujours imaginaires [a kind of developed parable whose heroes are not always imaginery]; [stories, in fact,] ' . . . qui incarnent pour ainsi dire en un exemple frappant, voire paradoxal, un enseignement théorique difficile et transcendant' [which as it were personify in a striking and even paradoxical example some theoretical teaching which is difficult and transcendant].[27]

These are definitions which describe a certain number, indeed a large number, of the known tales, but not by any means all of them. On the whole, they describe the earlier tales better than the later. Taking for instance Halkin's criterion of a tale as something with no attachment to any specific time, place or person, we would say that many of the early monastic tales *do* specify a person and/or a place (rarely a time,) but that somehow these are quite unimportant. These specifics could be changed at will and nothing of the strength of the tale would be lost. It is a characteristic of the later tales that this is not so often the case. The tales of Paul of Monembasia and of others who wrote the same kind of tales are far more wedded to precise times and places, with clearly identified personages taking part in them: though even amongst these latter-day tales there are exceptions. The story of the Proud Monk[28] is a case in point. And again, there is rarely much doubt about the object of the earlier tales; they have a 'religious' point to make and they make it very clearly, often leaving the reader something to ponder, something in which ever deeper meanings are to be discovered, very much like the dominical parables. With the later stories this is not so much the case. Generally speaking, they have a point to make (although perhaps not always; consider the Tale of the Converted Robber:[29] what is *its* point?) But it is usually a very simple one: priests ought not to fornicate; monks must not to be proud; people should confess their sins before they die, and so forth. It seems as though the later stories tend to become longer and more complex—and, to be honest, more entertaining. But they also become less subtle, less likely to be the vehicles of 'un enseignement théorique difficile et transcendant'.

It may well be that, in the last resort, the tales defy precise definition. If we take the easy way out and define them in terms of what (so far as we can discover) they are *not*—*i.e.*, neither hagiography on the one hand nor *apophthegmata* on the other—then it is clear that they have to be counted in hundreds. And it may not be far short of the mark to suggest that when all the records are in, there could be more than a thousand of them altogether[30] emanating from what might loosely be called Mediterranean and Levantine Christianity. If and when their Judaic, Oriental, and Egyptian ancestors are investigated, that number may have to be increased considerably. The known tales—so far about nine hundred of them—constitute a rich and fascinating literature which has something to offer everybody. It is a very conservative literature in some ways, always echoing its earlier stages, but one which nevertheless saw a development from the earliest, very simple tales of the late fourth century to sometimes highly complex *récits tardifs* towards the end of the tenth. Throughout that period (but not consistently) the tales-tradition flourished, and its flourishing is the more obvious for having taken place in a world, and even at a social level, in which literary activity was not particularly brilliant. The tales are the more attractive because they are so often spontaneous and sometimes naïve, even when they are shamelessly despoiling the common treasure-house of the tradition. This, in a measure, is what makes them so difficult to deal with.

Every scholar who deals with manuscripts is grateful for the fact that the scribes who wrote those manuscripts did so with the intention of making an accurate copy of the exemplar before them. Sometimes there was a discrepancy between what they sought to achieve and what they actually accomplished, but there is rarely any doubt but that the copyist's intention was to do his work accurately. Except, that is, when it comes to the beneficial tales. For when dealing with tales, the copyist—or rather many copyists—had no such intention, and this is something of an enigma. It seems to have been the case that many a scribe who set out to copy a tale felt at liberty to do almost whatever he wanted to do with the text. Names could be changed, phrases re-written, passages introduced or omitted, stories conflated—the list could go on and on. Even a scribe who is known to have produced accurate copies of other documents would then proceed to produce a version of a tale which bore scant resemblance to any other known text of it.

Why scribes allowed themselves this 'double standard' is something of a mystery. It could have been because they learned the tales by a double medium: written and oral. For consider: if the tales were used to instruct the less sophisticated members of the monastic community and its associates, then they would have been passed around by verbal transmission, with all that this entails. At any time, therefore, a scribe might have both a written form before his eyes and an oral form (or forms) in his head: proof in itself that there was no 'fixed' text. And if he considered the version in his head preferable to the one in the book, would he not be doing posterity a service in bequeathing the superior product?

The situation was further complicated by the fact that there were copyists who applied different kinds of treatment to their texts. There was, for example, the copyist who wanted to 'improve' the quality of the language. What the

Metaphrast did for hagiography, this kind of copyist did for the tales, no doubt adding his own contribution in the process. On the other hand, there was the scribe who felt that the language of his exemplar was too difficult and should be 'vulgarised'. Hence, there is variation among three styles, high, medium, and low, with several gradations along the way. Thus it comes about that there is such a wide variety of manuscripts for nearly every tale. There is an equally bewildering variety so far as the collections of tales are concerned, and for the same reason. Copyists seem to have regarded tales' collections as dossiers rather than as fixed books: dossiers which they were at liberty to augment or diminish, revise or combine as they felt fit.[31]

The tales of Paul are no exception. They are found in many manuscripts and there are almost as many discrepancies among them as there are manuscripts. By and large (but not exclusively by any means), the later the manuscript the further the devolution from the original text; more recent manuscripts tend more and more towards one of the versions of 'demotic'. Our task was to try to rescue the text in a form as like the original as possible. It is a task which was easier in the case of some stories than of others; and it was facilitated in some way by the very inconsistency of the copyists themselves.

The manuscripts of Paul's stories fall into three classes: Category I—those which are faithful *grosso modo* to the exemplar; Category II—those made by 'retouchers'; and Category III—complete re-workings of the text. In one sense it is a straightforward matter to divide the manuscripts into these three classes, but to do so is to conceal the fact that not all scribes were consistent even in their treatment of successive tales. A scribe might faithfully transcribe one tale, retouch another, and completely rework a third. He might sometimes show the same variation from section to section (or even from phrase to phrase) of a given story; see, for instance, the description of Cod. Paris. suppl. graec 28 (below). It is therefore often necessary to add a number of supplementary observations after assigning a manuscript to one or other of the three categories. This, in fact, is the procedure that was followed.

By far the greater proportion of the extant manuscripts falls into Category III.[32] These need not detain us long, for they were of little use. Many of them contain only one or two tales; most of them are very late manuscripts and all have transformed the text into something almost unrecognisable, either by vulgarisation on the one hand or by quasi-atticisation on the other. There is, however, one exceptional manuscript in this category worthy of note: the Codex Mediol. Ambros. M 83 'sup' (Graec. 529). It is a thirteenth-century manuscript, which makes it only a little younger than the oldest known Greek text (**I**). It contains the fourteen tales of Paul found in the present edition, but in the following order (the obliques signal the presence of other items:) 12 // 13 14 // 1 2 3 4 11 5 / 6 7 8 9 10. (*cf* the order of the tales in **M**, below.) Clearly the original order has been severely disrupted, but not to the extent of destroying all trace of it. The text, however, has been subjected to a thorough revision and is probably best described as a neo-metaphrastic version of the original. Had space allowed, this text would have been included in the Paris edition of the tales.[33]

The most useful manuscripts were undoubtedlty those of the first category, those that are the work of fairly accurate copyists. Of these there are four main ones:

I. Cod. Athos Iviron 408 (Lambros 4528) is a miscellany of ascetical and hagiographical writings written at the end of the twelfth or the beginning of the thirteenth century. It contains stories Nos. 1–12 (ff. 4–39) in the order 1–4, 11, 12, 5–10, but Nos. 8 and 9 have significant lacunae, due to the loss of a folio. Other tales follow No. 10, but these are in no sense attributable to Paul and are thus of no interest to this present study. The copyist of **I** did not attempt to revise the text, nor was he very careful; there are also mistakes which he would have avoided had he been alert and intelligent. The only available microfilm of this manuscript was not of the best quality. In places, especially in the titles of the stories (written in red in the original), it is illegible. Nevertheless, in spite of these deficiencies, it is good enough to be used as the base text for stories Nos. 1–12.[34]

A. Cod. Athen. B.N. 513 is a rather complex collection of ascetic and monastic texts dating from the end of the thirteenth century or the beginning of the fourteenth.[35] There are only five of Paul's tales in this codex, and they are found in a section reserved for women (ff. 195–283v) entitled: 'spiritually beneficial *logoi* concerning honourable and holy women'. Presumably our No. 5 qualifies by virtue of the leather-worker's wife. The five tales of Paul are items 23, 40, 41, 42 and 57 of this section, ff. 218v- 221v, 241–247, 264–266. They appear in the order 12 /// 13 1 4 // 5. For these five stories the copyist has used an exemplar very similar to the text of **I**, but he has either corrected or avoided the faults of the **I**-text. It should however be pointed out that while praise is in order for the fidelity of the **A**-copyist so far as the stories of Paul are concerned, the same copyist has presented a thoroughly revised version of another text, the story of Sergius, the *dêmotês* of Alexandria (No. 16 in the present edition). It may, of course, be what he found in his exemplar, or it may be a good indication of the inconsistency of copyists where tales were concerned.

M. Cod. Venet. Marcian. app. II 101 is dated to the year 1592.[36] It contains a section (XII, ff.110v *et seq.*) of twenty-five spiritually beneficial tales, twelve of which might be thought to be the work of Paul. They appear in the following order: 12 // 13 14 // 1 4 11 5 / 6 8 9 10. The name of Paul is never mentioned here, not even at the end of the fourteenth tale. Only with hesitation was this manuscript admitted to category 1, for the scribe has touched up the text here and there. But for the most part it is only a question of changing the order of words, of replacing verbs with participles, leaving out redundant expressions, inserting doxologies and so forth. And in spite of these changes, it often gives excellent readings which agree very well with those of **A**.

V. Codex Vaticanus Archivio di S. Pietro graec. C.149, dated 1611, '*collectio narrationum et apophthegmatum sat confuse congesta*' has 421 folios.[37] It contains all fourteen tales of the present edition in the following order: 1 2 3 4 11 12 5 6 7 8 9 10 /// 13 14. The reader is given the impression that all the twenty-three tales of the first section (ff. 5–98) are by Paul of Monembasia, but this is certainly not the case. For the fourteen which might possibly be attributed to Paul, one has the impression that the copyist had two exemplars before him, and that when he noticed faults such as **I** contains, he attempted to correct them. He was a conscientious worker who obviously did his best to restore the text rather than to 'improve' it; he has earned and received the gratitude of the present editor. It should be added that in so far as it has been possible to check (which means on the basis of the beginnings and endings of the tales translated by Sauget) it would appear that **V** resembles the Arabic text of the tales more closely than any other of the known Greek manuscripts.[38]

It was hoped that with the aid of **I A M** and **V** a common ancestor could be discerned. But in spite of the fact that they often agree with each other, this was not possible. It rapidly became apparent that long before these copies were made, the tradition had suffered so many distortions that any hopes of recapturing the *ipsissima verba* of the Bishop of Monembasia were doomed to be disappointed. This meant that, much as the editor wished to respect the scientific principles of his craft, in reality he was often reduced to making more or less arbitrary choices between the readings of his witnesses.

And doubtless, not everybody would have made the same choices. But if the editor's choices are unsatisfactory, readers may make their own by consulting the *apparatus criticus* of the Greek text. The fact of the matter is that the text of tales was never stable in the sense that other texts were. The scribes of former generations made their own choices; let the readers of today feel free to do likewise.

Whatever the virtues of **I A M** and **V** might be, only the last of the four contains the complete text of all fourteen tales. And only four of the fourteen are to be found in all four manuscripts: Nos. 1, 4, 5 and 12. Six of the tales are found in three of the four manuscripts: Nos. 6, 8, 9, 10, 11 and 13. Four tales are attested only by two of these four manuscripts: Nos. 2, 3 and 7 (**I** and **V** only,) No. 14 (**M** and **V** only.) For these last four tales, and especially for No.14 (which presents some problems which remain unsolved) it was obviously essential that at least a third witness be found. With the exception of No. 3 (which is very short and of no great interest) other witnesses have been found by searching through the Category II manuscripts. This could have been a lengthy and time-consuming process, for the codices which contain one or two tales of Paul in various redactions and adaptations are legion. In the end it appeared that the most useful manuscript in this respect was also one of the most bizarre:

P. Cod. Paris. suppl. graec. 28 is a fifteenth-century manuscript. Towards the end (ff.340v–345) it contains six of Paul's tales presented without interruption in the following order: Nos. 1, 2, 9, 6–7, 13. It is impossible to place this text in one of the three categories, for the copyist (or his predecessor) worked in a most irregular way. Tale No. 1 has been completely rewritten; No.2 has been lightly retouched; of No. 11, the first and last paragraphs have been transformed, but the rest of the text is in fairly good order; and Nos. 6 and 7 are presented as one tale, possibly on account of the loss of a folio at some time. The resulting narrative is a nightmare of incoherence which could scarcely have benefitted anybody's soul. Of No. 13 there remains little more than the basic idea on which a dramatic story has been constructed and which bears little or no resemblance to the text as it appears in other manuscripts.

The other manuscripts used in the preparation of the edition, each one for what it was worth, are as follows:

C Cod. Paris. Coisl. 378 (14th-15th cent) ff. 157–158 (No.4)
Q Cod. Paris. graec. 1613 (15th cent) ff. 17–19 (No.7)
D Cod. Paris. Coisl. 381 (*anno* 1609) ff. 155–156v (No.14)[39]

THE COLLECTION

Reference has been made to 'tales which might reasonably be attributed to Paul'. Which tales are these, and in what order are they to be placed? Since answers to both these questions were proposed in the first pages of this book, it is high time to see how they were arrived at. It must be said at the outset that there is not much to add to what Sauget wrote on the matter twenty-six years ago.[40] He pointed out that the oldest known manuscript of the Tales of Paul is not the Athonite Codex (hereafter **I**) which dates from *ca* 1200 AD, but that of an arabic translation, Codex Paris Arab. 276 (Arab.). There are good reasons, palaeographic and others (he wrote), for thinking that this manuscript was copied around the beginning of the eleventh century. Sauget believes that the translator was a monk named Anthony from the Monastery of Saint Symeon the Wonder-worker, in the region of Antioch, and he cites evidence that this Anthony was at work as a translator before and after the year 989–900. It will readily be perceived that this is scarcely a generation later than the time of the supposed florescence of the author of the tales himself. It is beyond the competence of the present writer to judge the value of the arabic text, but in this it is very useful: it gives a unique testimony of a very early shape of the collection—not necessarily, however, as we shall see, of its original shape.

Several manuscripts, none of them very old, attribute thirty and more tales to Paul of Monembasia. Of these, as Sauget has demonstrated, twelve at least can immediately be discounted, either because they are known to belong to collections already in existence before the tenth century (such as *Pratum Spirituale,* for instance) or because they have other known origins. Of the seventeen remaining tales, three (which are included in this book) will easily be perceived—even in the english translation—not to be the work of the same man who composed Tales Nos. 1–10. They are the tales of: *The Naked Nun* (No.15,) *Sergius the dêmotês of Alexandria* (No.16) and *The Proud Monk* (No.19.)[41]

The arabic translation in Cod. Paris. Arab. 276 offers in all fifteen tales attributed to Paul: Nos. 1–10, 13 and 14 of the present edition, two tales of which no greek text is known,[42] and the tale BHG 1319, W507: *de Theophili paenitentia.* Greek manuscripts of the last tale are known, but so far as Sauget knew (and I can discover) none of them attributes the work to Paul. It should be added that the tale itself presents a good deal of internal evidence suggesting that it was written by a hand other than Paul's.

As we have already seen, the oldest known greek manuscript of the tales is **I**. It was copied approximately two centuries after the time at which Sauget believes the arabic translation of the Tales was made and about one century later than the earliest extant manuscript of the arabic translation. Yet **I** contains only twelve pieces which might be attributed to Paul. Ten of the twelve, our Nos. 1–10, correspond exactly to the first ten pieces in the arabic collection, and they appear in the same order in **I** as in the arabic manuscript—*except* that between the fourth and fifth items of the arabic collection **I** interposes two tales of which these are the earliest known texts in any language: our Nos. 11 and 12.

There is, therefore, a remarkable consonance between Arab. and **I** so far as the order of the tales is concerned, even though the order is interrupted in **I**. Traces of the same order, further interrupted, have already been noted in some of the other greek manuscripts too. It was for these reasons that Sauget reached the conclusion that in these tales Nos. 1–10 is to be discerned 'le noyau primitif', the original kernel of the collection.

> Tout se présente donc comme si une section bien déterminée s'achevait avec le IX [everything tends to suggest that a well-defined section comes to an end with item IX,—*i.e.*, with our No. 10]. Ce fait est d'autant plus sensible dans le Paris arabe 276 où cette pièce est terminée par une doxologie beaucoup plus développée que dans les autres Histoires. On peut par conséquent se demander si IX [=10] n'était pas la dernière histoire du noyau primitif de la collection [This is even more noticeable in Cod. Paris. Arab. 276 where this item terminates with a much more developed doxology than do the other stories. One might well suspect that IX (our No. 10) was the last story of the original core of the collection].[43]

Sauget's contention is borne out by a study of the greek manuscripts; there is now very little doubt that No. 10 is indeed the first tale which terminates in a well-developed doxology. Both the first and the fourth tales end in an abbreviated doxology, but in both cases an interpolation is suspected. No. 1 has no doxology in the arabic translation, and the reading which gives a doxology at the end of No. 4 is, to say the least, somewhat doubtful. None of the other tales, until the tenth, ends with a doxology (unlike many later tales,) so it is quite possible that the doxology to No. 10 was meant to serve for all ten tales, and thus to round off the collection. Careful attention should also be paid to the concluding paragraph of the tenth tale. There is nothing like it in all that has gone before, for it is a small homily in its own right. One inevitably suspects that it was meant to be a reflexion on all that has been said before, in *all* the tales up to this point, rather than a comment merely on No. 10. In short: it does indeed look as though tales Nos. 1–10 constituted the original collection.

What then of the additional tales, Nos. 13 and 14 which are found in the arabic manuscript but not in **I**, and Nos. 11 and 12 which are inserted between Nos. 4 and 5 in **I** but are not to be found in the arabic text? Even though the original collection might have ended with No. 10, it is not impossible that the bishop himself, or for that matter his literary executor, might have added genuine Pauline stories to the collection. So the first question to be asked is: can the hand of Paul be discerned in these 'additional tales'? The question is particularly apt in the case of tales which in all probability found their way into the collection before the end of the tenth century, Nos. 13 and 14. Yet it should be noted that the fact of their absence from **I** rather suggests that their incorporation took place *after* the collection had left its author's hands and when the tradition began to branch out in different forms. So let the four additional tales be considered together, for there are certain factors common to three of them which rather lead one to think that they are *not* the work of Paul.

Leaving No. 12 aside for a while—for it is quite a different kind of tale—let us note that Tales Nos. 11, 13 and 14 deal with a number of subjects which are almost entirely ignored in Tales 1–10: relics, for example,[44] icons, sacred objects, and visions of the Mother of God. These are all commonplaces in byzantine sacred literature and predominant elements of byzantine spirituality; and yet, curiously enough, they are all notoriously absent from Nos. 1–10. Certainly, nothing is to be deduced from silence itself, but the marked disparity in this respect between 1–10 and the three tales under examination (in which these commonplaces recur in their customary profusion) is surely eloquent. And the very silence of 1–10 in matters so dear to the latter-day Romans tempts one to ask certain questions, even though there is not much hope of finding any definitive answers to them. For instance: is it possible that the spirituality and theology of the author of Nos. 1–10 might have been a little different from those of his contemporaries? Could it be that we detect here the conservative influence of Latros, still distinguished by its supposed Palestinian origins? It does indeed seem that Tales Nos 1–10 indicate a piety on the part of their author which, while it sought to approach the divinity by sacramental paths, as one would expect, these paths are significantly more direct than those which went *via* relics, icons, visions and so forth. Tales Nos.11, 13 and 14 betray a very different (and more customary) kind of piety; so much so that it becomes rather difficult to believe that they are by the same writer.

Affinities between the earlier and later stories, on closer examination, are mostly apparent rather than real. No. 13, for example, bears striking resemblance to No. 2 in some ways, both in content and in form. But there is also a very important difference which almost renders it unthinkable that they are the work of the same author. In the next world as portrayed in the second tale, the protagonists are a heavenly eunuch and some *aithiopes*, 'black-faced ones'. But the next world of No. 13 is a very different affair: only angels have to do with the heroine of that story. Now the byzantine church had no precise eschatology, to be sure. Within certain limits, individuals were free to form their own opinions about death, judgement, heavenly rewards, and infernal punishments. Not surprisingly, a great variety of beliefs sprang up concerning 'the last things', and nowhere is this variety better illustrated than in the 'spiritually beneficial tales'. Yet even though one can find radically different ideas about the after-life from one tale to the next, is it likely that these would change in a series of tales written by the same person? Is it not far more likely that, having once adopted one set of notions of what became of a person at and after death, he would remain faithful to them *grosso modo*, possibly until his life's end? Obviously we cannot be sure, but it would seem that a discrepancy (and a significant one) where these matters are concerned is a strong indication of diversity of authorship.

Of the other additional tales, it should be noted that No. 11, *'The Man who Confessed to an Icon'*, is also completely devoid of any monastic element—which would be surprising for a tale of Paul. But it is No. 14, the tale of 'The blessed Abbess Martha' which, in spite of its strongly monastic element, is probably the furthest removed from the spirit of Nos. 1–10, and is therefore the most suspect. It very likely owes its incorporation solely to the fact that it has to do with Monembasia and its citizens. There are two more tales in the arabic translation of which exactly the same is true (see note 42 above) for both describe events which took place in that city. What could be more simple or more natural than for a scribe to add to a collection of tales by a bishop of Monembasia those tales he had to hand which were located in Monembasia? (In fact, not one of Paul's tales is actually located in his see-city, though No. 2 begins in it.)

Tale No. 12, *'The Woman Discovered on an Island with her Son'*, is a different matter, as we have already indicated. It resembles in so many ways that one is loth to reject it, even though it is not found in the arabic translation. It is undoubtedly in the spirit of Paul, but more than that, it so closely resembles one of his stories (No. 1) that one wonders if it is in fact an alternative version of the same tale. The resemblances are truly astonishing: they include the use of the same quotations, almost identical phrases, and even the very structure of the tale. As we note below, both No. 1 and No. 12 draw on a common heritage in some ways. It is of course possible that No. 12 is a deliberate imitation of Paul, but somehow the imitation is too good to be an imitation. It is just possible that Paul himself made two versions of this story, one for use at the capital, the other for the provinces; and that, being the excellent story-teller he obviously was, he was not going to spoil the effect of the collected stories by including two versions of the same tale. The manuscript would have to have lain undiscovered until after the arabic translation was made, and then have entered the greek tradition. That at least is what *could* have happened; whether it *did*, we may never know.

At this point it may well be asked: why then, when there are all these reservations concerning their authenticity, have the additional tales been included in the edition and the translation? The answer is simply that the reservations are only that; they are not proofs. It is not possible to say with certainty that these are *not* Paul's work. Even the absence of Nos. 11 and 12 from the arabic translation proves no more than that the translator either did not know them or chose to ignore them. On the other hand, the fact that he *did* know and *did* translate Nos. 13 and 14 means, if Sauget has correctly identified the time when the translation was made, not only that they are tales which certainly go back almost to the time of Paul, but also that within a generation of his florescence, they were being attributed to him. Obviously the same cannot be said of Nos. 11 and 12, but the consistency of the greek manuscripts in attributing them to Paul is evidence of a tradition of respectable age which cannot be lightly set aside. So the first reason for including these four tales in a modern edition is that we cannot be sure they are *spuria*. The second reason for admitting them is probably the very reason which led to their inclusion in the original collection and the reason which accounts for the presence of so many other narratives in the present volume: they are good tales; the sort of stuff that can 'hold old men from the chimney corner and children from their play', to use Sir Philip Sidney's definition of a good story. The third reason is equally valid: whoever their author might have been, they are undoubtedly true *reliques de Byzance,* and as such, they merit our attention every bit as much as the *genuina* for what they have to say of life in the Empire in its 'golden age'—as Ostrogorsky designated the macedonian era. But for all that, these four stories must be set a little apart from the first ten, perhaps in a compartment inscribed *Pauli Monembasiae episcopi, opera dubia*. For the fact remains that their authenticity is in doubt.

THE VALUE OF THE TALES FOR THE HISTORIAN

To appreciate the full historical value of the tales, we must set them in their context as precisely as possible. Account must be taken not only of their date and place of origin, but also of the literary *genre* to which they belong. And to set them in perspective, we must compare them with other documents which are likely to be of similar service to the historian. The reasons have already been given for believing that—with the exception of Nos. 11 and 12—the tales were written in the second half of the tenth century. The chances are that 11 and 12 appeared not long after the rest. It is also no secret where Paul worked: he obviously divided his time between Constantinople and Monembasia. The greater part of his tales derive from things he had heard (or claims to have heard) at the capital, that great 'queen of cities' in which he seems to have been completely at home. So it is very likely that it was at the Capital that he did his writing, although it would be wrong to suppose that Monembasia was a town of illiterates. There is in the Vatican library a codex which was the property and (apparently) the creation of one Leo the *taboullarios* [notary] of Monembasia. He signed his name in it on Monday, 28 August 898. He expressed his relief in the colophon for coming to the end of the text, stating that for scribes the last verse is as sweet as a calm port for sailors.[45] But Paul somehow conveys the impression that the calm port he most preferred was the Golden Horn. That in all probability is where he spent most of his time and did most of his writing. A copy of the 'original kernel' could have made its way to Monembasia, more than likely taken there by the author. It would be easy to see how at Monembasia, tales No. 14 and Arab. Nos. xiii and xiv would be added to that manuscript, just as Nos. 11 and 12 might have been added to a Constantinopolitan copy—but this is speculation bordering on outrage.

It is much less easy to identify the literary context of the tales, for the simple reason that Paul seems either to have invented, or to have worked with, a newly-invented subgenre which is typical of the tenth century, the *récit tardif*. In a general way, of course, his tales belong to the genre of the 'spiritually beneficial tale'. As we have already noted, the *diêgêseis psychopheleis* have a long history reaching back into the fourth century at least, and probably (it may eventually be discovered) much further back still. Their known origins, however, are monastic and oral. Together with the *apophthegmata*, they are the lore of the deserts, primarily of the deserts of Egypt, but also of Syria-Palestine. They circulated amongst the desert fathers and their disciples to their friends, many of them originally in Coptic, Syriac, or some other language. They are known to us today because eventually somebody—in most of the known cases a person of monastic sympathies living at least partly 'in the world'—set them down in writing, usually in Greek. Thus they were passed 'into the world', and began to take on a secular character. The period of this literary activity lasted from just before 400 AD to shortly before 700 and then it came to quite an abrupt halt. It would be saying too much to describe it as a period of literary creativity, for although there is no doubt that Palladius, for instance, or John Moschus contributed something to his work, on the whole (at least so far as one can tell) collectors of monastic lore merely set down what was told to them, duly noting (as no doubt the oral version noted) by whom or of whom each story was told.

Although they made their appearance a quarter of a millenium after the close of the first phase of story-writing, the tales of Paul (including the *dubia*) are very closely related to the fifth-seventh century tales-tradition. The writer betrays familiarity with some of the known primitive tales, or if not with the tales themselves, certainly with the oft-recurring themes which are found in so many of them—and which he uses to good effect in his own tales. Paul also strives to recapture the primitive form of the tales, re-echoing their formulae. The most striking example of this is the way he will begin, just as do so many of the old tales: 'Such and such a person coming from the monastery of such and such a holy father, told me/us that abba N. once heard abba M. tell how . . . .' One should not, however, take this too seriously, for in more than one instance, having begun thus, Paul continues to write a series of things which he could just as easily have read in one of the old books called *paterika* or *gerontika*, collections of tales which are known to have been in existence centuries before Paul came along. In other words, unlike the collectors of the primitive tales and no matter what he might say, Paul—at least some of the time—is not reporting things that were told to him by holy fathers. He is a literary artist who sets about synthesising the themes of a venerable tradition into something at once both venerably old and brand new. It is true that, on occasion, he can tell a tale every bit as simple and straightforward as those found in the *Lausiac History* or *The Spiritual Meadow*. But he is equally capable of putting together a fairly complex one where very ancient elements are blended with fairly new ones. Unfortunately, it is not possible to say with certainty whether this was his own doing or that he merely wrote down what he had heard, for it is clear that he was not the only person indulging in the 'synthetic tale'.

Annexed to the tales of Paul (and, perhaps, of Pseudo-Paul) in the present volume are nine more tales—some of them published and all translated here for the first time—which are, each in its own way, further specimens of the *récit tardif*. Even at the first glance, it will be immediately apparent that, in common with some (but not all) of Paul's tales, these are far more substantial pieces of writing than the great majority of earlier tales.[46] It will then emerge that, for the most part, like Paul's, these stories have been constructed out of the 'stuff' of the old tradition, from which their writers have produced distinct creations, certain of which resemble the more adventurous creations of Paul in some ways. But the reader will go on to discover that some of the supplementary tales are considerably more advanced than Paul's, displaying a degree of craftsmanship on the part of their anonymous writers which is never discernible in his writing. *The Tale of Sergius*, the *dêmotês* of Alexandria ('the Sergius'),[47] is undoubtedly the outstanding example (see the introductory note to Tale No. 16 below,) but *The Converted Robber* (No. 18) and *The Proud Monk* (No. 19) rival it very closely. Only by a careful analysis of these tales, revealing the ways in which the old themes have been blended together, can their craftsmanship be revealed. The question inevitably arises of whether Paul was the inferior practitioner of a literary tradition which was already extant, or the pioneer of one which others took to greater lengths after his time. Unfortunately, with the exception of Paul's, all these later tales are anonymous, and none of them can be dated with any greater precision than 'prior to the earliest known manuscript', which, not surprisingly, usually indicates the tenth century.

Even if we assume that the other *récits tardifs* can be taken into consideration, it is not difficult to set Paul's tales in the context of similar contemporary work which might be of comparable service to the historian, for the simple reason that there is very little of it. By and large (especially in historiography) the tenth century was a time of intense literary activity at Constantinople. It has bequeathed a legacy of mounting sophistication—even in hagiography, that erstwhile quasi-popular Byzantine literature. This means that in the tenth century literature became increasingly the prerogative of an exclusive elite. Paul is almost the only writer known by name who was not swept up in the fashions of the tenth century, but who wrote in a simple, unpretentious style which could be understood by almost anybody. We will therefore seek in vain to discover anything of kings and palaces in Paul's tales. But of the lower ranks of Byzantine society, those who are little known to us, we may hope to learn something here, and something of unique value. For relatively unsophisticated literature is very rare indeed in this period. Apart from Paul's tales, which probably constitute the only extant collection of *récits tardifs*, there are at most only about twenty tales which might reasonably be said to be more or less contemporary products.[48] There are two or three *Lives* of saints to be added to the list,[49] and that is about all the historian has to go on in trying to gauge the customs and the mentality of the ordinary Byzantine folk in the Macedonian era.

Who were these Byzantines? For whom was Paul writing his tales? Obviously a monk himself, he seems primarily to have envisaged a monastic audience, for in fact some of his tales are wholly concerned with the affairs of the cloister and would have had little to say to men 'in the world'. But others of his tales are addressed to the clergy, possibly the clergy of Monembasia; in other words, the secular clergy. And there are a few which are apparently addressed to the laity. Possibly these are tales which he used in his sermons; perhaps he used one or other of them depending on the kind of audience he was addressing. But it is equally possible that he usually spoke to a mixed audience and that he quite indiscriminately used whichever of his stories came to hand—the way they seem to have ended up in the collection. His may have been a world in which monks, secular clergy and laity were not sharply distinguished from each other. It is well known that in the tenth century the cloister was beginning to project itself upon 'the world': this is clear from the way in which, from this time, the episcopate began to transform itself into a monastic prerogative.[50] This means that one cannot blindly accept all that Paul says as evidence of 'popular' mentality. It could just as well be interpreted as an effort to project monastic mentality onto the laity.

Fortunately, it is for once possible to check this hypothesis, something which is extremely rare in the case of tales. There has come down to us a document of the early half of the tenth century, written at Constantinople in a style equally simple as Paul's, which is both one of the most curious and one of the most fascinating *reliques de Byzance*: *The Life of Saint Andrew the Fool*.[51] It is a *pot-pourri* of fiction and of tales borrowed from the tradition of the *diêgêseis psychôpheleis*. Obviously aimed at a popular audience, it is the work of someone who calls himself Nicephorus, 'priest of the Great Church'. He seems neither to have been a monk himself nor to have been the friend of monks. On the contrary, he seems to have been hostile to monks.[52] So by comparing the Tales with the *Life* it should be possible to detect which elements in the former arise from the cloister and are not truly endemic to the populace.[53] To come to the heart of the matter, the value of the tales rests in the light they can shed on the social, intellectual and spiritual condition of the mass of the people who are so little known. They also have something to tell us in a wider sense of the world as Paul knew it.

The world he knew from personal experience probably extended only from Monembasia and the Peloponnese to the monasteries of Asia Minor. But by hearsay, he knew a much wider world, extending in three directions: across southern Italy to Muslim Africa; across Asia Minor to the Holy Places; and even as far as a distant and uncertain *Scythia* to the north where slaves came from. Paul's world, unlike the world of the early tales, is essentially the north-east Mediterranean world, dominated by the Capital. In other words, it is exactly the byzantine world of the tenth century except for eastern Anatolia: a world on the threshold of a major expansion. This is the stage on which his little dramas take place.

Onto this stage the bishop of Monembasia projects a rich variety of characters so clearly delineated that they arrest the attention of the reader and excite the historian's interest. Yet one would search in vain for a representative cross-section of byzantine society here. How could it be otherwise? The author is no simple citizen at 'grass roots level' who can view society in its entirety without respect of persons. His bishopric might have stood ninety-eighth in the order of precedence, but Paul was nevertheless a bishop and therefore a person of high rank. In a society which made little distinction between church and state, this meant a high *social* rank, but not the very highest. He probably ranked among the lesser aristocracy which did not have the direct access to the imperial presence which the grandees of their caste enjoyed. Not surprisingly, when telling his tales, Paul speaks of the kinds of people best known to him. It may be worth while seeing what kind of people they are.

In Tales Nos. 1–10 (the *genuina*) we read more of monks than of any other kind of person; many times of monks as individuals, but also of five communities of monks. This is easily explained if Paul were himself a monk. After the monks, the petty aristocrats play the principal roles: three imperial administrative officers (or even four if the heavenly eunuch of the second tale is included;) two aristocratic widows of whom one seems to be illiterate; one magnate and one muslim governor. After these distinguished personages, the slaves are mentioned most often. Whether these are all truly slaves in the fullest sense of the word or merely very dependent servants is less than clear, for the terminology was in a state of transition in the tenth century as slavery slowly faded away. Amongst this servile class we note two male youths, one of them a Slav. The impression given is that, after the persons of his own rank, slaves/servants were the people Paul knew best, they being perhaps the ones with whom he came into the most frequent contact. His references to them therefore deserve careful study. Next to them it is the priests who are most frequently mentioned. There are surprisingly few of them, considering that the author of the tales was a diocesan bishop, therefore *pastor pastorum*, shepherd of the shepherds. This may indicate that he was more often *pastor in absentia* than *pastor in parochia*. Altogether only seven priests are mentioned and of those only one (Pardos, the future monk Peter of Tale No. 2) served a parish. Two of these priests serve in private oratories[54] and one is the priest of a monastery. Three of the seven are at fault, two of them in grievous sin.

Seven women are mentioned (plus the implied *fornicatrix* in No. 7)—no less than might be expected given the general title of the work ('tales . . . concerning godly and virtuous men *and women*.') In fact, only two of the ten tales are primarily about godly women (Nos. 1 and 4). The woman in No. 2 is noted only for being cheated out of her slave, but the leather worker's wife in No. 5 is clearly associated with his godliness. This may seem rather meagre, but it is a much more generous allocation of space to women than is found in the primitive tales. There they tend only to be mentioned either as occasions for sin or as disguised as monks.

Little though the author might seem to have to say about women, what he does say reveals quite a lot about their status in life and the liberties they enjoyed. The sad tale of the woman discovered on the island with her son (No. 12), which we have reluctantly placed amongst the *dubia*, contains a particularly touching story on the plight of one woman, but this should be read with care, as it has a long string of antecedents.

After the women it only remains to mention the dying man in Tale No. 2—whose mother once possessed a slave—and the poor couple in the fifth tale—the leather-worker and his above-mentioned wife. At first glance their story looks like the one and only chance we have of catching a glimpse into the way the vast majority of Constantinopolitans lived, *i.e.*, the very poor. But in fact, it is a striking example of the snares and pitfalls which await the unwary user of these tales. Far from being typical city-dwellers of the tenth century, this couple is a recurrence of some personages who are very well known in the repertoire of the beneficial tales from several centuries earlier. One need only recall the Alexandrine leather-worker to whom Saint Anthony the Great is sent in Nau 490, W638 (*cf* Nau 67, W538) or Deusdedit *qui calciamenta solebat operari*, mentioned by Gregory the Great.[55] Their *mariage blanc* is a very familiar hagiographical *topos* of which at least eight cases are to be found in beneficial tales.[56] What Paul has done is to 'recycle' the existing stock characters and some of their story to suit his own purposes. The would-be interpreter should therefore set his gaze not so much on the characters as on the ways in which they have been transformed by Paul.

In view of what has just been said, it must be obvious that Paul does not by any means present a representative selection of the population of Byzantium or of the Empire; there are no farmers in the stories, no peasants, no workmen, no merchants, no representatives of those unfortunates who are known to have been numerous in the city: the indigent unemployed. There are no soldiers, no lesser civil servants, no members of the professional classes, and so forth. In fact, when one begins to think of the absences, Paul's selection seems to be significantly *un*-representative of the whole, and this is in itself deserving of consideration. Yet in another sense Paul's selection runs the gamut from the slaves and the poverty-stricken leather-worker and his wife to the Patriarch of Constantinople (in the sixth tale) who occupied the next place to the emperor in the byzantine lists of precedence.

But if Paul fails to provide the complete picture of byzantine society we would like to see, he does supply something else of considerable importance which is otherwise difficult to find. He (and the other writers of tales) shed considerable light on the relationships between the various kinds of people of whom they write. We learn a great deal from them, for instance, about marital relationships, class relationships, the relationships between parents and children, masters/mistresses and slaves/subordinates, clergy and laity, priests and bishops, rich and poor, monk and father-superior, monastery and the tax inspector. There is also plenty about the relationship between people and the beings they anticipated encountering in the the next world. Even more curious than all these is what the eighth tale has to say about the relationships between Muslims and Christians in the tenth century, not to mention some of the amazing attitudes expressed on both sides.

In the final analysis, the main historical value of these tales is the light they shed on the way in which certain sections of byzantine society cohered, and this perhaps is the most valuable thing there is to discover about any society. It is a great thing to isolate and analyse its constituent parts, but what has been accomplished if we do not understand what held those parts together? Byzantine society undoubtedly had many flaws, but lack of cohesion was never one of them. Indeed, the tightly-knit nature of it might well be the principle feature which distinguishes it from the disintegrating society of the end of the twentieth century, and it certainly goes a long way to accounting for the remarkable longevity of the later Roman Empire. These tales not only reveal that cohesion to have been a highly complex network of relationships; they also show something of the underlying assumptions on which those relationships were built. They make it abundantly clear that this was a people which had relationships, not only with each other, but with an invisible world which in many ways was far more important to them than the perceptible universe they inhabited. If we are to believe the tales, their relationships with each other were predicated on and largely conditioned by their relationships not only with the divinity, but with a whole company both of heaven and hell, a company which they expected one day to join and at whose mercy they would be. The relationship of humans with saints and angels, demons and 'black-faced-ones', far from being imaginary, appears to have been even more 'real' than merely human relations. Relationships which have to do with heaven and hell, God and death are the controlling ones, because on these depends each person's eternal condition.

It would be denying the obvious to pretend that these presuppositions did not lead to a fear-ridden society which, by modern standards, seemed to consist of people largely determined to torture themselves (and others) in various ways for their souls' health. Many readers will find some aspects of these stories depressing. But that is largely because today we are on the one hand very conscious of the fears and the suffering of those people Paul and the others portray, while on the other, we have largely lost any awareness of the hopes to which they aspired and the rewards they anticipated. It is only by restoring to these people the full range of their expectations that we can see them as the writers saw them (and wished us to see them,) and thereby learn all that they have to tell us about the world in which they lived and the one for which they strived.

A Note on the Translation

Throughout the following texts the greek word *anthrôpos* has consistently been rendered *man*, pl. *men*. This has been done partly to avoid ugly and inaccurate circumlocutions, but mainly because the first meaning of *man* according to the *OED* conforms exactly to the prime meaning of *anthrôpos*: 'I.1. A human being (irrespective of sex or age.)' Thus, when *man* occurs in the texts, it is to be understood to mean a man *of either sex*. This is particularly to be noted in the many phrases which speak of the *philanthrôpia* of God, which has been translated as his 'love of *men*', meanings persons of either sex or any age. Hence the oft-recurring phrase ὁ ἀγαθὸς καὶ φιλάνθρωπος Θεός, consistently rendered 'God the good, the lover-of men', to be understood as equally ambiguous. It is in fact first uttered by a woman (see Tale N°1, lines 75–76).

The *numbers* in the english text refer to the line-numbers in the Greek-French edition to which note 1 (above) the *Foreword* refers. A superscript n (^{n}) draws the reader's attention to the fact that there is a note on that word or line in *Notes on the Texts*, pages 165ff.

NOTES

1. The 'W'-numbers refer to John Wortley, *A Répertoire of Byzantine 'Beneficial Tales'*, [διηγήσεις ψυχωφελεῖς] (forthcoming.)

2. The exception to this rule is also the oldest extant Greek manuscript of the tales, *I* (see below,) which disconcertingly attributes them to a *Peter* of Monembasia. The *Synodikon* identifies a Peter as eighteenth *arch*bishop of Monembasia who was present at the Seventh Oecumenical Council (Nicaea) in 787 and who cannot therefore have been the author of the tales. Thus Haris Kalligas, *Byzantine Monemvasia*, an (as yet) unpublished Ph. D. dissertation (London: King's College, 1987) VI.ii. See the note below on the title of the first story.

3. See V. Laurent, 'La liste épiscopale du synodicon de Monembasie', *Echos d'Orient* 32 (1933) 145, and J. Gouillard, 'Le Synodicon de l'Orthodoxie', *Travaux et Mémoires* 2 (1967) 117. There is a thorough discussion of the *Synodikon* in Kalligas, *Byzantine Monemvasia* VI.i.

4. Monembasia is on the east coast of Lacedaemon, the most easterly of the three prongs of the Peloponnese. It faces out across the Aegean towards the Sporades. By the tenth century it had both a great past and a great future. It was originally founded by refugees from the nearby Epidaurus Limera, who turned the promontory of Minos into an island and fortified it. It then rapidly developed as a fortress-harbour. The Emperor Maurice (582–602) is said to have raised it to the dignity of a metropolis with its own archbishop (Phrantzes 4.16.) Under the Comnenian emperors in the twelfth century and under the Franks from the thirteenth it would become one of the principal fortresses and commercial centres of the Levant, famous for the distinctive wine of its hinterland: Malmsey. The Franks called the town Malvoisie. See Kalligas, *Byzantine Monemvasia* II, i-iii.

5. Gouillard, 'Le Synodicon', discussion on pp.144–145, and see N. Bees in *Vizantinski Vremenik* 21 (1914) 107–108. Kalligas (*Byzantine Monemvasia* VI, ii,iii) is largely convincing in her arguments that Monembasia had been an archbishopric but was demoted to the rank of a suffragan see of Corinth, probably at the beginning of the tenth century. This was probably the result of (a) the declining fortunes of the town, subject to attacks from the Cretan Arabs; and (b) an ecclesiastical re-organisation consequent upon the incorporation of the Illyrian dioceses into the patriarchate of Constantinople, believed by Kalligas to have occurred not (as was formerly thought) during the reign of Leo III, but at least a century later.

6. V. Laurent, *Le Corpus des Sceaux de l'Empire byzantin* V/1 (Paris, 1963,) *item* 528; Gladys R. Davidson. *The Minor Objects, Corinth XII* (Princeton, 1952) No. 2735 and plate 130.

7. *Vita Sancti Pauli iunioris*, ed. Hippolyte Delehaye, *Analecta Bollandiana* 11 (1892) 19–74, 136–181. In the introduction to this text Delehaye collected together a considerable amount of information concerning the monks and monasteries of Mount Latros; nobody seems to have added much to what he has to say on those subjects.

8. K. Krumbacher, *Geschichte der Byzantinischen Literatur* (Munich, 1896) 194.

9. *Vita sancti Pauli junioris, c.* 44; ed. Delehaye p.163. There is a striking similarity between this event and John Moschos' account of the death of Symeon the Stylite near Aegaeon in Cilicia: 'Abba Julian told his disciples to burn incense, not at the accustomed time. The disciples said to him; "Tell us why, father". He said to them; "Because brother Symeon of Aegaeon has been struck by lightning and is dead. Behold, his soul is departing with great gladness". They were twenty-four miles from each other.' *Pratum Sprituale* c. 57; *PG* 87:2912 AB; CS 139:45.

10. The intimation of the death of a person over a great distance at the exact moment of his death is found very early in monastic literature: for instance, when Anthony the Great saw the soul of Amoun the Nitriote

carried to heaven by a great crowd (*Vita Antonii c.*60; *PG* 26:929A) or when Pachomius saw angels taking away the soul of Silvanus (*Paralipomena de SS. Pachomio et Theodoro, cc.* 4, 13 ed François Halkin, *Le Corpus Athénien de Saint Pachôme, Cahiers d'Orientalisme* II (Geneva, 1982) 76–78. Later examples are numerous.

11. Nevertheless, his absence from his diocese at Christmas does create a slight suspicion that he might have been more often absent than present, rather like scottish bishops in the eighteenth century who 'wintered' out of their dioceses for months on end.

12. As for the mistaken belief, frequently expressed, that Paul was a native of Monembasia, see the note to the last line of Story No.14 (below).

13. In the ninth century the monks of Mount Latros (in Caria, south of Ephesus) seem to have been very poor (*Theophanes Continuatus* p.137; Cretan Arabs slaughtered them mercilessly in 841), but starting in the reign or Romanus I Lecapenus (919–944) they benefitted considerably from imperial munificence. Hence the need of an agent in the capital. 'Latros' (like Olympus and, later, Athos) connotes several monastic communities, not one only. By the middle of the tenth century it is possible to distinguish four distinct monasteries on the mountain: Karyes, the Saviour's, *tôn Kellibarôn* and the monastery of the pillar (*tou stulou,*) the lavra of Saint Paul the Lesser at the summit; thus Delehaye in the *Introduction* to the *vita* cited above.

14. Rufinus, *Historia Monachorum* c. 21, *PL* 21: 466A and note *e* ('Dioscorus . . . ad Episcopatus officium raptus est';) *Historia Lausiaca c.*38; *cf* the *narratio* Nau 132B = 'Pelagius and John' 20.12, *PL* 73:1010C -1011D. There is also Abraames the monk who was bishop of Carrhes (Theodoret, *Philotheos Historia* 17.1).

15. See Delehaye in *Analecta Bollandiana* 14 (1895) 130 - 166, especially p.132. The case of Bishop Nicephorus of nearby Miletus is deceptive, for it now appears that his episcopate *pre*ceded his profession at Latros in 987.

16. It is not impossible that Paul was Photeinos' predecessor as *antiprosôpos* at the capital; this would explain his close knowledge of the city and of its inhabitants.

17. The case of Abba Neophytus in the fourth story (title and line 7) may be an exception; but is it not implied that he, like the person relating the story, is also a monk of the monastery of Saint Arsenius the Lesser?

18. *Vita sancti Pauli junioris, c.* 6, *c.* 4.

19. See *Analecta Bollandiana* 54 (1936) 69, n.2, and 76 (1961) 35 n.1 *etc.*

20. See the Bibliography for texts and translations of these works.

21. It is not impossible that this, like some other known collections (*e.g. The New Paradise*) was such an unstable collection (*i.e.* that it was more of a dossier than a book) that no definitive dimensions can be identified. For this and other reasons it is extremely difficult accurately to assess the extent of the tales-tradition.

22. *The Stories of Anastasios the Sinaïte* are forthcoming (translation J. Wortley) from Cistercian Publication.

23. Heribert Rosweyde, *Vitae Patrum* (Antwerp, 1624; reprinted in PL 73) was in fact preceded by Aloysius Lippoman, *Historiae de vitis sanctorum* (Venice, 1558). The word *vita* [*bios*] in this context does not mean 'life' in any modern sense, but rather *an incident* in a life, or something significant done or said by such and such a father (*abba*).

24. *BHG* 247ff., ed. François Combefis, *Sanctorum patrum Amphilochii Iconiensis, Methodii Patarensis et Andreae Cretensis opera omnia quae supersunt* (Paris, 1644) 155–225. A critical edition of this collection is badly needed; there are known to be over two hundred manuscripts of all or parts of it.

25. Hippolyte Delehaye, 'Un group de récits 'utiles à l'âme'', *Mélanges Bidez* (Brussels, 1934) 257.

26. F. Halkin, 'La vision de Kaioumos et le sort éternel de Philentolos Olympiou (*BHG* 1322w)', *Analecta Bollandiana* 63 (1945) 56.

27. *Recherches et documents d'hagiographie byzantine; Subsidia Hagiographica* 51 (Brussels, 1971) 261, 303.

28. *BHG* 1450x, Nau 620, W629; Tale No. 19 below.

29. *BHG* 1450k, ka, kb; W861; Tale No. 18 below.

30. This is not counting more than a few of those 'historical legends' which occur so frequently in the chronicles and clearly overlap with the beneficial tales.

31. Thus, for instance, the eleventh-century Paul Euergetinos (see bibliography) refers to both collections of apophthegmata indiscriminately as *Gerontika*, a collection which contained several items not to be found in the existing editions, but could have been missing much which *is* in those editions.

32. For an almost complete listing of all the known manuscripts of tales attributed to Paul, see the article of Athanasio Kominis cited above (p. 13, note 2). The information listed below brings it up to date.

33. The extent to which it varies from the original text can been seen by consulting a recent edition of *BHG* 1318w: Bernard Flusin and Joseph Paramelle, 'De syncletica in deserto Iordanis', *Analecta Bollandiana* 100 (1982) 291–317. This article also contains a partial analysis of the codex in question, pp 295–297.

34. For full description of this manuscript see S. Lambros, *Catalogue of the Greek Manuscripts on Mount Athos* (Cambridge, 1900) *item* 4528.

35. For a detailed analysis of this cod. see Flusin and Paramelle, 'De Syncletico' (note 28 above) pp. 291–294.

36. For a complete description see Elpidius Mioni, *Bibliothecae Divi Marci Venetiarum Graeci Manuscripti* I.1 (Venice, 1967) 299–306.

37. See Paul Canart, *Catalogue des manuscrits grecs de l'Archivio di san Pietro, Studi e Testi* 246 (1966) 35–39.

38. Cod. Lugdun. Batav. 73B (*anno* 1613) containing tales Nos. 1, 2, 3,

12, 6, 9 and 10, resembles **V** so closely that it was considered pointless to include it in the edition.

39. It may be helpful to list and interpret here the main manuscripts mentioned in this book.

Cod. Ann Arbor 41
Cod. Athen. B.N. 513 *ca* 1300 *AD*, our **A**
Cod. Athos Iviron 408 (Lambros 4528), our **I**
Cod. Lesbos Monê Leimônos 148
Cod. Londin. addit. 28270
Cod. Mediol. Ambros. M 83 'sup' (Graec. 529)
Cod. Oxon. Holkham 43
Cod. Paris. Arab. 276
Cod. Paris. graec. 1596
Cod. Paris. suppl. graec. 28, 15th cent., our **P**
Cod. Paris. Coislin 126
Cod. Paris. graec. 1613, 15th cent., our **Q**
Cod. Paris. Coisl. 381, *AD* 1609, our **D**
Cod. Paris. Coisl. 378, 14th-15th cent., our **C**
Cod. Vatic. Archivio di S. Pietro graec. C.149, dated 1611 our **V**
Cod. Venet. Marciano II.101
Cod. Venet. Marcian. app. II 101, *AD* 1592, our **M**

The following remarks are intended for those who find the above listings rather puzzling.

Cod. is an abbreviation of *codex* (plural: *codices*) the latin name for a book as we know it, *i.e.* a set of pages which turn (as opposed to a scroll which has to be unrolled), often of parchment, but increasingly of paper in the later middle ages. Many *codices* are collections of works rather than books, in the sense that they contain many different works by a variety of authors.

When describing a codex, scholars customarily first to mention its location, sometimes simply in English, but more often by using an abbreviated form of the adjectival form of the latin name of the town. Athen. = Atheniensis = Athens; Mediol. = Mediolanus = Milan; Oxon. = Oxoniensis = Oxford—and so forth. This is sometimes (when there is any doubt) followed by the language of the codex; graec[us] = Greek, for instance. As there are cities which have more than one library in which ancient manuscripts are preserved, it is often necessary then to identify in which library a codex is located. B.N. = *bibliotheca nationalis*, the national library (this is 'default': if it is not stated, it is assumed.) The Vatican especially has several major collections within its walls, *e.g.* Archivio de Santo Pietro ('Saint Peter's Archive'). At Paris there are several discrete collections (*fonds*) of greek manuscripts even within the Bibliothèque Nationale, namely Coislin, Grecque and Grecque supplémentaire.

When all this information has been coded, then the *number* of the codex within its collection must be stated. With all that information, the manuscript can be retrieved. Even then, because libraries have sometimes been reorganised over the last centuries, it is sometimes desirable to add what the number of a volume used to be (*olim* G 29= formerly G 29, for instance). And to be absolutely sure, for instance when ordering a photographic reproduction of a portion of a codex, it is not uncommon to add its reference number in a well-known catalogue of the collection, *e.g.* in Lambros' great 2-volume catalogue of the manuscripts of the monasteries on Mount Athos. All that still remains to be stated is the number of the folios which one wishes to consult. Most codices are numbered by sheet (folio), not by page, and it is necessary to state *recto* or *verso* (front or back) to be specific. These are abbreviated thus: ff. 10^v–14^r. Translation: sheets numbered 10 (backside) to 14 (front side.) Default is *recto*.

Descriptive catalogues in a variety of languages now exist for all the major collections of greek codices but they are by no means of equal value. In many cases the only way to find out what is really in a codex is to examine it yourself, either directly or by use of photographic reproductions. Because manuscripts are *written by hand* (which is exactly what the word means,) they can be difficult to read and may contain many mistakes. The task of the scholar wishing to 'edit' a text which still only exists in manuscript is to discover, insofar as it is possible to do so from the extant copies, what the author actually wrote. It is not always an easy task.

40. J. M. Sauget, 'Le *Paterikon* du MS Arabe 276 de la Bibliothèque Nationale de Paris', *Le Muséon* 82 (1969) 363–403, and its appendix: 'Les *Histoires utiles à l'âme* de Paul de Monembasie', *ibid.*, pp. 395–404.

41. In the notes to these tales the reader will find further reasons for rejecting the possibility of their being Paul's work.

42. Arab xiii, 'Histoire de l'invention des corps des saints Valère l'évêque, Vincent le diacre et Eulalie (ou Anastasie) la vierge dans le Péloponnèse', ed. P. Peeters, *Analecta Bollandiana* 30 (1911). 301–304; Arab xiv, 'Narratio miraculi quod contingit in imagine sancti Cyri thaumaturgi [at Monembasia]' ed. P. Peeters, *Analecta Bollandiana* 25 (1906) 236–240.

43. See above, note 40.

44. Paul notes that miracles were a daily occurrence at the tomb of Peter-Pardos in 2/IV but that is the *only* reference to relics in 1–10.

45. Kalligas, *Byzantine Monemvasia*, II.iii.

46. It should however be noted that the sixth-century Tales of Daniel of Scêtê are also much longer than most early tales and so are some of those attributed (probably falsely) to the seventh-century Anastasios the Sinaïte.

47. *BHG* 1449i, W716.

48. In addition to the nine tales printed at the end of the present volume, we could probably count most of the tales found in the *M*-manuscripts of *Synaxarium Ecclesiae Constantinopolitanae* (*e.g. Cosmae vision*, *BHG* 2086

and the various tales of Nicetas Chartoularios, *BHG* 1322e, d *etc.*,) also *Theodotae filia BHG* 1317y.

49. *Vita sancti Andreae sali, PG* 111:625–888, for example, and *Vita sancti Basilii junioris, BHG* 264.

50. Occasional monk-bishops were of course known from very early times. See Rufinus, PL 21:456, *Historia Lausiaca* c. 38, and the Tale Nau 132B = 'Pelagius and John' 20.12, PL 73:1010C.

51. Until recently (see note 49), more or less everyone who had studied this *Life* was agreed that it was a fiction which appeared in the tenth century: thus (most recently) Lennart Rydén, 'The Date of the Life of Andreas Salos', *Dumbarton Oaks Papers* 32 (1978), 129–155. But then an article appeared pointing out certain indications that it might have appeared at the end of the seventh century. See Cyril Mango, 'The Life of Saint Andrew the Fool reconsidered', *Rivista di studi byzantini e slavi* 2 (1982) 297–313. Not everybody will find Professor Mango's evidence convincing, but for the time being we can no longer confidently attribute the *Life* to the tenth century.

52. The *Life* rarely mentions monks, and when it does, it is to discredit them: see especially cc. 106–113. But Epiphanios is described as 'philomonarchos' with approbation, c.88 and at the very end of the *Life*.

53. Unfortunately there is not yet available a reliable edition of the text of this *Life*, but it seems very likely that when there is and the comparison is made, it will almost certainly demonstrate that the tales we are discussing will shed considerable light on the social, intellectual and spiritual condition of the mass of the 'byzantine' people, who still remain one of great unknown *Untermenschen* of the middle ages.

54. Justinian legislated to inhibit private oratories (Novellae 58 and 131, c.8) but Leo VI (Novella 4) reversed this trend, not only allowing any priest to officiate in such a shrine, but also permitting persons to be baptised in one (Novella 15).

55. *Dialogues* 4.38.1. For another version of the same legend see *BHG* 1322g, W864. For the division of profit see the Story of Eucharistus and Maria, *BHG* 2125, W035 and that of Andronicus, *BHG* 121–122. W470, *etc.*

56. *e.g.* Amoun in *HME* 22.1, Magna of Ancyra in *Hist. Laus.* c.67, and for a western example, the priest of Narsia in Gregory the Great, *Dialogues* 44.12.2–3 ('presbiteram suam ut sororem diligens sed quasi hostem cavens.') One of the *Apophthegmata 'Berolinensia'*, *BHG* 1445v, makes the Emperor Theodosius II (408–450) say that for thirty two years he never slept with his wife (Athenaïs-Eudocia.)

THE SPIRITUALLY BENEFICIAL TALES OF PAUL, BISHOP OF MONEMBASIA CONCERNING VIRTUOUS AND GOD-FEARING MEN AND WOMEN[n]

1/I *BHG* 1449

THE THREE WOMEN WHO WERE DISCOVERED IN THE TIME OF THE EMPEROR CONSTANTINE[n]

1. A TAX-COLLECTOR told this story:

In the reign of the Emperor Constantine,[n] the son of Leo and of Zoê, the son-in-law of the Emperor Romanos the elder, I was sent to the Anatolic theme[n] in my capacity as tax-collector. I came to a monastery to collect what was due to the treasury.[n] It was summer-time and the higoumen came out to meet me together with his monks.[n] Having greeted each other, we sat down in the fore-court. There were different kinds of trees in that place, heavy with fruit. As we were sitting talking together, birds came and broke off branches from the trees. These they took away with the fruit still on them, making off with speedy wing. Seeing this curious sight, I asked the monks: "Why do the birds not eat the fruit, but instead carry it away on the branch?" They replied: "This is now the eleventh year that the birds have behaved like that at this season of the year." When I asked what this might mean, they replied: "We know nothing of it; we can only behold in wonder, for we are at a loss to explain it." With a flash of inspiration I said to them: "Bear in mind that birds are known to supply produce in this manner to certain monks who are in the mountains"[n]—and whilst I was still speaking, a crow came and made off with the branch of a tree bearing fruit. I told the higoumen and his monks to follow me, which they did with alacrity. The crow flew calmly on ahead of us, still carrying the branch. Then it came to a mountain where it laid down its burden, stretching its wings and scratching itself.

2. When we came up the mountain and got near to the crow, it seized its branch and went higher up. Then it went down into a ravine and, having deposited the fruit, rose up again carrying nothing; so it made off, caw-cawing. When we came to the edge of the ravine into which we had seen the crow descend, we threw some stones. Some voices cried out from below: "If you are Christians, do not kill us!" We said: "Who are you?" The voices replied: "If you wish to see us, throw us three tunics, for we are naked. Then, over there where the mountain is steepest, you will find a small track, almost impassable. It will lead you to us." At these words, three monks immediately divested themselves of their tunics, wrapped stones in them, and threw them down to those below. Following their directions we came down the mountain and found that difficult path which we were only just able to traverse. But then we looked, and behold, what did we see there but three women; they had seen us and were coming to meet us. They fell to the ground in reverence before us. We performed a similar act of reverence and offered a prayer, then we sat down. One of the women also sat down, but the other two remained standing.[n]

3. Then the higoumen said to the woman who was seated: "Where are you from, my lady mother, and how did you come to be here?" She said: "I am from Constantinople,

father. My husband, who held the rank of *protospatharios*,[n] died whilst he was still a young man. I was left a childless widow and I was young too, only twenty-two years old. As I mourned for him, lamenting my widowhood and my childlessness, it happened after a few days that a high and mighty lord heard tell of me. In thrall to the devil, the enemy of our souls, he sent his servants to carry me off by force. I politely refused their advances whilst, for their part, they went away promising to be back next day. They would then take me to their master, even against my will if necessary. Stricken with fear, I called upon our Lord Jesus Christ all night long to *give me words in opening my mouth*,[n] and that he would fend off that wicked man who wished to destroy me, body and soul. I resolved that if those men came back again, I would give them a good reason for not taking me away against my will. When they came next day to remove me forcibly, I said to them: "Ah sirs, do not I also rejoice at the prospect of coming to your illustrious lord? But I have a grievous disease. The symptoms are an intolerable stench and an ulcer, for which I am undergoing treatment.[n] You will have to be patient until I am healed; then I will come to him with all eagerness. What would be the use of my coming to your master whilst I have this stench about me? You would be disgraced and I reduced to shame. So be patient; it is my belief that in forty days from now I will be in good health." When they heard this they went away saying: "If that is the case, our master will expect you forty days from now."

4. As soon as they had left I set all my household [slaves/ servants] free, made them gifts and legacies and dismissed them. I retained none of them except for these two serving-women whom you see here. Likewise I distributed all my goods amongst widows, orphans and the poor. I summoned a Christ-loving relative of mine and bound him with the most solemn oaths to sell my estates and my house, distributing

the proceeds to those in need. Free of all concern about my property, I took these two sisters with me by night and went aboard a ship. As God was our guide, we came to this place and behold, it is now eleven years since we have seen a man except for you today. In time, our clothes fell into tatters and disintegrated."

5. When the higoumen heard this, he said to her: "But where do you get food from, my lady?" She answered: "God the good, the lover of men,[n] who fed a refugee people in the wilderness forty years, he himself sends food for us, his unworthy servants. Year by year, according to his will, birds bring us every kind of fruit, not only sufficient for but over and beyond our need. That is not all; although we are naked, he also shelters and warms us by his grace so that we feel neither the cold in winter nor the heat of summer. Here we are entertained as in a paradise of delight, glorifying with ceaseless hymns the all-holy name of the super-substantial and all-holy Trinity of the Father, Son, and Holy Ghost". When we had heard all this and were wondering in amazement at what was said, the higoumen asked her: "My lady, if you would like, I will send a brother to the monastery to fetch provisions so that we might share some refreshment with you." She replied: "If that is what you want to do, would you give instructions for the priest of the monastery to come here and to offer the unbloody sacrifice to the Lord God, so that we can partake of the spotless and life-giving mysteries of Christ our God? For since we left the city, we have never had the privilege of partaking of such sanctifying gifts.'[n]

6. Agreeing to this request, the higoumen sent a monk to the monastery to bring the priest and whatever else was needed. When the priest came, he celebrated the divine liturgy.[n] The lady and her two serving-women partook of the spotless mysteries and then shared some refreshment

with the monks. Then that blessed lady said to the higoumen: "I beseech your holiness to stay here for three days." He agreed to her request and promised to stay for three days. At dawn next morning the blessed one herself arose and prayed at great length; after which she went to meet the Lord. We prepared her for burial and laid her in a tomb with tears and psalms and prayers. Next day the second of the three went to the Lord and likewise the other on the third day. We laid these out and buried them too. Then we returned, singing hymns to Christ our God, the worker of marvelous and unusual *wonders of which there is no number*.[n] To him be glory for ever and ever, amen.[n]

2/IV *BHG* 1449c

THE MAN WHO WAS CALLED TO ACCOUNT THREE DAYS BEFORE HIS DEATH[n]

1. A PRIEST in the Peloponnese named Pardos came to see me in Monembasia[n] asking to be clothed with the holy monastic habit. Acceding to his request I catechised him, tonsured him and invested him with the clothing of the holy habit, changing his name to Peter. Whilst this blessed man was fighting the good fight he had to leave me at his father's insistence[n] and return to his native district, to a town named Eniklion.[n] There he fell seriously ill and departed to the Lord, leaving behind the fruits of his labours [. . . ?] A testimony of the freedom of his converse with God are the wonders which daily occur at his tomb.[n]

2. One day before he died I was speaking[n] with this ever-memorable one on the subject of the departing of the soul and of how it is called to account by unclean spirits.[n] In reply, he told me the following story:

A friend of mine fell ill, and when I went to visit him he said: "Unless I am mistaken, reverend father, I am very near to death. If you will allow me to do so, I will confess my deeds to your holiness." I said: "Speak unashamedly brother, for we have all sinned, goaded on by him who is the enemy of us all. But the multitude of our sins will not overcome the mercy of God, provided we come before him with genuine penitence."[n] At that he fell to pouring out his transgressions.

3. Later, after he had made his confession, some friends and relations came to see him. Whilst they and I were sitting there and the patient was talking to us, he suddenly turned to the other side of the bed and said: "God grant your excellence a long life." We were all thunderstruck with amazement and fear, thinking that he was seeing some kind of vision. Looking intently on whatever it was he was seeing, he said: "Yes indeed, your excellence, I did do that, but I admitted it to the priest." Then again he said: "Those things also I did, but I confessed them." Then again: "They are lying, your excellence; I did not do those things. They are accusing me falsely." He said a great deal more in the same vein; that some things he had done and had confessed, whilst others he had not done and was being falsely accused. Then he said: "So far as the document of which they speak is concerned, the Lord knows, your excellence, that I did not want to take it. Others as feeble-minded as I am led me astray. "Steal it from your mother" they said "and give it to the slave. He will give you a gold piece[n] and you will have your reward from God." That is the truth, your excellence.' Again he said: "They are lying your excellence; they are accusing me falsely. Make enquiries and kill me if what they are saying is true." Then he said: "You mean to go away and come again after three days, your excellence? For the love of God, if you have come to take me, take me now, for I cannot face three days' torment." And a little later: "Let your excellence then go his way. I will

expect you three days from now, and may God grant you a long life."

4. As we all listened to this we were stricken with fear and trembling, astounded at that awesome and invisible reckoning. The patient turned to us and I said to him: "What was it you were saying, brother, and to whom were you speaking?" "Are you thinking that I was besides myself and not in my right mind?" he rejoined. "Are you blind and could not see that imperial personage and the illustrious men who accompanied him? Nor the black-faced-ones[n] who were standing at the door?" I said: "What imperial personage?" He replied: "That eunuch who was speaking with me just now, whose face was brighter than the sun and whose clothing glistened like light. When he came here with his illustrious terrifying men, there came some evil-looking black-faced-ones with eyes like fire and they stood at the door. They were accusing me, saying what I had done and what I had left undone. When the imperial personage asked me whether what they were saying was true, so far as those things which I was aware of having done were concerned, I said: "Yes, your excellence, those things I did do, but I confessed them to the priest". But as for those things which I knew I had not done, I said: "They are lying; those things I did not do. They are accusing me falsely."'

5. Then I said to him: "The document you mentioned, what was that? You said nothing to me about it." He answered: "I did not think it was of any importance, so I did not confess it." "Well, what was it?" I asked. He replied: 'My mother had a slave and she made out a document granting him his freedom, but she kept it in her own possession, saying: "After my death, this is to be given to the slave and he can go wherever he will, a free man." Now this slave was an extremely cunning fellow. He got some persons who were as weak-minded as I am to coerce me into stealing

the document from my mother and giving it to him. It was agreed that in return I would receive a piece of gold. Under their malign influence, I did steal the document and give it to the slave; but I never saw the piece of gold! And once he had laid his hands on the document, he would no longer perform any service for my mother. She, having searched in vain for the document, angrily denounced the thief and, although I often heard her complaints, I did not confess to the theft. This is what the black-faced-ones were saying; but they also spoke of many things which I did *not* do. When the imperial personage asked me about these, I answered: "They are lying, your excellence; they are accusing me falsely. But make enquiries and kill me if what they are saying has any truth in it." He then chased the black-faced-ones away and said to me: "Go, prepare yourself," and replying to me a second time, he said: "Go, be tonsured and put on the holy monastic habit; in three days I will come and take you away." But I said to him: "If it please your excellence, take me now, for I cannot endure three days' torment." He said to me: "No, no; go and do as I say. In three days I will come to take you away." Then I responded: "May God grant your excellence a long life' and he and his companions immediately went their way.' On hearing this from him we were all astounded, trembling at the thought of how terrible an end awaited us. For his part, having set all his affairs in order, after putting on the holy monastic habit, three days later he went to the Lord.

3/VII *BHG* 1449f

THE MAN WHO MADE HIS CONFESSION TO A HOLY ELDER ON MOUNT OLYMPUS[n]

A DEVOUT MONK from Mount Olympus whose name was Sophronios told me a story similar to something that is written in the holy *Book of the Ladder*.[n] This is what he said:

There was a virtuous and godly elder on Mount Olympus whom several brethren visited to hear some salutary saying from him. As they were sitting [with him] and the holy elder was speaking of those things which are conducive to the salvation of the soul, a layman came up, made an act of obeisance and stood [there waiting.] The elder looked at him and asked what need had prompted his visit. He replied: "Reverend father, I have come to confess my sins to your holiness". The elder said to him: "Do you wish to tell me your sins in private or in the presence of these brothers?" He replied: "If you like, holy father, I will tell them before all these people." "Then speak out unashamedly my child," said the elder. The man then began to speak of such things as are improper either to be heard or to be set down in writing. When he had tearfully told all, he stood there downcast, with a broken and contrite heart. The elder remained engrossed in thought for some considerable time, then he said to the man: "Child, do you want to be clothed with the holy habit?" "Yes, holy father," came the reply, "and I have the necessary garments in my baggage," whereupon the elder catechised him, tonsured him, and invested him with the holy habit. He then dismissed him saying: "Go your way in peace, my child, and sin no more."[n] The man took his leave, made an act of obeisance and went away glorifying God.

The monks were amazed and said: "When he confessed such things before us all, reverend father, how could you not give him a small injunction or a penance?"[n] He replied: "My dearest children, did you not see that most awe-inspiring and exceedingly glorious man who stood there, whose face was like lightning and his raiment white as light? In his hands he was holding a document in which were written the sins of the man who was making his confession. He also had pen and ink; as the man told out his transgressions to my insignificance and before you all, this person crossed them out with the pen. If God the merciful, the lover of men, has forgiven his sins, who am I, sinner that I am, to lay injunctions and penances on the man?"[n] When the monks heard this, they were stricken with terror. They made an act of obeisance to the venerable elder, giving thanks for the goodness of our Lord Jesus Christ and for his goodness towards men. Then they went their way in great wonder and amazement at the extraordinary deeds of God the merciful.

4/XII *BHG* 1449m

THE WOMAN WHO CAME TO CONFESS TO ABBA NEOPHYTUS[n]

1. THE RENOWNED EUTHYMIUS, that virtuous monk and priest of God[n] who led a life of asceticism at the monastery of our father amongst the saints, Arsenius the younger,[n] told me of the wife of a certain illustrious personage. After the death of her husband she gathered her thoughts together and took stock of her sins. Having in mind the awful hour of death and the terrible judgement, she went to Abba Neophytus. Making an act of obeisance to him, she said: "I come to your holiness in faith, honoured father, to confess my transgressions to you." But he refused her saying: "My child, it is beyond my power to lend my ear to women's doings." She replied: "Holy father, our Lord Jesus Christ, the true God, having put on our nature, sat at table with publicans and sinners.[n] And when he was eating in the house of Simon the Pharisee, the Lord did not send away the prostitute who tearfully embraced his spotless feet whilst confessing her

sins.[n] And yet you send me away, me who wish to repent and be saved!"

2. When the monk heard this, he replied: "Since you speak like this, child, and since you have come to my unworthiness in faith, let us go into the church together. Tell your deeds there to God the merciful, the lover of men. Do it with a broken heart and a humble mind, and I, the unworthy one, will listen in." On hearing this, she went into the church of God together with the virtuous elder. But having prayed and worshipped, she simply stood there in silence, stupefied. He was surprised and said to her: "What then is this, child? First you urge my lowliness to receive your confession, and now you have nothing to say." She replied: "Honoured father, I dare not declare [my sins]; I am constrained by a variety of evil thoughts." Said the elder: "If this is the case, my child, and your thoughts constrain you to the point of not wanting to say anything, then write down [your sins], if you know how to write,[n] and I will read them out before the Lord our God who knows the secrets of our hearts[n] and pardons our transgressions according to his great mercy and boundless love of men." She said: "I cannot do that either." After thinking about this for some considerable time, the elder said: "If you are not even prepared to write [your sins] down, I will myself mention the sort of things that occur in life. Have you done this, or that, or so-and-so?"—to which she responded: "By the grace of God and through your holy prayers, honoured father, I have done none of the things you mention. Mine are other transgressions." He said: "If your transgressions are other [than these,] I am not one who can look into the heart or discern the secrets of men."[n] "Pray for me, holy father. If it pleases the Lord, he will resolve my difficulties," she cried.[n]

3. With these words, she made an act of obeisance to the elder and went her way. As she passed through a certain arcade

she saw an aged monk lying on the ground, covered with ulcers.[n] Nobody was paying him any attention whatever. She said to him: "Would you like me to take you to my house and take care of you there, so that you can intercede with God for my unworthiness?" He replied: "Indeed, lady, would that you might take pity upon my wretched and sinful self." She then went to her house where she set a small room in order and prepared a bed in it.[n] Then she sent her domestic slaves to purchase some monastic apparel and instructed them to take the monk with the ulcers to the baths and wash him.[n] After that, they were to dress him in the clothes, bring him home and put him into the bed which had been made ready for him. When all this had been accomplished, she herself waited upon him. She treated his wounds with dressings and cared for him in many ways.

4. When the great and holy Thursday of [the week of] the saving Passion came round, she said to the elder: "There is something I want to do for you, father, but you must undergo it without saying anything." "Do whatever you like, my lady" he replied. When the time came for the Divine Liturgy and the priest was celebrating it in the chapel[n] of her house, the priest began to read the holy Gospel thus: "When Jesus was in Bethany, in the house of Simon the Leper, there came unto him a woman with an alabaster box of myrrh of great price" and so forth.[n] At that point, the woman took up a flask of myrrh and coming to the monk, poured it over his feet, kissing and watering them with tears. And she wiped them with the hair of her head,[n] confessing her sins. Whilst she was doing this, there was an alarming earthquake, not throughout the entire city, but only in that house. And after the earthquake, there came a voice saying: "Your sins are forgiven you".[n] This voice having made that pronouncement, the monk arose, completely cured, with not so much as a scar on his body. He was continually glorifying and

praising our Lord Jesus Christ who works terrifying and great wonders. Having received forgiveness of her transgressions from God's inexhaustible and unspeakable love of men, that blessed woman spent the remaining time of her life in repentance. Then she went to the Lord, leaving behind her a fine example to those who wish with all their hearts (in repentance and confession) to draw near to God, the lover of men, who *wills all men to be saved and to come unto the knowledge of the truth.*[n] To him be glory, for ever and ever. Amen.

5/XIV *BHG* 1075d

THE POOR MAN WHO PRAYED AT THE CHURCH OF THE ALL-HOLY MOTHER OF GOD AT CHALCOPRATEIA[n]

1. AN IMPERIAL secretary[n] told the following:

I went into the Church of the all-holy Mother of God at Chalcoprateia to take part in the vigil of praise which was to be held there.[n] As Saturday begins to dawn,[n] while I am standing and singing there in the church, I see a poor man dressed in rags. He is praying fervently, with tears in his eyes and he kneels down over and over again. I was wondering at such fervent devotion when he left the church, about cock-crow. I also immediately went out and followed him. When he came to the doors of the Church of Saint John the Evangelist and Divine called Diïpion,[n] he knelt down three times and prayed, whereupon the closed doors of that holy temple opened of their own accord. In he went, leaving me standing outside (out of sight), astounded by the wonder which had just taken place. When he had prayed, he came out again and the doors of that holy temple closed of their own accord. The man then made his way to the lower arcade of the Great Church, with me still following him. He went into one of those miserable hovels in the arcade of which poor people have the use,[n] and shut the door. I put a mark on that door and returned home. Saturday and Sunday I was occupied with certain responsibilities and did not go in search of him.

2. On Monday I went along and found the mark I had made on his door. I saw a woman sitting there and I asked her: "Where is the man who lives here?" She replied: "You mean my husband, sir?" I said: "I mean the man who lives here; I don't know whether he is your husband or not." "Nobody lives here except me and my husband," she replied. "He is a leather-worker and he has gone to market to sell his wares. Why are you looking for him, sir?" For want of something to say, I improvised: "I want to place an order with him to make some footwear." "If you would like to wait for him until he returns, he will do whatever you wish," she said. I took out a small piece of gold[n] and gave it to her, saying: "Go and buy some provisions so that I can eat here with you." At this, she asked: "Does my lord wish to eat amid this stench and in this miserable hovel?" I said: "It doesn't matter to me; my house is a long way off and I cannot go there and come back here again." Off she went, bought what I had stipulated and brought it back.

3. When her husband came and found me there he made an act of obeisance and asked: "What can I do for you, my lord?" "I came to place an order with you to make footwear for my men," I replied. " But my lord," he said, "I am not the sort of craftsman that can produce work which will satisfy you." I responded: "I told you, it is for my men that I want you to make footwear, no matter what it is like. But first let us eat; we can come to an agreement after taking refreshment." "How can you stoop to eat in this lowly dwelling of ours, my lord?" he asked. Again I said: "It is nothing to me and

this is where I want to eat today." So I ate together with the man and his wife and when the meal was over I said to the woman: "Go somewhere else for the time being; I have something to say to your husband in private."

4. When she had left us I said to him: "When I was at the vigil on Saturday in the Church of the very-holy Mother of God at Chalcoprateia I saw you praying persistently. When you went out about cock-crow, I came out too and followed you. When you came to the doors of the venerable Church of [Saint] John the Evangelist and Divine, I saw how you bowed yourself down to the ground three times and the doors opened up to you of their own volition. In you went, and after you came out, the doors closed again of their own accord. What I saw made me realise that you are a servant of God. As you fear him, do not conceal your virtues from me, for I would study to emulate them and so gain pardon for my many transgressions." He blushed on hearing these words and after a period of reflection replied: "My Lord, I am a stranger to all virtue. But since you condemn me to speak of those things which I do by the power of God, I will not conceal them from your honour. But I adjure you by the Lord not to tell anybody about me until God releases me from earth.[n] As you can see, my lord, I practise the trade of a leather-worker. Whatever I earn, I divide into three parts: one for our own needs, one for my brethren the destitute, and the third to buy what I need for my work. We fast every day until evening, I and she your servant, eating nothing but bread and drinking only water, and we pray all night long. It is now twenty-seven years since we were married and the Lord God has preserved us in virginity." When I heard this, I glorified God; and after his death, I delighted in telling this story for the benefit of those who heard it.

6/VII *BHG* 1449g

THE PRIEST SUSPENDED BY HIS BISHOP[n]

A PRIEST WAS SUSPENDED by his bishop from performing his priestly office. Having received this censure[n] the priest chanced to go into another city to attend to his personal affairs. But while he was away, it chanced that the bishop died. Because he was still under excommunication, the priest was afflicted with anguish and distress, not knowing what to do. He went up to Constantinople and approached the archbishop, to whom he explained the matter. The archbishop said: "Tell me your fault and, if the bishop acted unreasonably in excommunicating you, I will obtain your release from excommunication." The priest told him: "My bishop sent me to perform a certain task and it was beyond my capabilities to accomplish it. He was angry with me and he suspended me from the performance of my priestly functions." The archbishop replied: "As you describe it, my child, your fault is nothing and your bishop excommunicated you unreasonably. Yet even if such be the case, I think it is not fitting that one should bind and another should loose.

But the Lord will arrange things for you according to his will."[n] Then the archbishop took the priest and went into a monastery. He said to the higoumen and to the brethren: "Such-and-such befell this man. I beg of you, holy fathers, for the Lord's sake, to labour this week long in fasting, vigils and prayer. Perhaps, on account of your holy prayers, the Lord will have mercy on the priest who has been unreasonably suspended." They replied: "For your holiness' sake, we do as you command." The archbishop remained there with the priest, fasting and praying with a contrite heart. When the week had run its course, at the early-morning worship, the bishop who had suspended the priest appeared among the holy fathers, standing there and singing. When the archbishop saw him, he said to the priest: "Do you know the man who is standing there?" The other replied: "Yes, my lord; it is my bishop." "Go then," said the archbishop, "fall down before him and receive absolution." The priest accordingly went and fell on his face, saying: "For the Lord's sake, forgive me, my lord," to which the bishop replied thrice: "May God forgive you; may God forgive you; may God forgive you," and so saying, he disappeared. Having seen the wonder that had taken place, the archbishop and the fathers glorified God who performs great and unsearchable *wonders of which there is no number*.[n]

7/XVII BHG 1449nb

THE PRIEST WHO FELL INTO FORNICATION[n]

1. BY THE MACHINATIONS of the devil, a priest of Constantinople fell foul of the sin of fornication. Some days later he perceived the enormity of his own fault. Thinking of the fearful hour of death and of the day of judgement he lamented his condition and said: "Ah, wretched creature that I am, to have defiled both my body and my soul! What am I to do to obtain pardon for what I have done?" God the good, the lover of men who *wishes no man to be destroyed*[n] put it into his heart to go to Mount Olympus and to confess his transgressions to a father. He went there and found an holy elder to whom he confessed all the faults of his life, including that of fornication. The elder asked: "Do you mean you presumed to perform the priestly functions even after falling into such a grievous sin, my child?" The other replied: "Yes, holy father, that I did, treading my own conscience under foot."[n] The elder said: "Know then, my child, that if a priest fall into sin so grave as that, there is

no other remedy. Let him abstain from the sacred liturgy and let him approach God the lover of men in complete penitence. But if he presume to perform the priestly office after falling [into such sin], in my opinion, there is no pardon for him." The other asked: "If there is no repenting of such a transgression, am I then to despair of my case?" The elder said: "Forgive me, my child, for the Lord's sake; for who am I to hear such things as these or to distinguish between them? Would indeed that I were capable of lamenting my own evils!" At these words, the priest made an act of obeisance and went his way, downcast.

2. As he was returning he met Abba Peter who, when he saw him downcast, said to him: "What is the matter with you, my child?" The priest replied: "I went to that elder, reverend father, and told him what was on my mind; and he reduced me to despair." The wondrous Peter said to him: "I think, child, there is no sin which can overcome the love of God for men. So come into my cell with me and show me plainly how things are with you. God will surely arrange things for you according to his will." So the priest went into the cell with him and immediately acknowledged the sin of fornication, to which the elder responded: "What that holy elder told you is true: this is a grave sin in a priest and it is unpardonable. Yes, that is a fact; but since this has happened, what is to be done? Never again will you perform the office of a priest. You are to be tonsured and clothed in the habit of a monk and in that way you will make a sincere repentance. We trust in the goodness of our Lord Jesus Christ that he will deal mercifully with you, as he does with all who repent." At these words the priest fell down at the elder's feet and said: "As the Lord God has delivered me into your holy hands, I will not go away from you." Seeing his tears and his broken spirit, the elder said to him: "If it please you to stay with me, I will not send you

away, my child, for the Lord said (as you well know): *he who comes to me I will in no wise cast out*"[n] So some days later he catechised and tonsured the priest, clothing him with the holy monastic habit; and he was with him in repentance and fastings and tears, propitiating God.

3. Now the elder had an underground cellar and some time later the ex-priest urged the elder to order him to live in the cellar. Acceding to his request, the elder granted him the cellar. The other went and made a chain. This he fastened around his neck and secured the end of the chain to the cellar-wall. When he had not come out to the elder three days later, the elder went down to him. When he saw the man secured with the chain he said: "What have you done, my child? How can you get out to perform the needs of the body when you are chained up like that?" The other replied: "Holy father, I have known the delightful fragrance of musk and of many perfumes and incenses. Henceforth I must perform my bodily functions here, fastened up like this, so that whereas I formerly delighted in fragrance, I may now experience the stench which comes from my own self. If God so guide your holiness, do you provide me with a little bread or water every second or third day to keep body and soul together." The elder agreed to his request and provided him with bread every second or third day. This the man moistened with his tears and ate. After he had persevered three years in this utter repentance, it was revealed by God to the elder that the man's penitence had found acceptance and that he was about to pass from this life. The elder went down and approached to release him from the chain, telling him: "You are about to die." The other begged not to be released, but rather to die as he was, but the elder said: "No, my child, it is not fitting for it to be so." So he released him and told him to offer a prayer, but while the prayer was still on his lips, the man surrendered his spirit to the Lord.

8/III *BHG* 1449b

THE THREE MONKS TAKEN PRISONER IN AFRICA[n]

1. IN THE DISTRICT of Calabria[n] there is a monastery inhabited by pious and virtuous monks, one of whom found a child for sale. He purchased the child and raised him with care. He also taught him how to read and write in the hope of tonsuring him and clothing him with the monastic habit.[n] One day three of the monks decided to go down to the sea to fish and as they went along, they took the child with them. When they came to the sea, some Saracens from Africa were there with their ship and seized them. When the higoumen and fathers of the monastery learned of this, they suffered no small grief, especially the monk who was master to the boy. After some days, the higoumen said to the monks: "Fathers, it is not right that our brothers in barbarian captivity and enslaved to impious men should be forgotten. But whoever amongst you has courage enough to do so, let him go to those who know mercy and the love of Christ and ask them for alms. If the Lord lead him in the

straight way, perhaps he will collect a little gold so that it will be possible to redeem at least one of our brethren." When the higoumen had said this, the master of the boy replied: "Father, with your holy prayers I will go and ask for alms. And if the Lord God sends anything into my hands, I will set out for Africa in search of our spiritual brethren." And so he left the monastery, making his way to those God-fearing persons who benefit their own souls by almsgiving and he collected a hundred pieces of gold.[n] With these he departed for Africa.

2. As he was walking through the market place, his child came face-to-face with him.[n] Taking and embracing him, the monk asked him with tears in his eyes: " Oh, child! What has become of you?" The child replied: "Worthy father, a man who is an enemy of God purchased me. He abuses me every day, coercing me to become a Moslem. But my trust is in God and in your holy prayers that I will not do that, even if I have to die." As he was saying this to the monk (his former master) behold, the Saracen (his present master) comes along! When he saw the boy engaged in conversation, he reviled the monk and raised his hand to strike him. But at that very moment, his hand froze in the air, paralysed and ineffective. Another Saracen came up and tried to do the same, but his hand was immobilised too.[n] When the rest of the Saracens saw the miracle which had taken place, they seized the monk and took him to their ruler, whom they call in their own language *Amir al-Muminin*, "Prince of Believers".[n] They said: "This monk is a magician, and by his magic he has paralysed the right hands of those who wanted to strike him." When this came to the ears of those elders who sat in council with the Prince of Believers (distinguished by their beards and short cloaks, men also known as "the sole witnesses")[n]—when they heard these things, they replied: "If he is a magician, he will be incapable

of curing paralysed hands. If he will now offer a prayer in our presence and restore them, we will know that this is a servant of God." Saying this, they invited the monk to offer a prayer. Kneeling down, he stretched out his hands to heaven and said: "Lord Jesus Christ, who did perform fearful and mighty wonders upon earth; who did raise up the dead, did cleanse lepers, open the eyes of the blind and cure paralysed hands; give ear to me, thy sinful and unworthy servant, and heal the paralysed hands of these persons."[n] When he had said this, he made the sign of the honourable cross over their hands and restored them to health.

3. When the barbarians saw the miracle which had taken place they were beside themselves and said: "Truly this monk is a servant of God". Then the Prince of Believers summoned him and said: "What did you come looking for in this place, good old man[n]?" He answered: "Three monks of our monastery were taken prisoner together with a youth; I came in search of them. Would you be so merciful as to surrender them to me?" The Prince of Believers replied: "And have you any money to give, with which to purchase them?" The monk said: "I brought with me one hundred gold pieces received from friends of Christ. If there is mercy in you, take the money and give me the prisoners." The Prince of Believers replied: "Since it has been made known to us that you are a servant of God, we will surrender the three monks and the youth to you free of charge. This we do so that you will remember us too in your prayers to God. Give your hundred gold pieces for the purchase of other prisoners." Having said this, the Prince of Believers sent and fetched the three monks and the youth whom he then gave to the monk. When he received them, the monk thanked the ruler, offered prayers on his behalf and went his way. He purchased prisoners too by means of the hundred gold

pieces. Then he came back to the ruler and said: "I have purchased prisoners according to your instructions, but how am I to take them away from here, since I have neither vessel nor supplies? The ruler said: "For the sake of your prayers I will do this too". Then he ordered a boat of the type they call *monerion*[n] to be made ready and stowed all the necessary supplies aboard her. He summoned the man who was in command of the ship and said to him privately: "Take charge of these monks and prisoners and conduct them to whatever place they will. But do you and the Saracens note the behaviour and comportment of the monk who worked the miracle of the paralysed hands, so that when you return you can tell us whether he is truly a servant of God." Having heard this, the Saracen left his presence. He called together the Saracens who were the officers and crew of the vessel and went on board, taking with him the monks and the prisoners.

4. They set out from Africa and, as they sailed along, the Saracens were astounded to see the monk fasting every day, praying and delivering words of salvation to the other monks. Then they came to an island totally devoid of water; and because a contrary wind was blowing, they stayed there for many days. When the water in the vessels which they had with them in the boat was exhausted, they were left burning with thirst for three or four days. When the monk saw that everyone was in real danger on account of thirst he said to them: "Fill all the jars from the sea[n] and bring them to me." When they had filled them and brought them to him, he knelt down and prayed, saying: "Lord Jesus Christ, Son and Word of God, who through thy holy prophet Elisha did sweeten bitter water and again at the time of thine holy incarnation did turn water into wine; do thou now sweeten this water so that those who are with me, faithful and infidel, may be amazed when they drink of it, magnifying thy power

and glorifying thine awful and holy name, together with thy Father who has no beginning and thine all-holy, beneficent, life-giving Spirit." After offering this prayer, he made the sign [of the cross] over the jars filled with sea-water and they were immediately sweetened. When they all drank, prisoners and Saracens, they glorified God—and they went on drinking it for some days.

5. When it was exhausted and the contrary winds continued to blow, they all came to the monk again asking him to take pity on them, endangered by thirst. Once again he ordered the jars to be filled from the sea and, when they had done as he commanded, again he prayed and made the sign [of the cross] over the jars and they were sweetened. The Saracens were amazed and they regarded this monk as an angel of God. A favourable wind now blew so they left the island and took the monks and the prisoners to their homes. When they returned to Africa they told the Prince of Believers everything that they had seen. He listened to everything they had to say in amazement and, clapping his hand to his forehead, he declared: "What have I done! God sent such a man as this into my hands and I did not hold onto him so that I could witness the extraordinary deeds he accomplished!" So he immediately wrote a letter and sent it to the monk, beseeching him to come to him and promising that he should be given as many prisoners as he wished. When the monk received the letter he said: "What I did in leaving the holy monastery I did out of necessity, in compassion for my spiritual brethren in captivity. The Lord will not permit me to leave the monastery in future, until the day of my death. If the Prince of Believers has it in mind to benefit his soul, let him do so by all means. Let him release as many prisoners as he will; but let him not hope to see me." The Saracen delegation returned empty-handed and told the Prince of Believers what the elder had said. Both he

and all [120]the Saracens were amazed at the virtuous conduct of the monk. Even though they were unable to forsake their deception and turn to the true and correct religion of the Christians (because they were ensnared by the devil in his own will), they were amazed and wondered at the elder's freedom of access to God.

9/VI *BHG* 1449e

THE CHILD WHO HAD A VISION AT HIS BAPTISM

1. IN THE DAYS of the Emperors Leo and Alexander[n] there was a governor in the Peloponnese[n] who purchased a child, a Scythian[n] by race. He handed the child over to the priest who served his domestic chapel,[n] to raise him and to teach him the sacred letters. While he was being educated, the child also provided such services as the priest required. When he was twelve years old, his master asked him whether the Scythians from whom he originated were Christians. The child replied: " No, my lord, they are not Christians; and so far as I know, I have not been baptised."[n] His master said to him: "Then how is it that you receive the communion[n] if you have not been baptised? I thought you were a Christian, and that is why I never stopped the priest from giving you the life-giving body and blood of our Lord Jesus Christ." The child answered: "It was in my ignorance, my lord, that when I saw the other children receiving communion, I also received."

2. The governor then summoned the priest and directed him to baptise the child. The priest baptised him and performed the divine initiation. When it was accomplished, the child came to the master, candle in hand. The master said to him: "Go back and invite the one who baptised you." Going back to the chapel, the child found the priest just at the point of setting the holy gifts in order.[n] He returned and said to his master: "The one who baptised me is not there, sir." The master was surprised that the priest should have left the chapel so quickly. Again he said to the child: "Invite him who baptised you, as I told you." So the child went again, saw the priest and returned saying: "He who baptised me is not there, sir."

3. The governor, very surprised by this, sent another child to invite the priest. This one found him setting the holy gifts in order and invited him. When he arrived, the governor saw him and asked the baptised child: 'Did I not tell you to invite the one who baptised you, and did you not go and come back saying "he who is baptised me is not there"? Who then is this?' The child replied: "This is not the one who baptised me, my lord.[n] He who baptised me had a face which shone like lightning; it was he who performed the divine initiation. While that light-bearing person was celebrating the service, this priest was standing outside the chapel, naked, and bound hand and neck with a chain held by two fearful and stinking black-faced-ones. When the one who shone like the sun had completed the divine initiation, I came to you, my lord, while he was still in church. When you sent me to invite him, I went but did not find him."

4. When he heard this, the boy's master was struck with wonder and fear at the child uttering such words. He took the priest by the hand and went into his chamber.[n] Then he said to him: "Oh man, what is this the child is saying?" The priest fell weeping at his master's feet. "Since the Lord God

has revealed my situation, I will not conceal it from my lord. While I was in my native country, my lord, by the machinations of the devil, the enemy of our souls, within me, I fell into sin.[n] When my bishop heard of this, he suspended me from performing the priestly duties. But I am a poor man and I could not live without exercising my priesthood; so I left those parts and came here. You, my lord, taking pity on me as an alien and having compassion on my utter destitution, received me into your holy house. And I, wretch that I am, I trampled underfoot my own conscience. Turning a blind eye to the righteous judgements of God and the dread eternal punishments, I have been exercising my priesthood until this day. Since the Lord God has revealed my situation, from this time forth I am unworthy to look upon you, my lord."

5. On hearing this, the master said to him: "Oh man, it were better for you to have endured destitution than to have trampled on your own conscience for the sake of the things of this world, than to have slain your own soul by violating the untouchable and awesome divine mysteries. If, as the divine apostle says, these are *things the angels desire to look into*,[n] how could you in your unworthiness presume to lay your hand on them? However, since ours is a God who loves men and who receives those who come to him in unfeigned repentance, get you off into a monastery and sincerely repent for the remaining time of your life. The Lord will be gracious to you even in such a sin as this; for in my opinion, there is no worse sin than when an unworthy priest presumes to administer the divine mysteries." With these words he sent him away.

10/IX *BHG* 1449h

THE MONK IN THE CAVE

1. A DEVOUT MONK whose name is Gregory[n] told me this:

There once came over me a longing to go to Jerusalem, to revere the [site of] our Lord's resurrection and all the holy places there. On my way there I came upon a place where there was a high precipice in which there was a cave, and below the precipice there was a monastery. The monks of that monastery told me this:

One of our brethren conceived a desire to live in the cave in the precipice and he asked the higoumen about it. The higoumen (who had the gift of perception) said to him: 'How can you live alone in the cave, my child, you whose reason has not yet mastered your carnal and animal passions? He who would live alone in silence must be a teacher, not one in need of teaching; how can you who have not yet reached that level ask my humility to allow you to live alone in the cave? It seems that you are unaware of the manifold machinations of the devil. It is much better for you to attend to the needs of the fathers and to nourish yourself by their prayers, joining with them in the appointed hours of worship and hymn-singing to the Master of all, rather than for you to be alone, struggling with unclean thoughts. Surely you have heard our godly father John, author of *The Ladder*,[n] saying "Woe to him that is alone, for when he falls into accidie or laziness, there is no man to raise him up. *Where two or three are gathered together in my name, I am in the midst of them*,[n] our Lord said.' " But even with these and other similar arguments the higoumen was not able to persuade him to shake off his soul-destroying notion. When he realised that the monk was not going to change his mind but instead persevered in his request to live in the cave, the higoumen permitted him to do as he wanted. With the prayers of the fathers, he entered the cave. At mealtimes a brother used to provide him with food. The monk had a little basket tied to a rope; he let it down to receive what was brought.

2. While the monk was in the cave, the devil (who is always fighting against anyone who wishes to lead a godly life) never relented from inflicting evil thoughts upon him by day and by night. After some days, he appeared to him disguised as an angel of light,[n] saying: "I would have you know that, on account of your pure conscience and your exalted, angelic way of life, the Lord has sent me to wait upon your holiness". The monk replied: "What good have I done that angels should minister to me?[n] "The devil answered: "Everything you have done is great and exalted. You forsook all the delights of the world and became a monk; you persevered in vigils, fasting, and prayer. And then again, you forsook the monastery and came to live here. How should angels not serve your worthiness?" With such words the soul-destroying dragon led him up the path of pride (to which he was naturally disposed), appearing to him every day.

3. One day a man whose house had been burgled came to the monk. When he saw him coming, the unclean demon who was appearing to the monk as an angel and leading him astray came and said to him: "The man who is coming to you has had his house rifled by burglars. The stolen items are such-and-such and they are lying in such-a-place; now tell him to go and get them." The man came and made an act of reverence below the cave. Said the monk, standing above: "Welcome brother; I know you are in trouble, but do not be distressed. Thieves entered your home and made off with such-and-such. They then hid them in such-a-place. Go there and you will find everything that was stolen, and pray for me." When the man heard this he went and found the stolen goods; he was puzzled and amazed. He then broadcast it throughout the region that the monk living in the cave was a prophet. An innumerable host of men and women flocked to him and they were awe-struck at the things he said. For, tutored by the devil, he told each person what had befallen him in the past and often what was going to happen in the future.

4. When the higoumen and the monks heard this, they were amazed that in so short a time the monk had acquired the ability to tell past and future events. On Monday of the week of the Ascension of our Lord Jesus Christ, that abominable demon appeared to the man who, for some considerable time by now, had been led astray and said to him: "I would have you know, worthy father, that because of your blameless behaviour and angelic life other angels are going to come to you with the intention of carrying you bodily up into the heavens so that, with all the angels, you might behold beauty which is invisible." Having spoken thus, the unclean demon disappeared. Now God the merciful, the lover of men, *not willing that any should perish,*[n] put it into the heart of the monk to report all this to the higoumen. When

the brother came as usual to bring the necessities of life he peered down from on high and said: "Tell the higoumen to come here, brother." When the brother told this to the higoumen, he dropped what he was doing, rose up quickly and came. He climbed up the ladder to the monk and said to him: "Why did you want me to come up here, my child?" He replied: "Holy father, what can I give you in return for all the benefits you have conferred upon my unworthiness?" The higoumen said: "What benefits have I conferred on you?" The other replied: "But yes, holy father, many benefits, both great and exalted. It was through you that I was found worthy to be clothed with this holy and angelic habit. Through you I came to dwell in this cave. Through you I am found worthy to see angels and to speak with them. Through you also I merited the gift of perception and prophecy." The higoumen, astounded at what he was hearing, replied: "You see angels, wretched one? You have merited the gift of perception? Oh, miserable, wretched man! Did I not tell you not to come up into the cave and be led astray by unclean demons?" When the higoumen had said this, the other cried: "Do not speak so, reverend father. It is through your holy prayers both that I see angels and that on the day of the Ascension I am to be lifted up bodily into the heavens by them. I want your holiness to know this: that when I come up on high, I mean to ask our Lord Jesus Christ that the angels might bring you up into the heavens too, so that you can be with me in the glory which is there."

5. When the higoumen heard this he clapped his hand to his brow saying: "You have fallen prey to demons, wretched one; you are out of your mind! Yet since I have come up here, I will not go down. I will stay here until I see what happens to you. Those filthy and impure demons whom you call angels will not be visible to me, so tell me if you see them coming."

He then looked down and told them to take the ladder away. He remained in the cave with the deceived monk in fasting and prayer, ceaselessly reciting the psalms verse by verse. When it came round to the day on which the deceived monk hoped to ascend into the heavens, he saw the demons coming and exclaimed: "Father, they are here!" Thereupon the higoumen seized him in his arms and cried out with a loud voice: "Lord Jesus Christ, Son and Word of God, help your servant who has been led astray. Let not the unclean demons have dominion over him." Even as he said this the demons were tugging at the demented one, trying to snatch him out of the hands of the elder. When he frustrated them in their efforts, they seized the pallium[n] of the deceived one and disappeared with it. He saw the pallium rising higher and higher in the air until it was lost to sight. Then, some considerable time later, it came back down again and fell to the ground. The elder said to the deceived brother: "You see what the demons did with your pallium, miserable half-wit? That is what they wanted to do to you. They wanted to bear you up into the sky like Simon Magus,[n] so they could drop you to destruction and deliver your soul into evil." The blessed elder called the monks and told them to bring the ladder. He then brought down the deceived monk and appointed him to serve in the kitchen and in the bakery and to attend to the other needs of the monks. This was to humble his spirit and and enable him to make a fitting repentance.

6. Take note, my brethren, of the cunning trickery of the unclean demons. Behold what enemies beset us, immaterial and invisible, who labour night and day to destroy us,[n] even as they tried to destroy the monk of whom we have been speaking. Let us be on the alert and take every precaution in our hearts[n] to ward off the evil thoughts with which they inflict us. Let us rather protect ourselves with other thoughts, such as the recollection of death and of

eternal punishments. And let us not pass the days of our sojourning in laziness and carelessness,[n] but in fasts and vigils, prayers and tears, and all things which are virtuous in the sight of the Lord God; so that, having lived our lives in a way which is pleasing to him, we may attain eternal benefits, together with all the saints in our Lord Jesus Christ, to whom, together with the Father and the Holy Spirit be glory, now and for ever and unto the ages of ages. Amen.

THE MAN WHO CONFESSED TO THE ICON OF OUR LORD JESUS CHRIST

THERE WAS A MAN of considerable prominence who had great faith in the holy high priest John Chrysostom.[n] Happening to fall ill, this man ordered his domestic servants to take him up and to bring bring him into the venerable temple of the Holy Apostles where the healing tomb of the divinely inspired father, Chrysostom, is located. He came into the venerable temple and prayed with tears in his eyes. Then he lay down on the bed which had been prepared for him on the ground. Lying there, racked with pain, he called upon Christ's holy apostles and our holy father Chrysostom to be merciful to him in his critical condition. Then there came to his mind the improper deeds he had done. As he thought over these sins, he lamented and said: "Woe is me, the wretched impenitent! How can I set out on that journey from which there is no return? How will I withstand the reproach of the fearful judge who is no respecter of persons? How endure those eternal and unbearable torments?" Such, and more beside, were the things he said in his wailing. About the sixth hour, when everybody else had gone out of that venerable dwelling, he was left alone. He looked intently into the dome of that holy temple and saw there the icon of our Lord Jesus Christ,[n] to which he began to address words such as: "Lord, if I quake and fear at the sight of your icon which came into existence through human hands, how will I be able to look upon you, the fearful judge—wretch that I am!—when you come to pass judgement on all creation? Oh Lord, I am a sinner. Forgive me, for I have not kept your commandments." Then he began openly to confess his sins to the icon. Yet, having said all, he then recalled another, yet more grievous, sin which he had committed. At that he began to say: "One other sin I have committed, Lord, but I dare not name it aloud. I dare not, lover of men; I dare not, oh merciful one." While he was saying this there came to him a voice out of the holy icon: "Speak!" When he had named this last sin, there came another utterance: "Your sins are forgiven". This awesome voice having resounded, the man rose up in good health. He fell on his face and offered up hymns of thanksgiving in a loud voice to the God who loves men and *desires not the death of a sinner*,[n] but who awaits his return and repentance; the God *who will have all men to be saved and come to the knowledge of his truth*.[n] He then made an act of reverence before the healing tomb of the divinely-inspired father Chrysostom, and went home. He lived the remaining time of his life in sobriety.

Brethren, we see [here] the power of repentance and confession. Let us not therefore be ashamed to confess our own sins to the all-merciful God and to spiritual men. For even though one might feel some shame when confessing in this world, [this is how] one is released from condemnation and shame before angels and men in the next.

12/II *BHG* 1449a

THE WOMAN FOUND ON AN ISLAND WITH HER SON

1. THE BLESSED and saintly monk Mark, founder of that illustrious monastery close by the [church of the] holy martyr Agathonicus[n] in this God-guarded city of Constantinople, told me that a most devout priest-monk related this story:

As I was returning to this queen of cities from the older Rome, we came to an island. As contrary winds were blowing, we remained several days at that island. One day I disembarked and went for a fairly long walk on the island, in the course of which I saw something in the distance which looked like the shadow of a naked man. I ran with all haste and came near to the apparition. Then I heard a voice saying: "Man of God, if you wish to see my insignificance and to accord my humility the benefit of your prayers, throw me one of your garments; for I am a woman and naked, as you can see. It would be quite improper for me to show myself to your priestly perfection." On hearing this, I took off one of my garments and threw it to her. She took the tunic and put it on. Then she turned to the east, knelt down and stood up again. She stretched out her hands to heaven and said with a loud voice: "Glory to you, my Lord Jesus Christ, Son and Word of God; for you have fulfilled the desire of your unworthy servant and condescended to allow me to see your priest." This said, she turned to me and made an act of reverence. I did likewise, and when we had prayed together, we sat down.

2. I then said to her: "Where are you from, my lady? How did you come here and how long have you been living on this island?" She answered: "I am of the Helladôn country[n] most worthy father, from the city of Larissa,[n] the daughter of poor parents. When they died and left me an orphan, one of the ruling class took pity on me and received me into his house. He nourished me and raised me with care as though I were his own daughter.[n] When I came of age that Christ-loving man married me to his only son as his wife, paying no attention to my poverty and lowly birth. When this was done, my husband's kinfolk and friends reviled him daily, saying: "What is this your father has done to you; a woman of your own social standing was never found for you; and he has given you this penniless and low-born wife?" The son would answer: "I am pleased with whatever my holy father has done for me. Since he raised her and knew her to be [a woman] of great value and beauty, his first considerations were not riches and noble birth, but virtue which is attractive to God; and that is what he gave me." But even though my husband answered his kinsfolk like this, they did not stop reviling him. When I saw him day after day being reproached like this by his friends and relatives, I said to him: "For the love of God, my husband, let me go into a monastery and you take a distinguished and illustrious wife of your own rank." He said: "I set no account whatever on their foolish talk. I am

pleased with what my holy father did for me." Yet for all he answered me and his taunters in these words, they still went on making their foolish and contemptuous remarks to him.

3. Seeing him being persecuted by them like this, I decided to run away, and that is what I did. Unknown to anyone, I got up during the night and fled, all alone, taking nothing with me but the clothes I stood in. I came to the shore and found a boat[n] in which I embarked. With God's guidance, I came to this island—without having realised that I was pregnant. I have strange and wonderful things to tell you, man of God: how from the time of my arrival here (suffering from fatigue and hunger) I gathered plants as food for this miserable body. In that way I just managed to stay alive and to nourish the child in my womb. But who can narrate the mighty and remarkable wonders of God?[n] When the nine months had passed by I gave birth to a male child. I cut up the clothes I was wearing to make swaddling clothes for him and I raised him, by the unspeakable mercies of God who makes and directs all things according to his will and desire. [The child] is now just thirty years old and naked, as am I. Every day, together with me, he offers hymns to God with his thoughts turned to heaven, himself a reflection of divine beauty. Every day I have implored God to have mercy on my humility and to send a priest to illuminate my son by holy baptism. And behold, the Lord has not refused my prayer, but has sent you, his servant, to fulfill my desire. I beseech your holiness, reverend father, go back to the ship and bring your priestly vestments and some bread to illuminate my son, and to celebrate the liturgy so that you can permit us to communicate of the worthy and honourable body and blood of Christ our God. I ask this also of your holiness: that you would bring a tunic for my son to put on after the holy baptism, and also that you not tell anybody

about me. I will wait here until you return so that we might go together to my son."

4. Having heard what she said, I made an act of reverence and went down to the ship. Without a word to a soul I collected my vestments and bread for the holy mystery. Going back up, I found her where I had left her. She said: "If it please you, father, let us now go to your servant, my son." As we approached [him,] when he saw his mother in the distance, clothed and with me, he hid himself in the thicket and forest. When his mother came near, she said to him: "What are you doing, my child? Did I not tell you every day to pray, beseeching our Lord Jesus Christ to send a priest to baptise you? Behold, the Lord God has heard your petition and has sent his priest to fulfill your desire. Come out, child, and reverence the one who has come to baptise you." On hearing this the son came out and made an act of reverence to me. I did the same, bowing low before him. Then his mother said to me: "If it please you, let us go to the spring so that you might illuminate him." We came to the spring with her leading the way for me and her son. I catechised him and performed the rest of the rite, baptising him in the name of the Father and of the Son and of the Holy Spirit. When I had celebrated the divine mystery, both of them partook of the spotless body and blood of Christ our God. When all was accomplished, we ate a little of the food I had brought and then that blessed lady said to me: "When you go back to the ship, for the Lord's sake, say nothing of what you have seen.[n] When (with God's help) you return to Constantinople, if you want to speak of what the Lord has revealed to you, then do so; but withhold the [name of the] island, lest by hearing the story, some persons might come and find us. For in thirty years we have seen no man except for you, today." So saying, she made an act of reverence to me and asked for a prayer. Then, together with her son, she

withdrew to the innermost part [100]of the island. With tears in my eyes I worshipped the God who works strange and remarkable things beyond number and makes provision for those who seek him with their whole heart and keep his divine precepts. Thus I returned to the ship and said nothing to a soul until I came back to this great City.

13/XIb *BHG* 1449k

THE WOMAN WHO DIED AND CAME BACK TO LIFE AGAIN

THERE WAS A WOMAN at Constantinople named Anna, the lawful wife of a man with whom she lived in devotion and sobriety. This woman fell seriously ill and broke out in abscesses and died. Whether she truly died or merely became as one possessed is something which is known only to God. Her mother and sisters began to weep for her. They sent to tell her husband to come with haste to be there for the funeral, for he was somewhere else, attending to some personal business. As he was late in arriving, they were weeping for the dead woman all the day long. Towards evening, the little finger of her right hand began to move. Then she stretched out both her hands and cried: "Glory to you, my all-holy Mother of God". As the two brothers-in-law were sitting there together with her mother and sisters, she embraced them. Everybody was awe-struck and amazed, but she had not the strength to tell them anything. Some of her relations who knew me sent asking me to see her next morning. When I came to see her I asked her what had happened to her. She replied: "I cannot tell you what I have seen." When I pressed her to tell just a little of what she had seen, she began very reluctantly to say in a scarcely audible voice: 'What am I to say to you? I had broken out in abscesses and I was fighting for my life like all dying persons. I could hear the lamentation of my mother and sisters, even though I could not utter a sound. Some time later I could hear their voices as though they were a long way off, and all at once, I saw two awesome men coming. No human tongue could describe how large, how illustrious and impressive they were. They took me and bore me up into the sky. They were aware of whatever came into my mind and I could tell what they were thinking. For my part, I was recalling that I was a sinner and that they were going to do me great evil. They were thinking of leading me off into the lower regions. When they bore me up into heaven, I saw an innumerable host of glorious angels, all of whom were worshiping and crying "Holy, holy, holy Lord of hosts; heaven and earth are full of thy glory". The angels who accompanied me instructed me to fall down and worship, and when I was doing that, I heard a voice saying: "Take her off to the lower regions", but I did not see whom we were worshiping.

2. 'It seemed as though the angels laid hold on me and led me down below the earth to a dark and fearful place where they left me, and went their way. There was an innumerable host down there, [and] much weeping and wailing and ceaseless gnashing of teeth. And I too, being imprisoned with them, wailed with them saying: "Woe is me, wretched and impenitent one that I am. Who will come to my aid, to speak up for me and to deliver me from this affliction, so that I can repent? Dives greatly implored Abraham to send Lazarus to his father's house to bear witness to his brothers so they would repent—and his request was not granted.[n] Who then will have mercy on the wretch that I am? All-holy

Mother of God, have mercy on me and deliver me from this gloomy predicament so that I might escape and repent in sincerity." Those who were with me in the same situation said to me: "You have come here too, wretched one? But you listened to what the holy Scriptures and the holy gospels say, did you not? For our part, we paid no attention to that but lived out our days heedlessly; so why are you [here]?" While they were saying those things I saw those holy angels who had taken me down approaching, and they said: "You are informed that the most spotless and all-holy Virgin, the mother of our God, has acceded to your request and has spoken on your behalf, that you might return to your body, to repent in sincerity and to make peace with your brothers. In two months' time we are to come again and take you." So saying, they took me and brought me and placed me back in my own body. I beg of you, father, that if with God's guidance my husband comes, you will speak to him about letting me go into a convent to weep for my sins, since I am to die again in two months' time.' I said to her 'What then was the evil which occurred between you and your brothers?' She replied: 'There was such hostility and malice between us that I neither wanted to see them nor they me.'

3. While she was speaking to me, her husband came in and was overjoyed to see her talking. I said to him: "Something has happened to your wife, the like of which I never saw before. She has made some terrible pronouncements and she says she is going to die two months from now. She asks you to let her go into a convent.' When he heard this he replied: 'It is improper for you to say such things, father, asking me to let my wife (who is not yet twenty-two) become a nun and leave me to my fate.' 'But' I said to him, 'according to her, she will die in two months.' The husband said: 'She will not die and there is nothing wrong with her. She was possessed and having hallucinations; she does not know what she is

saying.' That is what he said, and he did not let her go to the convent. When two months had gone by she died. After her death, her mother said: 'From the time when she [70]had that terrible vision, she fasted every day. In the evening she would crumble a few morsels in a vessel with some hot water and eat them; no other food whatsoever did she take. Every night she would make innumerable genuflexions with tears in her eyes; that is how she spent the two months.'

14/XVI *BHG* 1175

THE BLESSED MARTHA, ABBESS OF THE CHURCH OF THE MOST HOLY MOTHER OF GOD IN THE GOD-GUARDED CITY OF MONEMBASIA, BELOW THE CHURCH OF THE HODÊGÊTRIA IN THE SAME STRONGHOLD, ABOVE THE RIVER BLYCHAROS[n]

1. IN OUR FOREFATHERS' time the blessed Martha was abbess of the lower monastery of the most holy Mother of God, a woman of such virtue that her like was never again seen in the stronghold of Monembasia. She suffered from a haemorrhage, and because of this affliction she remained in the balconies of the same church. One day an elderly monk came to that monastery and asked to see the abbess. When the nuns told her that a strange monk was asking to see her, she said he was to come up into the balconies. When he came up, he asked for one of her garments to be given to him. She said to him: "Believe me, father, I possess two tunics. One of them I am wearing, as you can see, while my handmaid has just now been washing the other one. I can then put that one on and she can wash the one I am now wearing. [This is necessary] because of the disorder with which, for my sins, I am afflicted. But if you like, I will request a garment from one of the nuns and give that

to you." When the elder heard this he fell on his face and said: "I adjure you by Christ our God who was born of the holy Virgin Mary, give me one of your own garments." When that blessed woman heard him say this she told her serving-girl to give the newly-washed tunic to the monk. This he took, and even as he was going down from the balconies, the haemorrhage of that ever-memorable lady dried up. When she became aware of the miracle that had happened to her she sent some nuns running to invite the elder. They went out of the monastery and looked hither and thither, but there was nothing whatsoever to be seen of him.

2. At the same hour of that very day this elder, who looked like a monk, appeared to some men of Monembasia who were then in Thessalonica attending to their personal affairs. He said to them: "Do you know the lady abbess of the lower monastery of the most holy Mother of God in Monembasia?" They replied: "Most certainly we know her, and she is a relative of ours." He said: 'I was there just recently and she gave me this garment. When you return to Monembasia, say to her: "Many things await you.' " So saying, he left them. They ran after him, wanting to question him closely about this matter, but he became invisible to their eyes. Wondering at this occurrence, they made a careful note of the hour and day when he appeared to them. When they returned to Monembasia, they came to the blessed abbess and learned from her that it was at the same hour and on the same day that her haemorrhage had dried up. Wondering and praising God they came to the conclusion that he who appeared as an elder was John the evangelist and theologian.

3. When they were celebrating the feast of the Dormition of the most pure Mother of God, while the nuns were singing Matins, from up in the balconies the same blessed Martha saw the all-hymnable Mother of God sitting on the throne within the sanctuary of that holy church, and as

[the abbess] beheld that vision, she wept without ceasing. Towards the end of Matins, the nuns began to sing with loud voices, at which point the vision of Our Lady the Mother of God became invisible and was lost to the eyes of that ever-memorable lady. She immediately cried out saying: "Oh, what have you done?" The nuns, in their amazement, asked her (when Matins was finished) why she had cried out. She told them of that awesome vision and stipulated that in future they were to sing quietly and with a humble heart. "Those who wait upon an earthly king—a mortal man who suffers as they do—do not dare to turn this way and that. They give him their full and undivided attention, with eyes downcast, lest they offend his majesty. How much more so then should we, who wait upon the heavenly and fearful King, the immortal and eternal Demiurge of all creation, visible and invisible, —how much more should *we* attend with humble hearts, lest we give offence and become liable to eternal punishments?" She greatly benefited the souls which were entrusted to her with these and similar admonitions; and at the end, having run the ascetic race with distinction, she went to the Lord from whom she received (together with others) the eternal reward of the ascetic life and of patience.[n]

15 *BHG* 1449x

THE NAKED NUN

AN ANCHORITE told the brethren this:

One day, when I was living in the desert going down from Arnona, I became somewhat discouraged. My thoughts said to me: "Go out and walk around in the desert." I came to a dried-up streambed. It was well on in the evening and as I looked into the distance I saw, by the light of the moon, a hairy creature sitting on some rocks. As it seemed to be a lion,[n] I hesitated to make my way towards it directly. Then I thought to myself that even if it were a lion I need not fear it, but rather trust confidently in the grace of Christ.[n] So I approached the rock, in which there was a narrow opening. As soon as the creature saw me from afar off it fled inside, into the opening. When I arrived on top of the rock, I found a basket full of beans and a vessel full of water. Realising that the creature was a man, I began calling to him, saying: "Servant of God, do me the honour of coming out that I might receive your blessing". He was silent, but I stayed there and when I had repeated my request several times, he replied, saying: "Forgive me, abba, I cannot come out."[n] When I asked why this was, he said to me: "Excuse me, but I am a woman, and naked". At these words I rolled up the cloak I was wearing and thrust it into the opening in the rock crying: "Here, cover yourself and come out". This she did and out she came. When we had offered a prayer and sat down, I asked her saying: "Of your charity, amma, tell me about yourself. When did you come to this place? How did you get here, and how did you find that little cave? She began to tell me, saying: 'I used to be a nun [*kanonikê*[n]] in the service of the Holy Sepulchre. One of the monks who had his cell at the gate made my acquaintance. As we were frequently in each other's company we fell into sin. I used to go to him and he used to come to me. Well, one day I was going to his cell as usual and I heard him weeping before God and confessing. I knocked at the door and, knowing that it was I, he did not open to me; he just went on weeping and confessing to God. When I saw that I said to myself: "He repents of his sin, but not I of mine. He groans over his own faults; shall I not also lament?" I returned at once to my cell and put on some worn-out clothing. I filled this basket with beans and this vessel with water. I went into the Holy Sepulchre and prayed, saying: "Oh great and wonderful God who *came to save what was lost and to raise up the fallen*,[n] you who *delight in those who call upon you in truth*:[n] show mercy upon me, the sinner. And if my repentance and conversion are acceptable to you, bless these beans and this water; let them last me for all the time of my life. Thus my ceaseless hymn of praise will never be interrupted either by the needs of the flesh or by hunger." I came to holy Golgotha and prayed the same prayer there. Laying my hands on the covering of the holy rock I invoked the holy name of God there. I came out from there and placed myself in the hands of God.

'Then, having come down to Jericho, I crossed the holy Jordan and journeyed along the shore of the Dead Sea, for at that time the sea had not risen so high.[n] Crossing the mountains and wandering in the desert I came across this stream-bed. I climbed up the rock and saw this opening. In I went and fell in love with the place, thinking that it was given to me by God to repent in. Thirty years I have been here now and have seen no man other than you this very minute. The basket of beans and the vessel of water have lasted until now without failing.[n] My clothes wore out with age but as my hair grew I covered myself with it like a garment and I suffer neither from heat nor from cold by the grace of Christ.'

So saying, she invited me to partake of the beans, for she perceived spiritually that I was very hungry. We both partook of them and drank. When I was satisfied I looked at the basket and saw that there remained as many beans as before, and likewise for the water. I was glorifying God! I wanted to leave her my old cloak but she refused, saying: "Bring me some new clothes".[n] I was delighted to hear this and I asked her to wait for me in the same place. When we had prayed, off I went, marking the path I trod. I went to the church of the neighbouring village and explained the matter to the priest. He announced to the people that there were some of the saints going naked and that anybody who had superfluous clothing should bring it. The friends of Christ brought many garments without hesitation. I took what was needed and went joyfully on my way, hoping to see the sacred face of that spiritual mother. I went this way and that and wore myself out without finding the cave. And when at last I came across it, I did not find that divinely-inspired woman [there], which greatly distressed me.

A few days later some anchorites paid me a visit. They reported to me,[n] saying: "When we two were coming down to the other side of the sea, by night, we saw an anchorite with flowing hair sitting eating on a rock. But when we ran up to him in the hope of receiving a blessing, he fled from us and went into a little cave which was nearby. When we made to approach the entrance, he called out saying: "Trouble me not, oh servants of Christ. Look, the basket of beans and the vessel of water are on the rock; please be so kind as to help yourselves." We offered a prayer and when we approached, we found it was as he had said. We sat down and ate all the beans there were and drank all the water. The rest of the night we remained silent. In the morning we arose [expecting] to be blessed by the anchorite, but we found him asleep in the Lord. We also discovered that it was a naked woman, draped with her own hair. When we had received the blessing of her mortal remains we rolled a rock into the mouth of the cave, offered a prayer and went our way." Then I realised that she was that holy mother who had been one of the nuns. So I told them what I had heard from her and together we glorified God, to whom be glory for ever. Amen.

SERGIUS, THE DÊMOTÊS[n] OF ALEXANDRIA

A MONK whose name was Ambakoum told me this:

I found an ancient book at Tamiathaïs[n] and when I unrolled it, I found this passage:

A monk whose name was Elpidius was besieged in his cell by the devil which is the source of all evil, otherwise known as the demon of accidie. As the siege was of long duration he arose and went towards the inner desert which is called Helos.

As he travelled about in that place he saw a naked man with white hair who, when he saw him, fled towards the inner desert. When Elpidius the monk had pursued him vigorously for a considerable distance, beseeching him [to stop], he did stop and offered a prayer. After the prayer he said to [Elpidius]: 'Who are you brother, and how do you come to be here? Why do you put yourself to so much trouble?' In reply, the other said to him: 'I was besieged by the demon of *accidie* in my cell, reverend father. I arose, went out and wandered in the desert, all the time offering prayers to

God, the lover of men, that he would rid me of the demon of *accidie*. I had also this thought in mind: that perhaps I might find a servant of God who would be obliged to intercede for me. And behold, overlooking my sins, the all-merciful God has sent me your holiness. For the Lord's sake therefore I beseech you, father, to pray for me, the sinner. And, at least if you deem it proper to do so, allow me to stay with you.' The father embraced him and, after offering a prayer, said to him: 'It is impossible for me to receive you and to let you stay with me, child, for it is not given to you by God to do so'. Elpidius said to him: 'Then, for the Lord's sake, reverend father, please will you agree to tell me how you came here, how long ago, and what kind of grace God has bestowed on you?' The other willingly responded: 'As for the how and the why of my coming here, it was simply as a sinner desirous of salvation that I came to be here, with God, the lover of men, guiding my humility. I have been in this place seventy years more or less, never seeing a man's face until this day. Some time ago my heart was puffed up by the machinations of the perverse demon into thinking that I had attained a stature superior to that of all the fathers leading the ascetic life in the desert. By the providence of God, there came to me another idea: that I should beseech him to let me know with whom I had my portion and whether by chance my equal was to be found on earth. For seven days I prayed continuously to God and on the seventh day an invisible voice came to me saying: "You have your portion with Sergius the *dêmotês* of Alexandria". Much distressed on hearing this, I said to myself: "So much the worse for you, miserable Pyrrhus! Look at all those years you have spent in the service of God, with so many and such severe privations, only to be set in the same rank as a *dêmotês*!" To my pride-inflated imagination the voice I heard seemed to have been that of the adversary, and thus I fell to disbelieving it. I spent a further seven days praying in the same way and then

I heard the same voice saying to me: "I told you that you have your share and your portion with Sergius, the *dêmotês* of Alexandria." Then I said to myself: "If this is how it seems to God the good, the lover of men, I am determined before I die to see who this man is and what kind of deeds he does." So I set out immediately and came to the city of Alexandria. When I enquired as to the whereabouts of such a man, they pointed him out to me, sitting in a tavern,[n] rollicking and dallying with whores. There were prostitutes coming in and going out, for this Sergius was the supervisor and director of all the prostitutes.

'When I entered the tavern and asked him whether he were Sergius the *dêmotês* he said: "Yes, I am." Then I said to him: "Brother, I wish to make your acquaintance today and to have a friendly meal with you." He said: "As you please, abba. Sit down, anyway." Then at Sergius' bidding the host brought all those things that are usually consumed in taverns and, for love of God, I was obliged to partake [of those things] with him—after so many years [of abstaining from them!] For I reasoned with myself like this: "If this man has so pleased God that he had been ranked with me, ought I not to make his acquaintance and share his table?"

'When we had eaten and drunk and refreshed ourselves, the two of us stood up and went out together. Then I said to him: "Have you a house?" He said he had; "Then let us go into your house" I replied, "for I have something which I must of necessity say to you." He was secretly scandalised, thinking that perhaps I had been besieged by the adversary and that I wanted to sin. Examining me very closely, he condemned me in his heart and wondered to himself how one so advanced in years (and given his way of life) could have fallen victim to such temptation. All this he told me later on.

'We went off to his house and when I had offered a prayer, we sat down. Once we were seated I said to him: "For the sake of the Lord, brother, tell me about your [way of] life and what good you have accomplished."[n] Amazed and confused at my question, he replied: "Man of God, you found me in the tavern eating, drinking and making merry with whores. I am in charge of them, and without my consent, nobody can lay a finger on them. [A client] must speak to me and then I provide him with whichever whore he wants. And you have just told me you want to hear about my life? You have seen for yourself; what more do you want to learn of me?" I besought and adjured him still more insistently not to conceal it from me if any good deed had been accomplished by him. In the end I even told [him] of the voice which had been borne to me from heaven. In his amazement at the great love which God has for men, he heaved a great sigh from the depth of his heart and said to me: "If that is how the matter stands, reverend father, I do recall one day going into a certain tavern and seeing from there a pretty woman who was very beautiful, sitting in a weaver's workshop and working for wages. Filled with desire for her, I said to the hostess: 'Where is that woman from?' The hostess said to me: 'She is of this city.' 'Go and arrange with her for me to sleep with her' I said, but she told me: 'I cannot speak of any such thing to her; for although now she is in severely reduced circumstances, she is of very noble birth.' As I was desirous of knowing how she had come to fall on such evil days, the hostess told me that the woman's husband had borrowed a hundred pieces of gold from the governor of this city of Alexandria. When he had nothing with which to repay the debt, the governor had him arrested and thrown into prison, seizing [the woman's] two children for slavery.[n] That was why she found herself in such a state, slaving away night and day in the hope of setting them free.

" 'When I had heard this from the hostess, I said to her: 'Go and tell her to consort with me and I will give her the hundred gold pieces.' She replied: 'I cannot say a thing like that to her for I know that she is chaste and would never consent to such a proposition.' Again I said to the hostess: 'Go, speak to her and perhaps you will change her mind. If not, you are none the worse off.' The hostess gave in to me and went to speak to the woman; and she, albeit with sighs and tears, agreed to my proposition, saying to the hostess: 'I presume that as God is the lover of men, he will forgive me this sin which I am about to commit unwillingly; for he knows that until now I have had no knowledge of any man other [than my husband.] I have been toiling and labouring such a long time, night and day, to set those three souls at liberty, but it is beyond my capability. I am at the end of my tether with no strength left, and I no longer know what to do. It is better for me to bow to the necessity of delivering my body to sin for their sakes.'

" 'The hostess came and told me she had agreed. I went and fetched the hundred gold pieces, counted them out and gave them into the woman's hands. She arrived at my house with sighs and tears, and came into my chamber saying: 'Lord, you know my affliction; forgive me!' My heart was troubled when I heard this and I said to myself: 'Now if that is how the matter stands, why do I not go off to whichever I like of the prostitutes who are under my supervision and satisfy my desire? For it makes not the slightest difference with whom one performs the wrongful and unclean act.' Having said this, I absolved her of our agreement and dismissed her with the hundred pieces of gold of which I spoke. She went and gave them to the governor, thus releasing both her husband and the two children from his cruel hands."

'On hearing this from Sergius the *dêmotês* I exclaimed: "Glory to the only God, the lover of men. It is indeed with justice that I was ranked with you." Then he heaved a sigh and said to me: "If, as you say, this deed was truly pleasing to God the good, the lover of men; and if, reverend father, you have come from God to me who am indeed a sinner, I recall something even better than this. There came into the city of Alexadria a violent and sin-loving governor, an alien to the church of God. Every day he required of me two or three prostitutes. One day as he was passing one of the women's monasteries which are here, he chanced to see some good-looking maidens looking down from above. Seized with lust for them, he ordered soldiers to surround that monastery and to guard all the doors securely so that not one of [the inmates] could escape. He entered, gathered them together and counted them. He found there were seventy virgins in all and he handed them over to me with these instructions: 'Now they are in your hands. Do with them what you like, but send me each day as many of them as I require of you, up to the whole seventy of them.' With these words to me that perverse governor went his way.

" 'With a sigh from the depth of my heart I said to myself: 'Ah me, sinner that I am! How may years have these women preserved their virginity for the Lord's sake, wasting away their bodies with fasting, vigils and every kind of asceticism, in order to present them in spotless condition to the heavenly and immortal bridegroom, Christ who is God. and now, by my agency, the great toil they have endured for such a long time is going to be brought to nothing when they are defiled by that blood-thirsty and sacrilegious governor. God forbid that I should do any such thing to the spotless lambs and doves of Christ.' Much as I racked my brains, I could not think of a way of saving them from defiling intercourse with the iniquitous governor. In deep distress I begged God to give me some idea of how, and some means by which I might deliver them from such an abomination. The all-merciful God took pity on me, sinner that I am. He gave me a good idea. I rose and went to the prostitutes who operate in this city, those who were under my supervision. By distributing amongst them all my modest savings I was just able to persuade them to be tonsured and to dress themselves up in monastic habits. While I took them to the monastery and left them there, I took the virgins and hid them in another place. Each day I provided that wretched governor with some of the tonsured whores until the number of seventy was reached. Having had his seventy nuns (or rather whores) that evil demon of a governor promptly left the city. Then I took those virgin nuns and brought them back to the monastery, meaning to let the prostitutes go. But when they saw those servants and brides of Christ our God, they no longer wanted to leave that place. They said: "Since God has found us worthy to wear this habit, even though it were only in a masquerade, God forbid that we should ever return to that uncleanliness and the destruction of our souls," and they remained there wearing the sacred habit, well-pleasing in the sincerity of their repentance to God the all-merciful, the all-powerful.' "

'When Sergius told me this, yet more did I glorify Christ, the only helper and saviour of those who truly believe in him. I said to him: "In truth, brother, even though I have laboured mightily, I perceive that you are not only my equal, but that you are superior to me. For the Lord's sake, dismiss me with a prayer and let me return to my retreat." Sergius said to me: "You wish me to dismiss you with a prayer and let you go? By our Lord Jesus Christ, if (as you say) I have been ranked with you, I will not be separated from you, but I will come with you." He asked me to wait a day or two and, having given all his goods to the poor, he followed me [into the desert.]

'After spending three years with me he has now died in the Lord, just four days ago. Elpidius, my child, I know that it is by the providence of God that you came here, so that when the truly good Master, the lover of men, receives my soul, you might bury me with [Sergius]. But in the meantime, go away, I beseech you, and come back after three days, for there is something which I absolutely must tell you.' So I went away and came back again three days later, as I had been instructed by that holy elder. I found him dead in the Lord, so I buried him next to Abba Sergius as he had directed me. Then giving thanks to God for his exceptional wonders, I went my way, glorifying God.

17 *BHG* 1277a / 1449q

THE DRUNKEN PRIEST

IN THE DAYS when the great martyr Saint Mercury[n] endured martyrdom there was a priest in the same country who was a great drunkard. He spent all his time in taverns with wine-bibbers. One day a governor of that country sent his own female servant to the house of the priest where she found the priest's wife and said to her: 'Where is the priest?' She said: 'Don't you know? He's in the taverns.' The governor's servant said: 'My master sent me so he can have a liturgy tomorrow in memory of his parents.' She said this and went her way. Now the priest's wife also had a female servant and to her she said: 'I am going to my mother's house to sleep there. When your master the priest comes, lay him down properly in his bed because tomorrow he must celebrate the liturgy.'

When it was evening the priest came, very drunk, and lay down in his bed. The devil entered into his servant and she lay down close to the priest. He awoke and was intimate with her, thinking it was his wife. But she [his wife] found him [next morning] sleeping in the bed and said to him: 'Get up; sing your service because so-and-so the governor is having a liturgy for his parents.' The priest turned the other way and went back to sleep. The wife came and said to him again: 'Didn't I tell you to get up because you are going to celebrate the liturgy today?' The priest grinned and said to her: 'What are you saying, silly woman? Don't you know what we did this night? And you say I am going to celebrate the liturgy?' The wife replied: 'What did we do? So far as I am concerned, I slept at my father's house.' 'Well' said the priest, 'for my part I was intimate with a woman during this night. Who could it have been who ensnared me?' They questioned the servant and she said: 'Satan tormented me; I lay down beside him and he was intimate with me.'

The priest wept and lamented at some length. After that, he said: 'Keep quiet about this, to prevent it from coming to the ears of the authorities and [to keep] them from punishing us severely. It is clear that God is tender-hearted and full of mercy; I will propitiate him by confession.' So he sang his abbreviated office and, in fear of the governor, went off to celebrate the liturgy. After the oblation [*proskomidên*], when he was saying the prayer 'Oh God our God, the heavenly bread,' there came an angel to consecrate the holy gifts. When he saw the priest, he said: 'Oh, outcast of God! How dare you come in and celebrate the liturgy of the divine mysteries? Don't you know that you are vile [? *bibêlos*] and unclean on account of the sin which you committed last night? It is with profound reverence that we who are incorporeal and immaterial see the holy face of the blessed Divinity. We stand in fear and trembling, covering our faces with our wings. Yet you think so contemptuously of the holy gifts that you have dared to take them into your hands and are about to eat them with your mouth.' The priest replied to the angel: 'Since you make me an outcast like this, do you also be outcast!' And, oh, the wonder of it!—the angel immediately lost his wings and remained in the church as a man.[n] But the priest was not aware of this and after the liturgy he came into the governor's house, broke his fast that day and went off to his house.

Some days later a man died in that country and they invited the priests to sing over his mortal remains (for there were other priests in that district as it was a large one). They invited this priest too and when the priests were saying the prayer, he came to say the prayer; and—oh, the wonder of it!—when he said "For thou art the resurrection, the life and the repose", the dead man promptly sat up and said to the priest: "Even though you may raise the dead, you are unworthy to wear a stole or to celebrate the liturgy or to perform any priestly function". When the dead man had said this he lay down again. When all the other priests saw this extraordinary wonder they were flabbergasted. Then they said to the priest: 'What is this extraordinary and great wonder?' The priest confessed his own sin before them all. The rest of the priests said: "From now on we can have nothing to do with you; do what you will on your own."

The priest went to his house in sorrow and told what had happened. Then he said to his wife [*presbytera*]: "What shall I do now? I have no other skill; how am I going to support you? Let us go to another place where nobody knows about us and spend the rest of our lives [there]." They arose and went to another city where nobody knew them and he began celebrating the liturgy there. And—oh, the wonder of it!—he remained as he was when the angel outlawed him, except that his face turned black.

His wife [*presbytera*] and his children died and he lived alone three hundred and seventy years. There was at that time a truly remarkable and righteous bishop [*mêtropolitês*]. It came to the feast of Saint Mercury and one of the governors of that town celebrated the feast of this saint [as his name-day]. The governor invited the bishop [*archiereus*] and the priest was there too. At table the bishop [*archiereus*] told them the brief life [*synaxarion*] of the saint and explained it more fully to those who were at table. Then the priest spoke up and said: 'My holy lord, you know only the sufferings of the saint from the holy brief life [of him]. I know these things accurately because I was there and I had a good view of the martyr's passion and sufferings. He was my neighbour and we often used to eat together.' The bishop turned to the priest and said: "You are not yet forty years old and you know the saint? From the time when Saint Mercury endured martyrdom until now is three hundred and seventy years. You were not yet born [then] and you know these things?" The other replied with an oath: "I am telling the truth and no lie".

Then the bishop knew that there was something in all this, so he took him aside privately and said to him: "Tell me all about yourself and make a clean breast of it". The priest then told everything, whatever he had done: how he fell [into sin] with his female servant and how he and the outlawed angel remained unchanged.

The bishop then said to him: "I would have you know that you remain under the angel's ban [*dedemenos*] and are alive until now and will not die for endless ages. But go to the church where you laid the ban [*ton desmon epoiêsate*] [on the angel] when he was there at that moment, for [each] one [of you] laid the ban [*edêsen*] on the other." The priest said: "Holy lord [*hagie despota*], I cannot do that for the distance of the journey is great and I have nothing with which to pay [the expenses of the journey], nor is there a horse available to me which could ease [my path]." Then the bishop said to him: "If you do not go there, not only will you not die, neither will the angel regain his wings and go up into the heavens." The bishop, feeling sorry for him, said to him again: "Since you tell me you cannot [undertake this journey] I will be merciful with you; let us go together. I will give you a horse and I myself will bear the cost."

They took to the road immediately and travelled to where the priest used to live. But the place had been laid waste and they found nothing; not a house nor anything else. The bishop said: "This is where you lived?" "This is it, holy lord, and it has been laid waste," he replied. "Do you not know where the church was?" asked the bishop. The priest looked carefully and recognised some trees at a certain distance from where his place used to be. He said: "It seems to me that the church is over there where the trees are." They went there and found the church [*naos*] all broken down, except for a little bit of the sanctuary [*bêma*] which was still standing. They got off the horses and onto their feet and the bishop said: "Go into the sanctuary". The priest went in and found the angel standing there, and the angel said: "Are you still alive, wretched priest?" "Yes, I am still alive," said the priest, "and you are still standing in the same place." "Yes" said the angel; "you are welcome, for now we can forgive each other." "Bless the Lord, holy angel of God," said the priest; "please forgive me." The angel said: "I would rather that you forgave me first and then I you. For if I forgive you first, you are going to die at that very moment and I will be left under the ban." Then the priest said: "If I forgive you, you are going to recover your wings and go up into the heavens; then it is I who will remain under the ban." "I swear to you by the unshakable throne of God that I will not leave you under the ban," said the angel. (The bishop was hearing all this from outside.)

Then said the priest to the angel: "In the name of the Father and of the Son and of the Holy Spirit, may you be forgiven by me the sinner," and straightway—oh the wonder of it!—the angel received his wings and mounted up on high. Then the angel said to the priest: "Do you also be forgiven, oh priest," and before the angel had got the words out of his mouth, there were the priest's bones [lying] in a heap in the place where he had been standing.

Then said the bishop to the angel: "Oh holy angel, I beg you to grant me one request; sing an angelic hymn and let me hear it." The angel said: "That is not possible. The moment you hear the angelic voice you will pass from this world. It is impossible for mortal flesh to hear the voice of an angel and live. Yet, because of the trouble you have been to and your goodness to me and to the priest, wait a little for me to go up to the third heaven and sing there. You will hear, but scarcely be able to bear it." He mounted up to the third heaven and sang the alleluia. So sweet was the melody that the bishop fell to the ground as though dead [and lay there] for three hours. Even then he was only just able to come to his senses and get up.

The bishop, giving thanks to God, then returned to his diocese where he wrote this story of the priest for the benefit of many, so that we slothful ones, when we hear it, will turn over a new leaf and become attentive and studious, free of unclean thoughts and improper desires. When we perform priestly duties we must have no part [of such things]. So if anybody has a hankering after fornication [*porneia*] of for any other desire of the flesh—gluttony, drunkeness, covetousness [*philargyria,*] grudge-bearing [*mnêsikakia,*] vain glory or pride—these things make him unworthy of the priesthood and a despiser of the spotless mysteries. For this reason we are obliged when we are going to stand beside the holy table [. . . . .] and we accomplish the awesome sacrifice [*hierourgia*]. There are many who perform this act presumptuously, who neither make their confession nor sing the accustomed [preliminary] office, but rather perform their service [*diakonoumenoi*] as though they were immortal, the wretches (in my opinion) failing to recall that it was of us the Lord spoke: "He who knew the lord's will [. . .] and did it not shall be beaten with many stripes." In other words, the Lord stipulates that if someone discovers his will and does not do it, that man will be severely punished.

So then, look, my brethren; we have learned that there is nothing on earth greater than priesthood; not even kingship or any other thing. And a man who is unworthy [of priesthood] and does not desist [from the exercise of it], if death shall find him unrepentant, will be tormented with Judas Iscariot in the worst possible places of punishment. So let us now, readers and hearers of these things, coerce each other away from sin. Let us do the will of God, the lover of men, and be made worthy to stand at his right hand at his second coming, being made inheritors together with the righteous of eternal benefits in Christ Jesus our Lord, to whom be glory and power for ever and ever. Amen.

18 *BHG* 1450kb, longer recension

THE CONVERTED ROBBER

ONE OF THE HOLY fathers said that there is a ladies' monastery in one of the suburbs of Antioch with two hundred and sixty sisters in it.[n] It is encircled by a wall so that no one can enter. A band of twelve robbers held a meeting together with their chief to see how they could get in and despoil what was inside. The chief asked each one of them: "How can we get in, for the monastery wall is very strong?" And to each man as he replied, the chief said: "You have not spoken well". They said to their chief: "Look, we have spoken and you did not like what we said; so tell us what seems to be a good idea to you". He said: "I take the cowl of a lowly monk from distant parts and put it on, hiding my hair in it.[n] I attach my sword to my thigh and wear a tattered monastic broad-stole [*maphorion*]. In the evening I go and knock at the monastery door and they receive me as a poor monk from foreign parts. In the night, I open [the gate] for you; you enter, and we do what we will." And that is just what he did. He put on a monk's habit, hid his hair in a cowl and attached his sword to his thigh. He came to the monastery in the evening and said to the portress: "I am a stranger and it would not be proper for me to stay in the village because the women would be an occasion of sin for me. And I am ashamed to stay in the city[n] again because of the citizens. Therefore, of your charity and for a reward, tell this to the superior: just let me inside the doorway this evening; tomorrow I will greet you and go my way." The portress joyfully reported all this to the superior as though she had it from the lips of a holy father. The mother [superior] gave orders for him to enter and also for the wood [-en signal] to be sounded to gather all the sisters together.[n]When she had gathered them all together, they and she approached the arch-robber who was thought to be a monk, hoping to be blessed by him. She ordered a washing-bowl to be brought; she had the nuns stand in two choirs, and each one of them came by, washed his feet and was blessed by him.

Now one of those nuns was the attendant of a sister who lay paralysed on the upper floor. She took some of the water with which his feet had been washed and went up, saying to the sick sister: "A great holy man has come to our monastery; we all of us washed his feet and received a blessing from the water in which they were washed. I have brought you some of it so that you too can receive a blessing." On hearing this the paralysed sister washed her face and anointed her body with the water and, by faith, she was cured immediately. This came about that scripture might be fulfilled: "He who receives a prophet in the name of a prophet shall receive the reward of a prophet" [Mt 10:41]. As the attendant-sister was leaving to make her way downstairs, the sick one said to her: "Wait, sister, I will come down with you and I too will receive a blessing from this holy father, for behold! God has healed me through his holy prayers." She got up and went downstairs with the other sister. As she approached the man, all the sisters saw and were astonished at the extraordinary miracle. When they asked her how it had come about, she said: "As soon as I washed myself with the water which had washed this holy father, the illness fled from me." All the sisters, seeing the extraordinary miracle, glorified God and pressed about the man's feet more insistently, asking him to offer more prayers.

When the man heard these things, he was amazed, both at the miracle which had taken place and also that they should have such faith in him. In his astonishment he began shouting and saying: "Keep your hands off me, mothers, for, as God well knows, I am a very sinful man, unworthy to remain alive. It is *I* who beg *you* to make fervent intercession to the Lord on *my* behalf, praying him to reform me and of his love for mankind to save me." When he had said this to them, begging them to desist from their efforts, they thought that he had spoken like this out of humility; so they redoubled their requests to be blessed by him. Realising that they were not in any mood either to accept what he said or yet to be silenced, in his confusion the man threw back the cowl he was wearing and showed them the hair of his head. And loosening the sword from his thigh he cast it on the ground in the sight of them all saying: "*Now* will you believe me, that I am a sinner and the author of many evils? Desist now from your efforts to obtain favours of me. Rather, give thanks to God the good, the lover of men, that your prayers and sincere faith in him have brought about this extraordinary miracle in the case of the paralysed sister. I would have you know that I am a robber chief and it was by a ruse that I got in here. I have another twelve robbers who are coming to the monastery door tonight at my orders. But have no fear; pray rather that God will receive me as I repent of the evil deeds I have committed." When those worthy virgins heard this and saw the sword, they were stricken with terror and all stood [in prayer at the divine] office, singing psalms from dusk to dawn.

The twelve robbers came by night. Their chief went out and told them about the miracle that had taken place. He said: "From henceforth I fear God and I will have nothing more to do with wrong-doing. If it be the will of God, I would like to become a monk. So then, go away peacefully; you will no longer have me with you." When the robbers heard this they were stricken with awe. They said to him: "If that is how things are; if you, our chief, who are stronger than all of us, wish to be saved, then we too want to be saved with you and to become monks." This is what they said among themselves; and being of one accord, they rose up and went to a monastery, where, having renounced the world, they all became monks.

The father who told [this story] swore that he had himself been there and had learned from the monks who were living at the monastery that this is a true story; also that the robbers became monks with one accord and entered the same convent. Some of them became worthy of special gifts [*charismata*] from Christ. These things were written for the benefit and edification of those who hear and who wish to be well-pleasing to Christ our true God, who makes dispensations [to permit our] salvation. [They were also written] so that by hearing [them] and imitating [the virtues they illustrate] we might be saved, through the dispensations which come about in many ways.

19 *BHG* 1450x

THE PROUD MONK
[The conceited monk who wanted to be equal to Isaac]

1. THE ELDERS told us that there was a monk at Scêtê who asked God: "Lord, let me measure up to the stature of Isaac,"[n] who was one of the patriarchs of olden days. He prayed for many days, then there came a voice from God saying: "You are not able to measure up to the stature of Isaac the patriarch." So the monk said: "If I cannot be like Isaac, then let me be like Job", and the divine voice spoke to him again: "If you wrestle with the devil and conquer the adversary as Job did, you will be able to be like him." The monk promised to do it all and to fight with Satan and then he heard another message from the divine voice: "Now get yourself off to your cell and prepare yourself with manliness," and off he went to prepare himself for the fray. But some days later he forgot that he had promised to fight manfully against the temptations of Satan. Later on the devil disguised himself as an officer[n] and he came to the monk saying: "Father, I pray your holiness, be merciful to me, for I

am being sought after by my king.[n] Take these two hundred pounds in gold, that girl and the child.[n] Please keep all these safe by you in some hidden place, for I shall flee and go away to a remote region and hide there for some time. The monk, of course, did not realise that this was the devil spreading a snare for him. He said: "My child, I cannot take possession of them. I am a person of no social standing; how could I keep safe and conceal all these?" But the spurious officer began to constrain him until finally the monk said: "My son, go and hide your possessions behind that rock over there," for he did not know it was a deceit of the devil. But eventually he gave in and accepted the gold, the girl, and the child, having been completely taken in by the demon.

2.[n] Some days later bitter warfare invaded the soul of the monk on account of the girl. He rose up and violated her, then he felt bitter remorse for the deed he had done. His reason said to him: "Now kill the child so that he will not give away the secret of what you have done," so he killed the child. Now his reason said to him some days later: "Look, the officer is going to come and when he does not find the child he will kill you on his account. Get up and kill the girl and flee to a distant land so that you do not fall into the hands of the officer." And that is what he did. He got up and killed the girl, just as he had slain the child. He took the treasure and went off to a distant country; there he used the money to build a chapel and houses in which he dwelt. When the work was completed, the officer re-appeared, that devil in disguise, and he began to shout and cry: "Oh, quick! Help! That monk has put up these buildings with money I entrusted to him." The local inhabitants gathered around the spurious officer and drove him away from that place with all kinds of abuse. He went off hurting with indignation at the threats he had endured and saying that he would do utterly unimaginable things to the monk. In this manner he withdrew and went his way. The monk now knew no respite, neither by day nor by night, in the battle with his thoughts, until finally he talked himself into leaving that place. "For now my evil deeds have come to light" he said, "I will take what is left of the money and go to a distant city which seems good to me where the officer will not be able to come."

3. So now he went away to the city and there he met a girl who was the public executioner's daughter. Having spoken to her father, he took her for his wife. Some time later the girl's father died. Then the governor appointed by the king of that land decreed that the son-in-law of the executioner was to take his place. For it was the custom and rule of that region that when a person of military or patrician rank died, he who married the dead man's widow or his daughter should be appointed to discharge his duties. The governor enquired of the officials upon whom rested the obligation of performing the office of executioner according to custom. The official replied: "With us it is customary for the man who marries the wife or daughter of the deceased executioner to perform this service, even against his will." The governor said: "Is there such a one among you?" They replied that there was, a man who seemed to have been connected with the monastic order, whereupon he said: "Go and bring him to me." So they brought [the monk] to the governor and, against his will, he was appointed to serve as executioner according to custom by order of the court. And when they appointed him executioner, I cannot relate his iniquity without tears! For in all that land, whoever fell under punishment or chastisement, this man was his torturer and executioner. What can I say of a man who was once a monk, and is now a hardened, cruel torturer? Many times the governor ordered him to put people in boiling cauldrons, some to be roasted on hot-plates, others

to be cut in pieces or nailed up or to suffer various other torments. He even contrived to make each torture yet more excruciating, because he was recently appointed to the office and anxious to please.

4. Now it happened on a certain occasion that some persons answerable for their actions had charges brought against them, and the former monk, now become the executioner, was sent for (and believe me, I am so disturbed emotionally by this story that I cannot go through it with dry eyes). He was ordered by the governor to apply pitch or some other torture to those under examination. While the newly-appointed executioner was doing this, Satan came by, disguised as an officer. He began to shout with a loud voice and say: "Woe is me, wretch that I am; help me!" The sound of his voice attracted quite a large crowd; he was calling upon the governor to avenge one who had suffered an injustice. The governor responded, saying to the officer: "Calm down, man, and pull yourself together. Spell out in an orderly manner what has happened to you and stop this sounding-off like a barking dog". The officer said to the governor: "This executioner used to be a monk, and once when I was being pursued by enemies I entrusted to him a large amount of gold, two hundred pounds' worth, together with my child-slave and a virgin hand-maid. Make an injunction for me to receive back what I entrusted to him." When he heard the amount of the gold, the governor gladly heard this account of the affair in the hope of receiving a portion. With an eager heart he began to enquire of the executioner-monk whether the officer's words seemed true to him—this officer who had entrusted to him (and now sought the return of) his property. [The monk] replied: "It was all as he says. He brought me the property, but a little while later he came to take it away. I gave him everything without delay." The governor said to him: "So we have your

word that he brought the property to you; have you no written receipt for it, nor any witness that he took it back from you?" And the monk remained silent. At a loss for an explanation of what had become of that which had been entrusted to him, he finally (and unwillingly) confessed to murdering the child and the girl, also to spending the gold. When the governor realised there was nothing in it for him, he ordered the wretched executioner to be taken away to execution.

5. Now as [the monk] was drawing near the place where he would meet his end, the officer who had denounced him met him in the forum and said to him: "Do you know who I am, father?" He replied: "I think you are the officer with whom it was my misfortune to become acquainted and who entrusted to me the child, the girl, and the gold." The other retorted: "I am Satan, who deceived Adam, the first-made man; who wage war against men and, insofar as I am able, allow no one to be saved, nor to become like Isaac or like Job. Rather do I endeavour to make them all like that Achitophel, like Judas Iscariot, like Cain and like the elders of Babylon and their like. Go and join them, you too, for you failed to recognise our contrived chains of guile and deceit. Since you have not learnt to fight the invisible battle, you shall suffer as they suffer. For a proud person shall not be extolled beyond his capabilities, nor shall he presume to emulate better and stronger holy men. In the case of Job I was not remiss in assailing him with the devices I contrived against him, yet for all the great things I raised up against him, in the end I was conquered and weakened by him. In your case, however, not a single one of my great stratagems did I bring to bear; and you became such a devotee of all the evil I did to you and to all races of men! And look, you who set out to do battle with me: you have seen your strength and you have found a place befitting your worth, both

in this world and in the next." Having said this and much more beside, he disappeared. The poor wretch, the monk who became a torturer, suffered death by hanging, deceived by the demons through his pride and vain-glory.

So now, may we be protected from asking God for that which is beyond us, and from undertaking to perform that which it exceeds our strength to achieve. For it is better rather to travel the royal road by which, falling away neither to right nor to left, we will be able to be saved from this present wicked world, having humility in all things.

ANNA, WHO WAS RE-NAMED EUPHÊMIANOS

THIS, OUR HOLY MOTHER Anna, was born at Byzantium, [the daughter] of a devout deacon at the Church of our most holy lady, the Mother of God, at Blachernae.[n] Her grandmother was in a hurry to marry her, orphaned of her parents, to a very devout man, which she did. Then her uncle on her father's side, a man far advanced in the ascetic life and possessing the gift of perception to a high degree, came from Olympus. He had had his tongue cut out by the enemy of the icons, [the Emperor] Leo [IV],[n] but he spoke without impediment even after the excision. When he saw her married to a man, he said: "Why have you turned your eyes away from the way that leads to godly struggles and labours and have married a man?" He made intercession for her and went his way. Time passed by, and when that irreligious emperor was suffering torment in the galleries of Hades, the orthodox and [a25] most faithful emperors Irene and Constantine [VI], having learned of his sufferings under him who reigned before them, summoned that holy man. They received his blessing and availed themselves of his prayers. Then he, opting for those things which work together to be well-pleasing to God, took the road back to his own place. He then saw the blessed lady again. "Be bold and strong, my child" he said, "for many are the afflictions of the righteous. You know in your heart that the child in your womb will not be born before you have hidden your husband in the grave"—and that is what happened. In the sixth month of her pregnancy her husband died. Great was her lamentation and she wore herself out with grief. But she weaned the child and gave it into the hands of her other uncle. She prepared herself for those struggles, the like and the extent of which are known [only] to those who have been initiated into the mysteries and who have driven the ascetic road to its limit.

While she was so engaged, that most perceptive man came from Olympus. She fell at his feet and asked his blessing. "Be strong in the Lord," she heard [him say,] and: "where is the infant?" that wondrous man asked. She [replied]: "The one I entrusted to your own brother, my benefactor, together with God; the other one is with me." Having said these and no few other words of confusion and of a grieving heart, she stood both the children by that worthy elder; with tears streaming from her eyes she cried: "Pray for the children!" He [said]: "They have no need of prayers". Finding it very hard to believe her own ears, she heaved a great sigh. "Woe is me, sinner that I am," she said; "whatever else is going to happen to us?" The elder [said]: "Did I not tell you, child: many are the afflictions of the righteous? If we do not patiently endure, we will never be justified. It is seemly and pleasing to God that it should be so." "But surely, sir, it has not seemed good to the Lord that my tender children should go hence [into the next world]?" The wondrous man replied: "You have spoken correctly: very soon the Lord will receive them from you." As was her custom, she gave thanks [a45] to God, and fell at the feet of the honourable elder. Availing herself of prayer, she then began with both hands to make distribution of her possessions. Not long afterwards, the children died; she poured out tears for them and set what was left to her in the hands of the poor. She made the rounds of the churches praying, candle in hand, and taking her leave of them.

In the end, she encountered a monk from Olympus; by him she was tonsured and, in secret, she put on a man's habit, but with a woman's on the outside. Then, escaping notice, she appeared in the area of Olympus, having discarded the female habit. Coming to one of the monasteries and entering it, she spoke to the porter, telling him that she held it imperative above all other things that she come into the presence of the superior. The porter notified the superior in the usual way. He then presented that person (who had been invited [to follow him]) and went his way. The most honourable woman [a55] lay at the feet of the superior and requested the usual blessing. The man of God gave the blessing and then raised her up and said: "What brings you here, and what is your name?" She [replied]: "The reason for my arrival at this sacred monastery, holy father, is the number of my transgressions [*tôn eptaismenôn*], so that by keeping silence [*hêsuchasas*] for the remaining time of my life, even though I be unworthy, I might be found propitiating the deity in the day of judgement. My name is Euphêmianos." The elder said to her: "If that is the way you are thinking in your heart, child, and if you sincerely desire salvation, flee from speaking your mind [*parrêsia*]. The nature of eunuchs is easily ensnared in passionate-and-emotional thoughts [*tois empathesi logismois*"]. Having said this, he offered the customary prayer and enlisted her in the brotherhood.[n] Thereupon she so far excelled in all virtue and humility and exceeded those who were there that she became an example and pattern to all the monks living the ascetic life in the monastery.

When the steward [*diakonos*] in her household, chosen for this task by the saint, had administered everything as he was entrusted to do in this matter, he came looking for his mistress. It so happened that he met the monk who had tonsured her. He enquired of him if by chance he knew where she was who had abandoned earthly things [b20] in quest of the heavenly. [The monk] said to him: "I will not deny that, clearly, I did have something to do with her; however, I do not know where she is now. But let us go hence a little to such-and-such a monastery." When they arrived, they learned from the porter that the one whom they were looking for was within and they entreated that she be sent for. When she came, the monk indicated the steward and said: "Behold, your most faithful administrator [*oikonomos*] is here and he has been to great pains looking for you. Let us go to our lavra, if you please."

When the saint heard this, she went to the superior of the monastery and received a blessing both from him and from the rest of the brethren, then she went out from there. She went with the steward and in the company of the monk to the lavra. When she had been there some time, she was revealed as someone who was capable of producing boundless wonders by her own merits. Naturally, the rumour of the wonders spread around, and a great number of people who had kissed [the world] goodbye flowed towards the monastery. But the narrowness and smallness of the place hindered the devotion [b30] of those who arrived. So, by divine inspiration, the superior of the monastery reported the wondrous deeds of the monk Euphêmianos to the Patriarch of Constantinople, at that time the holy Tarasius. He also reported that, as the wonders became more widely known, no small number of men (having kissed [the world] goodbye) had flowed to the monastery, and that those who came could not be accommodated there because the place was altogether too small and incommodious. He found the holy patriarch was in agreement with his own idea; receiving from him the gift of a ruined place (which is now known as the Monastery of the Abramites), in a short time he built a monastery [*phrontistêrion*] on the foundations of it, for the salvation of many souls; and he equipped the saint to live out the rest of her ascetic career there. When [her transfer] was accomplished and her angelic way of life became well known to all, the secret gradually became known to such a degree that it is impossible to tell how many people came that way and were present there each day.

Then a trial [b40] befell the saint from one who wore the monastic habit, but who, to judge by his acts and deeds, manifested the principal characteristics of the malignant demon. This man, implacably undertaking the task, openly poured out against the saint violent and shameful accusations as if against a eunuch. She herself reckoned this to be of no account, but rather affirmed that what was being said against her should be to her credit. Now a certain god-fearing woman, hearing the wicked and evil utterances of that truly impure person (who afterwards turned out [b45] to be a murderer), said to him: "Take care brother, lest perchance she is not a eunuch as you say, not emotionally-passionate [*empathês*] as you imagine, but a woman, without passions [*apathês*]—and you have for a reward the hell of fire. For by deprecating passionlessness [*apathês*] you pollute those who hear. Some time ago, a woman divided out all her possessions and disappeared; perhaps she whom you say is a eunuch may be she, and you yourself conducting your soul into the pit of destruction." That evil and deceitful man then added this to his knavery: he abandoned his abusive railing and openly repeated these things [which the woman had said] to many people. He aimed to get the saint suspended in a sunken place so that (her garments being lifted up) he could see her naked and know for sure. He succeeded in doing this not long afterwards, but he saw nothing for by divine power she became half-withered [*hêmixêros*]. He rose up from there and went to his own [place] and there he was arraigned as an evil-doer on a charge of murder. His head having been inserted into a wooden branch as though in a noose, that fellow surrendered his wretched and filthy soul on what is locally known as "the fork" [= gibbet, gallows].

This brought some unwelcome publicity to the saint, so she fled from the scandal, taking only two monks with her. They ran away to the Stenos-district and, finding there a church with water and a garden, she took up residence there with the two monks, Eustathius and Neophytus. And setting out from there again after a certain time at the invitation of some monks in Byzantium in the [c45] Sigma-district, she lived out the remaining portion of her time in sanctity and in a way which is pleasing to God, conferring cures and no few wonders on those who came [there], and so she departed to join the Lord on October 27th.

[21] *BHG* 1322n

THE BOY CAST INTO THE FURNACE AND SAVED

1. ABBA BASIL, the anchorite-priest who became a monk of the New Lavra[n], told us that he had heard some friends of Christ recounting a wonder like this. In the land of the Palestinians there was a well-populated village in which there dwelt both Christians and Hebrews. They possessed large flocks and herds and this was their custom, handed down from [the time of] their forefathers: each day at dawn they used to gather the animals together at the gate of the village and each man would send either his son or his boy[n] with his own beasts. The young people would take the animals and also provisions for themselves. They would go out and stay in the field until evening. As the sun was setting, they would bring back [the flocks and herds].

2. Now one day, as they went forth as usual to pasture, they gathered together at meal-time and the children of the Christians said to each other: "Come, let us hold a Eucharist[n] like the clergy do in church". One of them took the role

of the bishop and he appointed one to be priest, one to be deacon, one subdeacon, and others to be readers. They set up one of the stones that was flat to serve as an altar and they offered the sacrifice [*prosphora*] out of the provisions they had brought along. Now with them there was a Hebrew, the son of the chief rabbi,[n] and he begged the children saying: "Let me [play] with you so that I can give [communion] like you do." They rejected him saying: "You cannot come with us for you are a Jew". He said: "I too can become a Christian". They said to him: "If you become a Christian, then we will accept you". When he agreed to this, they accepted him and the pretending bishop baptised him after they had found some water there. So they did everything in an orderly manner and offered the bread and, as they were completing [the service] and saying: "One is holy",[n] fire came down from heaven and consumed everything lying [on the altar]. [The children] were so afraid they fell down as though they were dead.

3. When evening came, the beasts went off, each to its own home. Early next day the neighbours went out and searched and they found the children lying half dead. Each one cared for his own child, and thus they brought them to their houses. They only just returned to their senses three days later; then their parents asked them what had happened to them. They confessed everything that had taken place, exactly as it is written above.

4. Bread was set before the chief rabbi's son and his father invited him to eat. But he would not agree to eat, saying: "I am a Christian and I will not feed [on this]." When that wretched fellow heard this he decided to hand his son over to bitter death. But God—who foresees [what will happen], who "tries the very hearts and reins," [Ps 7:10]—God, knowing the evil thoughts of that abominable [man], contrived for the magistrate[n] of the area, whom they call the emir, to

complain bitterly against the district bathhouse keeper for taking [his duties] too lightly and for failing to maintain the temperature of the bath [house] according to instructions. He said to him: "Just look how long you have been deceiving everybody! Whenever I come to bathe, I find it cold. I swear to you by the great god that if you do not obey instructions, and if [the bath] is found to be cold the next day [I come here], I will cut off your head." He undertook to do what would be of service to the emir.[n]

5. The father of the Hebrew child knew all about this. Convinced that [the child] was in the grip of a diabolical subterfuge, he sent to the bathkeeper (a man who was in debt to him) and said: "I am aware that you owe me ten pieces of gold".[n] "Yes, that is correct," came the answer. "If you will discharge the commission I am about to prescribe, I will excuse you this entire debt." 'In order to free myself of the weight of the debt, I will do whatever you require of me,' he replied. The lawless false priest said to him: 'I hear you have received an order from the emir to fire up the bath. I want you to tell me when the furnace is burning and you are about to close it up,[n] for I have a child who provokes me to anger. Then, no matter who it is I send to you asking, "Is the bath in order?" you are to seize him and hurl him into the furnace, shut it up and go away. This so that I may change his evil mentality." When the bathkeeper heard this, he agreed to do what was prescribed in the hope of gaining relief from his debt.

6. He came [to work] and, for fear of the emir's threats, he proceeded to make the furnace very much hotter than the usual heat. When he perceived that [it was time for] the furnace to be closed up, he sent a message to the chief rabbi who then sent his son saying: "Is the bath in order?" [The bathkeeper] said: "Master,[n] it is more than in order. If you don't believe me, look quickly"—and seizing the

child, he hurled him into the fire, closed up the furnace and went away.

7. The emir came to bathe and found the bath even cooler than on the former days. He called the bathmaster and said to him: "Did I not instruct you to heat the bath well? Why have you not obeyed, but have instead made it cooler?" He swore on his oath: "I laid out three times as much wood in my desire to please you and I just do not know why things are like this. If you do not believe my testimony, come and see the furnace and you will know from the number of coals that I am not lying." He went with him, fuming with anger, and when [the bathkeeper] uncovered [and removed] the slab of the furnace, he found the child sitting there as large as life. [The emir] said to the bathkeeper: "How does this child come to be here? How do you explain him having been thrown in there?" The bathkeeper explained everything to the emir and [suggested that] perhaps it was because the child had been unjustly thrown in that so great a flame in the furnace had died away.

8. The emir came to the conclusion that there was not a word of truth in what he was saying. He said to him: "Bring wood and heat up the furnace of the bath in my presence". While this was being done, the emir asked the child whose [son] he might be and why he had been thrown into the furnace. When he learned that this was because he wanted to be known altogether as a Christian and that he was unwilling to partake of Jewish food, he was beside himself with anger. Pouring derision on Christianity (for the fear of the Lord is an abomination to the sinner) *he* took the child and thrust him into the furnace saying: "Even if you put the fire to sleep by sorcery the first time, you will not escape from my hands now."

9. But God—who is always doing great and wondrous things, who is near to all who call upon him in truth—he

quieted down the flames of the furnace as before and kept the child safe. When the emir came back to bathe, the bath was found to be even cooler than before, as though it had remained a whole week without being fired up. Flabbergasted at this the emir went and opened the furnace of the bath and found the child sitting quite comfortably within. And there was not even the slightest smell of burning in the furnace. Utterly confused by the strangeness of this wonder, the emir went off at a run to make these things known to the person they call "the counsellor".[n] When he heard, he quickly came to the village, ordered the furnace to be fired up and the child to be thrown into it again, in his presence. He set a seal and guards[n] at the door [of the furnace] and went in to bathe. When he entered the bath [house], instead of the heat of the bath there was considerable coolness, so he came out immediately and opening the mouth of the furnace he found the child sitting in good condition. And there was no smell of fire in there. Then *he* questioned the child: whose son was he? When he learned that it was the false priest of the lawless Jews and what had happened [to the child] in the field (as it is written above) and that it was because the child had committed himself to and remained [faithful to] the confession of Christianity and would not allow himself to be polluted with the unclean food of his parents that he was delivered into such a deadly punishment of fire by his own father; [when he learned, furthermore,] that having already been three times hurled into the furnace of fire he had not been burned up but, on the contrary, it had comforted him just as the Babylonian furnace in ancient times [comforted] the three children, [when he learned all this], he brought the father of the child and said to him: "What excuse are you going to make to God for the devilish and filthy deed you have done? You thought you could escape the notice of God and of men. But God who knows your evil deeds and purposes did not grant his approval. On the contrary, he condemned the savagery of your soul. For if you were so heartless as to deliver the fruit of your loins to so bitter a death, what would you not have done if the right occasion had presented itself? Now, since you have committed this most evil deed and have contrived to make us accessories to your filthy undertaking, you shall suffer the death of evil-doers so that no other demon of like kind will work the same things in you [as this misdeed]." And saying this, he sent and ordered him to be beheaded outside the village in a desert place [and to be left there] as food for carnivorous beasts.

10. He summoned the children and learned exactly what play-acting had been done by them in the field. Then he put them in a monastery, making an allowance for each one according to the part he had played. To him who played bishop, a bishop's allowance; to those who played priests or deacons or subdeacons or readers, to each he ordered a support-allowance to be given approppriate to the rank of each one of them.

11. The God and Creator of all things was pleased to allow all this to happen for the help and support of us Christians, and to make known to all the peoples who oppose us out of evil intent the utter hatred of the lawless Jews for our Lord and God and his only begotten Son and for us who truly believe in him. For the prophecy of the Lord had to be fulfilled, [the one] which he made to those who lacked understanding: "I came in my Father's name and you received me not. Should another come in his own name, him you will receive and you will die in the sins of your evil deeds."[n]

[22] *BHG* 1318y

THE TWO BROTHERS

1. IN THIS GOD-PROTECTED city of Constantine there were two brothers, children of the same father and mother. By the machinations of the hostile adversary there arose such grudge-bearing [*mnêsikakia*][n] and hatred between them that the one had no wish to set eyes on the other.[n] While their mutual hostility remained still unplacated, it happened that one of the two died. When the other became aware of the sudden death of his brother, he was afflicted by terror more than man can bear. Confounded by mourning and lamentation, in self-deprecation he cried out: "Ah, wretched man that I am for never having kept so much as one of God's commandments, but having rather spent all my life in evil deeds. How can a grudge-bearing wretch like me, who did not forgive his own brother, go into God's temple, stretch out his hands in prayer and ask forgiveness of God the merciful, the lover of men?"[n] For many days he lamented bitterly, saying these and similar things. And then God the merciful,

the lover of mankind, *who wishes all men to be saved and to come to the knowledge of the truth,*[n] put into his heart the godly notion that he should go to Mount Olympus and declare all his transgressions (especially the sin of grudge-bearing) to one of the holy elders.

2. So he went and found a holy elder at whose feet he fell with great humility, and to whom he declared his sin of grudge-bearing. When the elder heard this he said: "Oh my child, have you not heard the divine words of the ever-memorable Ephraem[n] which he wrote concerning grudge-bearing, in which he states categorically that if two people bear a grudge against each other and one of them should chance to die while they are still in enmity with each other, they will find an implacable condemnation [awaiting them]. They will be despatched into outer darkness[n] as hated ones for having failed to heed the easy commandment which says: *love one another* and *forgive unto seventy times seven*".[n] When he heard this, the man said: "What am I to do, honourable father, that I might be acquitted of this charge before God the compassionate?" The elder said: "Believe me child, I am at a loss what to say to you concerning this matter. If you want to obtain forgiveness of this transgression, go to such-and-such a place on this mountain and there you will find what is called a chestnut tree. Wait there two or three days, for in the adjacent wilderness there dwells a holy elder, naked of body, who comes once a week to that tree to collect its fruit for food. Wait there in prayer and when the elder comes by, fall down and confess your transgression. Then do whatever he tells you to do and you will find pardon." When the man heard this, he made an act of obeisance to the elder and immediately made his way to the place which had been indicated to him.

3. He remained there three days as the elder instructed and on the third night a completely naked man came by. When

the one who was waiting saw him, he suddenly ran forward and laid hands on him, falling down at his feet and crying: "Have mercy on me, holy father". The other said: "Let me go; I adjure you by God, let me go!" Awe-struck and amazed, the man let him go, and the other, immediately turning in the other direction, said: "May God have mercy on you brother. All these years I have lived on this mountain and never suffered the like of this [affront]. Yet if you have something to say to my insignificance, throw me one of your garments to wear, for, as you see, I am a woman and naked." He took off a garment and threw it over his shoulder to her. She received it, put it on and came to him saying: "What do you want, oh man?" He said: "My holy mother, by the working of the enemy who hates all that is good, between me and my brother there came about a grudge-bearing so severe that we could not bear the sight of each other. While we were still bearing our grudges it came about that my brother died. After his death I perceived the enormity of my sin and came to this holy mountain. First I confessed my sin to a holy elder and he sent me to you, holy mother. Here in your presence I pray you to have pity on me, a sinner; and, if it be your will, to grant me absolution from my transgression." At these words that blessed woman said: "There is nothing I can do for you, brother. But return at once to the imperial city. Find such-and-such an arcade and the house of such-and-such a centurion. Go in and boldly confess your sin to him, then do whatever he says to you and you will quickly receive absolution." He replied: "Ah, wretched man that I am, my holy [mother], when you who serve God do not take pity on my miserable condition, but send me to a man of the world." But she said: "Go without delay, for you will hear no other word from me," and so saying she ran off towards the innermost part of the mountain.[n]

4. When he got to Constantinople he sought out the house of the centurion whom the holy woman had named. With

the help of God he found the man, who was busily occupied with his imperial responsibilities: the preparing and lading of transport vessels (for the emperor had ordered him to the western regions to supervise certain affairs). The visitor said to him: "I wanted to confess something to you, sir". The centurion replied: "You can see what toil and distraction assails me and you tell me such things. . . ." [The visitor answered] " . . . and I only wanted to say one thing to you, sir."[n] He said: "This evening, if I have time, you shall tell me what you want to." So [the visitor] waited around, and when evening fell, seeing the centurion at leisure, he told him all, including the enmity which he had towards his brother, his visit to Mount Olympus, his conversation with the elder and how the woman had sent him to the centurion. When the centurion heard this he replied: "You are deceived, brother; did you not just this day see what toil and distraction assails me? How can you say things like this to a man involved in secular activities and engaged in the imperial service?"[n] The visitor fell on his face and, grasping the centurion's feet, cried: "I will not rise until you take pity on me. Have mercy, for the sake of the God who said *Blessed are the merciful, for they shall receive mercy*".[n] The centurion said to him: "As I told you, I am a sinner and unworthy of heaven and of earth. But since you were sent by the holy woman and have come to me in faith,[n] come to the outer walls of the Great Church at the fourth hour of the night and you will find me there. The Lord will arrange things for you according to his will.[n]

5. As the centurion directed, the man came at the fourth hour and found him outside the sacred walls of the Great Church, standing in prayer. When he saw him, he made an act of obeisance to him; the centurion said to him: "Follow me". As he followed, they came to the outermost doors. Finding them closed, the centurion prostrated himself three times, at which they opened of their own accord. The [two

men] entered the temple without any of the guards being aware of it. The centurion said to the man: "Kneel down and pray". When they had both spent some considerable time in prayer, everything in that most sacred temple was bathed in light. Then, when they stood up from their prayer, another man was found there with them. The centurion said to his companion: "Do you know this man, brother?" Looking at him carefully, the other replied: "Yes, sir, it is my brother,"[n] and the centurion said: "Fall down before him and receive forgiveness from him." The other immediately fell on his face and said: "I sinned, brother; forgive me, for the Lord's sake." The brother said: "May God forgive you, brother." They embraced and kissed each other, weeping for some time; then the centurion said: "Are you now completely reconciled with each other? Very well then, since the Lord has arranged things for us according to his will, let us withdraw from this holy temple." As the two approached the doors of the temple to go out, the third, the brother who had died, became invisible to them. As they came through the innermost doors of the temple, these closed again of their own volition. The centurion said to the man: "Keep this to yourself, brother, and say nothing to anybody as long as I am living. After my departure from this life, do as you please."[n]

6. Now you see, my beloved brethren, it is not only those who embrace the monastic way of life and remove themselves from this life to dwell in hermitages and mountains who are well pleasing to God. Those also who live amidst worldly clamour and distractions, yet by good works and humility improve and rectify their souls, are most certainly distinguished in their service to God. In fact, whoever looks to his own soul's health and fears God is saved, in any place whatsoever. Glory to God the merciful, the lover of men . . . .[n]

[23] *BHG* 1442mb

THE JUDGEMENTS OF GOD
Mioni 6

THERE WAS A VIRTUOUS anchorite who called upon God saying: "Lord, make known to me what your judgements are". He demonstrated frequent [acts of] asceticism in support of this prayer, but God made it known to him that, for men, this was not possible. He still continued beseeching God by an ascetic mode of life; and as God wished to inform the elder, he allowed the idea to come to him of going to visit an anchorite who was settled not a few miles away. He got his sheepskin coat ready and set off. God sent an angel disguised as a monk who met the elder and said to him: "Where are you going, good elder?" The elder said: "To such-and-such the anchorite". The angel who was pretending to be a monk said: "I am going to [see] him too; we will travel together". When they had travelled the first day, they came to a place in which there dwelt a man who loved Christ. He received them [as guests] and put them up. Whilst they were eating, the man produced a silver dish [πατελίκιν, patella] and when they had eaten, the angel took the dish and made it disappear into thin air. The elder was disturbed when he saw that. Then going out together, they travelled the next day and in due course encountered another man who loved Christ and monks in the place where he dwelt. He received them as his guests, washed their feet and embraced them. Early next morning, he brought his son, the only child he had, to be blessed by them. The angel seized it by the throat and strangled it. The elder was flabbergasted, but he said not a word. The third day, although they travelled a great distance, they found nobody who would offer them hospitality. Then they found a long-deserted dwelling [αὐλή] where, sitting down in the shade of a wall, they partook of the dried-out crusts the elder had. And, as they were eating, the angel saw a wall about to collapse. Leaping up to safety, he began to take down the masonry and to rebuild [it]. The elder could bear it no longer; he swore at him, saying: "Are you an angel? Are you a demon? Tell me what you are; the things you do are not the sort of things a man does." The angel said: "What did I do?" The elder said: "Yesterday and the day before, those friends of Christ put us up. You not only made the first one's dish disappear; you also strangled the son of the other. And yet here, where we have found no rest, you stand doing the work of a labourer." Then the angel said to him: "Listen, and I will tell you. The first man who received us is one who loves God and manages his possessions in a godly way. That dish was left to him as the inheritance of an unjust man. I made that dish disappear, you see, so that he would not lose the reward of his other good [deeds] on account of it, and [now] his record is clean. And the other man who made us his guests, he is virtuous. Had that small child lived, it would have [grown up] to be an instrument of Satan, so that the good works of his father would pass into oblivion. So I strangled him whilst he was tender to ensure the salvation of the father, and that his record remain unassailable before God." The elder said: "And what about here?" The angel said: "The owner of this dwelling is a plague who seeks to harm many people; it grieves him that he cannot succeed in doing so. When his grandfather built this house, he put money into the masonry he was building. I restored the masonry, you see, so that he would not be able to harm those he intended to harm by means of the cash he would have found when the building collapsed; I deprived him of the means. Now go to [your] cell, for as the Holy Spirit says: *Thy judgements are like the great deep*".[n] Having said this to him, the angel of God disappeared. Then the elder returned to his senses; he went back to his cell, glorifying God.

NOTES ON THE TEXTS

Reference is made to each tale by number, then to the line of the greek text, *e.g.* 4/7 means the seventh line of Tale No. 4.

The 'W'-numbers refer to John Wortley, *A Répertoire of Byzantine 'Beneficial Tales,'* [διηγήσεις ψυχωφελεῖς] (forthcoming).

Except when it is expressly started to be otherwise, all the translations into English are the work of the author.

General title: This is found only in two manuscripts (**I** and **V**); the former, the earliest known Greek text, attributes the tales not to Paul, but to an otherwise competely unknown *Peter* of Monembasia. That this is an error on the part of the copyist is sufficiently clear from the facts that (a) whenever a bishop of Monembasia is elsewhere named as the author of tales (and this is frequently the case, even in manuscripts containing only one or two stories), the name of that bishop is never again any other than Paul. Moreover (b) the eleventh-century manuscript of the Arabic translation of the tales also names him Paul. Sauget renders the title thus: 'Histoires utiles qu'a racontées Bûlûs évêque de la ville de Mûnûfâsiyyah au sujet d'hommes et de femmes vertueux et soumis à Dieu' (Sauget, 'Le Paterikon', *Le Muséon* 82 (1969) 392, from Cod. Paris. Arab. 276, f.223).

spiritually beneficial tales [*diêgêseis psychôpheleis*]: the usual denomination of the genre (*narrationes animae utiles, récits utiles à l'âme*): *cf* John Moschos, *Introduction* to his *Pratum Spirituale*: 'The spiritually beneficial deeds of the fathers (*ta psychôphelê tôn paterôn . . . katorthômata*) *PG* 87:2852C). The teachings of Dorotheos of Gaza are referred to as *didaskalia psychôpheleis*; see *Dorothée de Gaza: Oeuvres spirituelles*, ed. and trans. L. Regnault and J. de Préville, *Sources Chrétiennes* 92 (Paris, 1963); *Dorotheos of Gaza: Discourses and Sayings*, translated by Eric Wheeler OSB (Kalamazoo, 1977).

men and women: in fact only Tales 1 and 4 of the ten which can confidently be attributed to Paul tell of godly women, but it is a feature of the later tales in general that they give far greater prominence to women than do the earlier ones. This tendency can already be noted in *Pratum Spirituale*, where there is significantly more mention of women than in earlier collections. There is evidence that attempts were made to isolate women's stories from time to time, *e.g.* Cod. Athen. B.N. 513 (*ca* 1300 ad)—our **A**, of which ff 195–283v is a section entitled: 'Spiritually beneficial *logoi* concerning honourable and holy women.'

Tale 1: *BHG* 1449, W701: THE THREE WOMEN WHO WERE DISCOVERED IN THE TIME OF THE EMPEROR CONSTANTINE [VII, Porphyrogenitus, 912–959].

It is to be assumed (though it is not said) that Paul heard this story at the Capital; and since (contrary to his usual practice) he does not say how it came to his ears, it may also be assumed that he did not hear it first hand from the *dioikêtês* (tax-collector) himself. Hippolyte Delehaye wrote of this story and of the remarkably close resemblance between this story and No.12 of the present edition (see *Mélanges d'hagiographie grecque et latine, Subsidia Hagiographica* No. 42 [Brussels, 1966] item 29, 'Un group de récits "utiles à l'âme'" [pp. 384–393]). He pointed out that the naked holy woman discovered in some remote place is a by no means uncommon *topos* in hagiographical literature. One of the earliest examples is to be found in *The Life of Saint Mary the Egyptian* (*BHG* 1042, *PG* 87:3697–3726) attributed to the Patriarch Sophronius of Jerusalem (*ob.* 638). Mary had an immoral youth; she went a-whoring to Jerusalem when it was still an imperial and a christian city, *i.e.* before 614. Then in repentance for her immorality she voluntarily withdrew into the wilderness where she remained until she was discovered forty-seven years later by a monk (note the resemblances so far to the 15th tale of the present edition, 'The Naked Nun', and *a fortiori* to its older form attributed to Cyril of Scythopolis, cited in the notes to that tale). From him she requests a garment to cover her nakedness; she asks for and receives Holy Communion and dies almost immediately afterwards.

However, if this is the distant ancestor of Paul's tales, there is a nearer one in *The Life of Saint Theoctista of Lesbos* (*AA SS Nov.* IV:224–233, *cf* Delehaye, 'La vie de sainte Théoctiste de Lesbos' in *Byzantion* 1 [1924] 191–200). This story was learned from an aged hermit by a certain Nicetas on the island of Paros, on his way to join Himerius' campaign against Crete in 906. Theoctista was a religious on the island of Lesbos; she was seized by Arabs whilst visiting her sister, but she was able to escape when they were on the then uninhabited island of Paros. After more than thirty-five years of living on the natural vegetation of the area she was discovered by Zosimus the hunter. She demanded of him a garment to cover her nakedness, for her clothes had disintegrated (*tôn rhakiôn moi dierrôgotôn*), and that he bring her the sacrament (*mian tôn achrantôn dôreôn*). A year later he was able to fulfill this second request; she then recited the 'Song of Symeon' (Luke 2:29–32) and so departed this life. Zosimus the hunter became Symeon the hermit and it was over thirty years later that he first divulged the story, to Nicetas. There are some expressions in this story which are echoed almost *verbatim* both in the first and in the twelfth story of the present collection. Delehaye (in the article cited above, 'Un group de récits') edited for the first time the text of yet another similar story ('The Two Brothers', *BHG* 1318y, W051; translated as No. 22 in the present collection) which shows even more striking resemblances to a number of Paul's stories.

For a useful study which touches upon the recurring theme of the monk who turns out to be a woman, see Evelyn Patlagean, 'L'histoire de la femme déguisée en moine et l'évolution de la sainteté feminine à Byzance', *Studi Medievali* s.III 17 (1976) 597–623.

Title: 'who were discovered'; the oldest greek manuscript (**I**) has *phôneuthentôn* ('noised abroad'?) but every other manuscripts which has been seen has *phanerôthentôn* ('brought to light') in some form or other. Sauget renders the arabic translation: 'dont la vie privée fut divulgée', ('whose private life became known').

The Athenian scholar, Christine Angelidi, has kindly supplied the very interesting variant reading of **A** (Athen. 513) here (absent from the microfilm, presumably because it is written in red:) 'Concerning the women who were found at the mountain near to Latros [*eis to oros plêsion tou Latrous*] in the days of the Emperor Constantine' (f.243).

1/1 Constantine VII Porphyrogenitus was born in 905 to Leo VI 'The Wise' (886–912) and Zoê Carbonopsina whom he married in 906. He reigned from 912 to 959, but from 920 to 944 he had as co-regent his father-in-law, Romanus Lecapenus, Romanus I 'the elder'. Constantine's son and successor was Romanus II 'the younger', 959–963.

1/3 *the Anatolic theme*: this was the largest and the most important of the original seven military and administrative districts (*themata*) of Asia Minor, consisting of almost the entire southern half of the anatolic plateau, bounded on the east by the Anti-Taurus through which the Cilician Gates opened. The western portion was reasonably fertile, but not so the eastern regions. This tale takes place in a mountainous region, hence in the east of the theme. It could not however have been too far to the east as this area became the separate theme of Cappadocia after 842. As the lady arrived by sea, the area to the east of Seleucia might be indicated for this is the only point at which the theme touched the coast (although this also became a separate *cleisura* after 842). The northern slopes of the *Toros Daglari* might be a likely location for this story.

1/4 The tax due: most monasteries had land which was farmed by peasants, and these had to pay the hearth tax (though until the time of Nicephorus I, 802–811, this was not always levied). See Theophanes, pp. 486–489.

1/5 Thus when Gregory of Nyssa came to Amissa, when the brotherhood heard of his arrival, 'the entire group of men came out of the monastery to greet me. It is their custom so to honour whom they are pleased to receive by going out to meet him'. (*Life of Macrina* c.16).

1/15 In 1/3 Kings 17:4–6 the Prophet Elijah is fed by ravens (bread in the morning and meat at night) at the Waddi Chorath where he was hiding. It is not unusal to find stories in which animals do the work of God, *e.g. Pratum Spirituale* c.21 (CS 139:15): 'Abba Gerontios, higoumen of the monastery of our holy father Euthymios, told me this: There were three of us who were grass-eaters [*boskoi*] living beyond the Red Sea, over towards Besimon. Once when we were walking around on the mountainside another grass-eater was walking along the shore of the sea below us. It happened that he met with some Saracens passing through the area. As they passed by him, one of the Saracens turned back and struck off the head of the anchorite. We saw all this from a distance as we were on the mountain. While we were grieving for the anchorite, suddenly a bird came over the Saracen, seized him and carried him up into the air. It then let him drop to the ground where he was turned into carrion'. Animals, and certainly black birds, are however sometimes demons in disguise: *e.g.* the two crows in *Pratum Spirituale* c. 105 (second part) which prevent an elder from entering the Holy Sepulchre (CS 139:84–85).

1/37 The relationship of the lady with her two former servants is clearly not one of equality if they stand and she sits; she calls them 'servants' (*therapainidai*-l. 65) and then 'these two sisters' (l.70). In *The Life of Macrina*, Gregory of Nyssa says of his sister when their mother joined her in her monastic life at Anissa: 'Having made sisters and equals of the slaves and servants that were with her . . .' (c.7). A little later (c.11) it is said that in that community they had all things in common, and there was no distinction of rank. Gregory has some hard things to say about slavery: see *PG* 44: 664B–668A. In his will, Gregory of Nazianzen left an income and two servants for Rusiana the virgin 'so that she might continue to live the life of a gentlewoman', (*Testament*, *PG* 37:392B, cited by Peter Brown, *The Body and Society* p. 264). Two servants would appear to be the necessary minimum for a basic standard of living for the gentry.

1/41 *prôtospatharios*: lit. 'first sword-bearer'; originally a commander of the imperial bodyguard, but later a high-ranking officer of the court.

1/49 'That utterance might be given unto me *that I may open my mouth boldly*', Ephesians 6:19.

1/55 *cf* the story of the maiden who was cultivating her virginity, but was accused of 'blasphemy' and of refusing to sacrifice to the gods. She was delivered to a brothel with orders that she was to be let out at three pieces of gold per day (3 x a *nomisma*; see note 2/34). She excused herself by claiming that she had 'a stinking ulcer (*elkos*, the same word Paul uses) in a hidden place. But wait a few days until I am well'. A young man came and paid four pieces of gold to have her for the night. He gave her his clothes in which to escape and he was subsequently put to death for his generosity (George the Monk, *Chronicon*, ed. De Boor pp. 479.13–480.14, but the story [*BHG* 1318h, W059] is in *Historia Lausiaca* cc.96–97 [see Butler's note] and elsewhere). In *Pratum Spirituale* c.205 [*BHG* 1445w, W370] a young woman (in Nau 52, a widow) excuses herself from sexual relations with a monk on the grounds of a bad odour, but no ulcer is mentioned (CS 139: 183–184).

1/76 'God the good, the lover of men' (*philanthrôpos*) is one of Paul's favourite expressions. The term *philanthrôpos* embraces men of either sex.

1/90–95 *cf* Theodoret, *Philotheos Historia* 19.4; Salmanes the recluse asks Theodoret the bishop to celebrate the Eucharist for him. Having commanded the necessary materials to be brought from the nearby village, using the deacons' hands in place of an altar, 'he offered the mysterious, divine and salvific sacrifice'. This instance is remarkable in that it is unusual; recluses do not seem to have built their devotional lives around the sacraments (but note Paul Euergetinos, *Synagôgê* 4.39.3, citing the Life of Saint Luke the Younger, † 953: 'How those who are in the desert are to partake in the absence of a priest'). Despatching someone to bring the wherewithal for the unbloody sacrice immediately before the death of a saint is something of a *topos*; thus did Barlaam despatch Joasaph (*Barlaam and Joasaph*, at the end of c. 39; tr. Woodward and Mattingly [London 1914 etc.] pp. 592–596) and *cf* Tale No. 12 below; also No. 16 although there the object of the quest is not specified nor the errand completed before the holy man dies.

1/95 The text makes it clear that it is the priest, not the higoumen—who might well not have been a priest—who celebrated the liturgy.

1/104–105 Job 34, 24 *LXX* (the Masoretic text varies widely): 'who understands things of which there is no trace, glorious and portentous matters *of which there is no number*'. *cf* Tale No. 12/101. The same phrase occurs at the end of *Pratum Spirituale* c.174 (CS 139:143).

1/105 The doxology is not found in the Arabic text.

Tale 2: *BHG* 1449c, W702: THE MAN WHO WAS CALLED TO ACCOUNT THREE DAYS BEFORE HIS DEATH.

This story is similar in some ways to No.13, below.

2/1 Here the author makes reference to his own experience as bishop at Monembasia, clearly indicating his close ties with the monastic life. Pardos-Peter is not encountered elsewhere.

2/5 It is curious that the will of his earthly father took precedence over his monastic obligations. A law of Leo VI (Nov. 6) allows a boy to become a monk as early as age ten, but he could not dispose of his fortune until fourteen, the legal age to do so. Were he to die before age fourteen, his slaves were to be freed and his property divided between his parents and his monastery. So there clearly was a period when the boy belonged (in a sense) both to the cloister and the world. But Pardos-Peter was already a priest when he came to be tonsured, so he must have been much older than fourteen; given the pastoral experience to which he testifies, probably very much older. On the whole, Leo's legislation made it easier to recover persons from the cloister: Under Justinian's legislation (Nov. 123, c. 35) a slave who became a monk without his master's permission could be reclaimed only up to three years after his profession. Nov. 10 of Leo VI abolished the three-year limit. But it may be going further than necessary to understand why Pardos-Peter returned home; it may have been no more than his willingness to obey the commandment 'honour thy father and thy mother'.

2/7 Eniklion: location unrecognised as yet.

2/9 The only reference to relics or to 'miraculous' healings in those stories which can reasonably be attributed to Paul.

2/10 It is understandable why Paul would want to keep with him a person with whom he could discuss such matters.

2/12 A revealing insight into the man's relations with one to whom he was both priest and friend.

2/18 That confession to a priest is a powerful agent against the powers of darkness is a favourite theme of Paul and of many tales.

2/34 A gold piece (*nomisma*): here and throughout these tales, as in all Byzantine literature from the fourth to the eleventh century, the *nomisma* (also later known as *solidus* and *bezant*) means a coin of 4.55 grams of gold.

2/52 The black-faced-ones (*aithiopes*) frequently appear in death-scenes, in the west as well as in the east. A small child expiring in its father's arms says he is afraid because 'black-men have come who want to take me away' (*mauri homines venerunt qui me tollere volunt*, Gregory, *Dialogues* 4.18; *cf quidam niger puerulus*, 2.4.2 and the *teterrimi vires* in 4.37.12). One could not begin to count how many times these evil *aethiopes* occur in the Greek tales, and this is very curious. Herodotus says that the Aithiopes (Ethiopians) are 'the largest and the most beautiful of all men' (3.20) and the most longevitous (3.114). Even though their name became a pejorative synonym for demons, it also continued to be used of them in its original sense: 'One could also see negroes (*aethiopes*) at that place practicing *askêsis* with the monks. Many of them excelled in the virtues. In them was fulfilled the text which says: "Ethiopia shall stretch out her hand to God' " [Psalm 68:31]—*Historia monachorum in Ægypto*, trans. Norman Russell, 8.35. It is tempting to wonder to what extent the opprobrium which was formerly associated with a dark face derived from this unfortunate misuse of the word *aethiops*, lit. 'black face'.

2/89 For a somewhat similar tale to this one, see *BHG* 1450m, W863: a notorious but reformed brigand falls ill in hospital (in the time of the Emperor Maurice) at Sampso. He weeps in penitence. His doctor has a vision of *aethiopes* who cast accusations in one side of a pair of scales whilst two angels set the man's tear-soaked sheet in the other side (*PG* 89:1112A–1116B, trans. J. Wortley in the forthcoming *Tales of Anastasios the Sinaïte* (Cistercian Publications) No. D02.

Tale 3: *BHG* 1449f, W703: THE MAN WHO MADE HIS CONFESSION TO AN HOLY ELDER ON MOUNT OLYMPOS.

Here Paul retells a story he heard from a monk named Sophronios from Bythinian Olympus. Bythinia is that land bordered by the Black Sea, the Bosphorus, the Sea of Marmora, and the River Sangarius, an area of mountains and forests opened up only in recent times. The highest point in a range of mountains covered with snow much of the year is that of Mysian (to give it its correct name) Olympus (2,280 m) which towers over Brusa and is often clearly visible from Constantinople, 112 km away. When restrictions on the monastic life were lifted after the Empress Irene became regent in 780, it appears that many men and women founded or entered convents in Bythinia in general (where many rich people had country estates) and on the slopes of Olympus in particular. It can therefore be safely assumed that it was at the capital or near to it that Paul heard this story, not in Monembasia.

3/4 In describing Sophronios' story as 'similar to something that is written in the holy *Book of the Ladder*' Paul has said nothing less than the truth. The text in question is in Grade VI of the *Scala Paradisi* (The Ladder of Paradise) by John Climacus (John of the Ladder), *ca* 570–*ca* 649 (*PG*88:681C–684C). There are important differences between the two. In the original story, which takes place in Egypt (possibly in Alexandria) a much more grandiose and formal confession is required of the penitent, and it is John himself, the author of the *Scala*, who questions the anonymous higoumen's decision to clothe him immediately. Sophronios' version reads very much like the re-telling of the original story by someone who had not listened too carefully to it, but had nevertheless retained a few phrases of the original *verbatim*. Had Paul actually known the *Scala*-version, it is doubtful he would have retained this one.

3/20 John 5:14, 8:11.

3/24 (and 31) penance(s) (*epitimion*, *-ia*). The same word is used in 9/44 to mean a suspension from clerical office. In *Pratum Spirituale* c.78 (*PG* 87:2934B; CS 139:61–63); Abba John, higoumen of the Giants' monastery [*sic*] at Theoupolis (probably Antioch,) says to a sinner: 'If you wish to be healed, tell me truthfully what deeds you have committed so that I can apply suitable *epitimia*. One does not apply the same treatment to a fornicator and to a murderer and to a sorcerer. Greed is treated in one way, but lying, anger, theft, adultery—each has its proper medication' (the last phrase is not found in the published Greek text, but it is in fifteenth-century Latin translation of Ambrogio Traversari, which was based on a better manuscript than the present edition). See also *Pratum Spirituale* c.192

where Gregory the Great is said to have laid upon a brother the penance of excommunication [*epitimion aphorismou*] for breaking a monastic rule which forbade the ownership of property (CS 139:165–166).

Tale 4: *BHG* 1449m, W704: THE WOMAN WHO CAME TO CONFESS TO ABBA NEOPHYTUS.

It is a curious feature of the *récits tardifs* that they use the title *abba*, father (which is common in the earlier tales and sayings) very sparingly. *Cf* Tale 7, 21, and 24, also Mark 14:26.

4/1 Note the care with which the person who told the tale is identified.

4/3 There was a monastery of a Saint Arsenios (or Arsakios) in Lazica, *i.e.* in the Caucasus (*Synax. CP.* 409, 42 and 889, 10) but this is unlikely to be what is referred to here. It is more likely to have been the house of a known Latronite monk of Constantinopolitan origins named Arsenios (see *BHG* 2046), probably in the vicinity of Miletos.

4/13 Luke 7:36ff In this tale the woman cites and acts out the Lucan version of the story, but it is the Matthean which is read out at the liturgy.

4/28 The abba does not think it improbable that she might be able to write; it is not clear whether she does not possess the ability, or simply cannot bring herself to write *these things*. In *BHG* 1318w, W009, (*de syncletica in deserto Iordanis*, believed by the editors to be sixth-century), the eighteen-year-old daughter of a distinguished Constantinopolitan writes two letters home explaining why she will not return. Two stories of sinful women who wrote down their sins have been preserved: *BHG* 258, W796, (in the Pseudo-Amphilochian *Vita Basilii*) and in the *Life* of Saint John the Almsgiver, c. 51 (*PL* 73:380–382, ed. Gelzer c. 59, ed. A.J. Festugière [Paris, 1974] 405–407, trans. 519–521). In both cases the paper is eventually found blank at the saint's intercession. The second story has some striking similarities with Paul's:

> 'If you really believe, woman, in God that by my unworthy intercession he will forgive you the crime of which you speak, confess it to me'. But she replied: 'O master, I cannot possibly say it, for no man could endure to hear it'. Thereupon the saint said to her: 'If you are ashamed to speak of it, go home and write it down, if you know how to write, and bring it to me'. She again replied: 'I really canot master'. Then the saint kept silent for a few minutes and afterwards said: 'Can you not write it down and seal it and bring it to me?'

which is what she did (trans. Baynes and Dawes, *Three Byzantine Saints*, c. 46 [London, 1948, Crestwood NY: SVS Press, 1977] 258).

4/29 1 Cor 14:25.

4/37 Rom 2:16.

4/38–39 *cf* Tale 6,13–14.

4/42 'covered with ulcers', *lelôbêmenos*. The word can mean either mutilated or leprous; in the latter case it seems to refer to a particular kind of leprousy known to Galen (see Liddell and Scott, *s.v*). That person so afflicted is cared for by a holy one is not uncommon in the tales; See *Historia Lausiaca* c.21: Eulogios the scholastikos took home a destitute man lacking hands and feet (*lelôbêmenos*) and cared for him for fifteen years. Then the patient started to rail on his benefactor. He was taken to Antony the Great who tongue-lashed him: 'Do you not know that it is Christ who waits upon you?' the saint asked. They returned in perfect charity, but Eulogios died forty days later and the sick man three days after him. In another tale, the Emperor Theodosius II is said personally to have bathed and cared for persons described as *kakoumenoi kai lelôbêmenoi* as a measure of his true holiness (whereas the lady in this story has her servants bathe the monk; but then she could hardly go into the men's bath house). See *BHG* 1445v, W512 *PO* 8:171–174. Daniel the Scetiote tended a *lelôbêmenos* in secret all his life long, in reparation for having once killed a man. But eventually he was seen feeding the unfortunate man (who had no hands) and wiping his mouth for him (*BHG* 2100, W460). When Naucratius, the younger brother of Basil the Great (and so of Gregory of Nyssa and Macrina) was twenty two, he withdrew to the river Iris with Chrysaphios his servant, where they served sick old men, sustaining them by their hunting skills, and this they did for five years until they (the young men) died, possibly in a hunting accident (Gregory of Nyssa, *Life of Macrina* cc.8, 9).

4/46 *Cf* 2/4 Kings 4, 9–10.

4/48 Generally speaking, bathing was frowned upon for monks. This is well illustrated by the following story from *Pratum Spirituale*: [c.80, 'A Spring Conferred on the Brothers of the Monastery Scopelos by the Prayers of their Abba, Theodosios]:

> We came to the monastery of Abba Theodosios at Scopelos. [Scopelos] is a mountain between inland Seleucia and Rossos in Cilicia. The fathers led us up beyond the monastery, about as far as an arrow could be shot. There they showed us a spring, saying that it gave a plentiful supply of excellent water and that it was a gift of God to them. 'It is not a natural phenomenon' they said, 'but a gift of God to us'. Our saintly father Theodosios the Great fasted at great length and poured forth tears, praying to God with many genuflexions that he would grant us the comfort of this water. In former times our fathers used to draw their water from the wadi. But God, who always 'fulfills the desire of them that call upon him' [Psalm 144:19], granted us the blessing of water through the prayers of our father. Two years ago some of the brothers asked the higoumen if they might construct a bath in the monastery. Our higoumen frowned on the suggestion, but he allowed it as a concession to the weakness of the brethren, but they only bathed in it the one time. For this, such a beautiful

> spring, which God had provided, promptly faltered and failed. It is no less than the truth when we tell you that we fasted a great deal and offered up a host of intercessions with many tears, yet no water came from the spring. It was dry for a whole year and we were in great distress. Then our father destroyed the bath and God gave us water again (CS 139:65).

This antipathy to bathing may explain why one of the great virtues of Isidore at the very beginning of *Historia Lausiaca* is that he never used the bath, but 'Poemen' (11) reproved a priest of Pelusium for defrocking some monks who bathed. There was no objection to using the bath in case of sickness, even for monks; *cf BHG* 1445n, and *BHG* 2102c W456 where Daniel the Scetiote severely reproves a brother in Alexandria for using the baths *when he was not sick*. The story goes on to show that the objection was not so much to the bath as to the nakedness which inevitably accompanied it. See Paul Euergetinos, *Synagôgê* 3.16: 'A monk should not take a bath without necessity nor should he remove his clothes' (eight extracts from various authorities are given to demonstrate this point). Thus:

> A brother was going to Scêtê, walking along the Nile. He was tired from his journey so, when it got to the hottest part of the day. he took his clothes off and went down into the river to bathe. A beast called a crocodile came in haste right away and seized him. An elder who had the gift of perception was passing and when he saw the brother taken, he cried out to the beast: 'Why are you eating the abba?' But the beast said to him with a human voice: 'I am eating no abba. I found a layman and I am eating him. There is no monk here'. Having made an act of obeisance to the [brother's] monastic habit, the old man went his way, deploring what had happened.

—Systematikon 18.53, translated from *SPD 3ème recueil & Tables* p. 106.

4/56 chapel [*euktêrion,*] lit. [house for] prayer. A private chapel with its own priest is mentioned again in Tale 9.

4/56 Matt 26:6.

4/61 Luke 7:36–50, John 12:1–3.

4/64 Luke 7:48.

4/73 1 Tim 2:4.

Tale 5: *BHG* 1075d, W705: THE POOR MAN WHO PRAYED AT THE CHURCH OF THE ALL-HOLY MOTHER OF GOD AT CHALCOPRATEIA.

This story has marked similarities to may others (*cf BHG* 1448z, W497, and *BHG* 1442m, W498 = Mioni 4 and 5,) but it so closely resembles *BHG* 1322g, W864 (*Synax. CP* 231.31–234.52) that it is difficult not to treat them as two versions of the same story. In the other, the characters are named: the pious and illustrious observer is John, the poor leather-worker, and his wife (Zacharias and Mary). The miraculous prayers take place only at the Great Church, and the poor couple live elsewhere (in one of the exceedingly small houses by the *martyrion* of Saint Julian). No meal is provided, but the *trimêsion* is mentioned (in a different context), likewise the *mariage blanc* and the division of earnings. There is a great deal about lights and the shining of them which is not to be found in Paul's tale. For further comment on this text see (most recently) Christina G. Angelidês, "'Ο Τσαγγάρης τῆς 'Αγίας Σοφίας" ("The Shoemaker of Saint Sophia,") *ΣΥΜΜΕΙΚΤΑ* 9 (Athens, 1994) 67–80.

5/1 The story comes from a very high-ranking civil servant, but the writer does not say he told *me* this. He could have heard it very indirectly—and it could have grown in the telling.

5/3 Far more churches at Constantinople (over one hundred thirty) were dedicated in the name of the Mother of God than in any other name and of these the church at Chalcoprateia was amongst the most illustrious. It was founded in the fifth century and was located a mere 150 m. from the Great Church. See Janin, *Les Églises et Monastères*, pp. 237–242. The *agrypnia* (vigil) could have been on any one of the twelve feasts of the Mother of God.

5/4ff The use of the present historic is very common in the tales. It is usually translated with a genuine past tense in English, but in this passage the translator has retained it as written to illustrate the lively effect the present historic can produce.

5/9 The Church of Saint John Theologos 'in the Diïpio' may have been founded by Heraclius in the seventh century. It was certainly functioning in the ninth and was significantly restored in the tenth. It survived the Turkish conquest, at which time it was turned into a menagerie. An earthquake ruined it in 1509. The exact location of this major shrine is disputed, but it appears to have been in the vicinity of the Great Church. See Janin, *Les Églises et les Monastères*, 2nd. ed., pp. 264–266.

5/15–16 There is a reference to 'workshops' (*ergastêria*) of the Great Church (Hagia Sophia) in Nov. 12 of Leo VI; these, it says, formerly provided services for the dead, but those are no longer needed. What services and why they are now redundant we cannot say, but maybe these abandoned premises are what is referred to here. On the other hand, the Novel says that the revenues of them still accrued to the Great Church, and as these amounted to 1100 (presumably *nomismata*) a year, either they were not by any means the dwellings of the indigent, or there were very many of them.

5/29 a small piece of gold, *trimêsion hen*. The *trimesion* was one-third of a *nomisma* (*solidus*), thus 1.5 gr of gold, probably six days' earnings for a moderately skilled worker. It was no mean allowance for supper for three. The coin ceased to be issued regularly after the reign of Constantine V (741–745) and the latest specimen in Warwick Wrath (*Catalogue of the*

Imperial Byzantine Coins in the British Museum [London, 1908] vol. I: p. xv) dates from the reign of Leo VI (887–912). H. Goodacre (*Handbook of the Coinage of the Byzantine Empire* [London, 1957] p. 12) says that, together with the *semissis* (half-*nomisma*), the *trimesion* went out of circulation in the tenth century. References to it are extremely rare in the tenth century: *cf Vita Sancti Andreae Sali* c.130 (*PG* 111:777C) and the note (45) of Janning. Other references to *trimesion* in the tales are in *BHG* 1448z, W497 W498; *BHG* 2102, W463; *BHG* 1322a, W529 (Nau 39) and *BHG* 1322g, W864.

5/59–60 *cf* Theodoret, *Philotheos Historia* 2.6 where Julian has slain a dragon. He tells James, his companion and successor: 'I will tell you how I slew it, but I forbid you to tell others until after my death because secrets of this sort cause pride and vainglory if they get out. But once I am freed from earthly passions, I have no objection to your telling what the grace of God can do'. See also *BHG* 1448za, pt.1, W275: *Pratum Sprituale* c.37 (*PG* 87:2888B; CS 139:27–28)

> Since he could conceal himself no longer, the bishop said to him: 'Give me your word that you will never tell anybody what you are about to hear from me as long as I am still alive and I will tell you about myself. But I will not tell you my name nor the name of my city'. The godly Ephraim swore to him: 'I will not tell anybody what you are about to tell me for as long as it pleases God to keep you in this life'. The the other said to him: 'I am a bishop. . . .'

At the end of Tale 12 (below) a similar injunction to silence precedes revelation.

Tale 6: *BHG* 1449g, W706: THE PRIEST SUSPENDED BY HIS BISHOP.

In the first five tales, the author very carefully indicates how he came by the narrative—a practice resumed in No. 10. But Nos. 6–9 have no such authentication, unless it can be assumed that the Peloponnesian governor in No. 9 himself told the story to Paul.

Tale 6 is one of a group of very similar stories turning upon the point that only he who bound can loose; *cf BHG* 1322 d, e, ea, W001, W005. In all these cases a deacon has been suspended by a priest who died. The reconciliation is effected by the intervention of a holy man: a naked desert father in one case, Nicetas Chartoularios in another. The structure is identical; it is not unlike the story given below of The Drunken Priest (No. 17). Two other stories are known which treat the same matter in a somewhat different way. *BHG* 1322v W040, ('Anastasius' 54): A priest banned by his bishop was martyred. The ruler of a city bought his relics [*sic*] and later a church was raised over the grave, but at the feast of dedication the coffin moved out of the church when the celebrant said 'Peace be to all'. Only when the original bishop absolves the dead man can the coffin be made to stay in the church. In *BHG* 1449s W039 a monk of Scêtê is condemned by his spiritual father for disobedience. His coffin departs at the words 'Let all the catechumens depart'. Only he who bound can loose, they say, and the spiritual father is summoned to set matters to rights. What makes the existence of these stories very surprising is that there is a precise regulation which seems to render them superfluous. It is the thirty-second of the so-called 'Apostolic Canons'. Only he who bound can loose, it says, *except* he [the one who bound] be dead. (Nothing is said though of one who dies under a ban, as in the two last cases mentioned above). It might not be impertinent to draw attention here to *Pratum Spirituale* c.192 where an unfortunate monk dies under the penance of excommunication [*epitimion aphorismou*] imposed by Gregory the Great (†604). The pope had a prayer of absolution read over the brother's grave. The same night the higoumen had a vision of the dead brother. 'Where were you until today?' he asked him. 'In prison, sir, and I was not set free until yesterday', came the reply. This assured everybody that the post-mortem absolution had been effective (CS 139:165–166).

The 'Continuator of Theophanes' (Theodore Daphnopatês?) writing after 961 but probably not long after, *i.e.* a near-contemporary of Paul of Monembasia, included an anecdote in his work which has something in common with this and other tales in the present collection. After being deposed and exiled to the island of Protê as a monk (in 945)

> the Emperor Romanos [I Lecapenos] saw two eunuchs clothed in white while he was asleep. Taking him by the hands they led him, naked, into the Tricymbalon [apparently a part of the Great Palace.] The ball-court was filled with fire and this was being spread around by many infernal beings. And he saw the Mother of God coming to him and telling the eunuchs about his [works of] mercy. The Mother of God clothed him and led him into the Tropicam. The Lord Constantine (who was slain) went by in bonds and so did Anastasios the Metropolitan [bishop] of Heracleia, both of them led by infernal beings. These handed them over and cast them into that fire. The day on which the emperor saw the dream, that same day both those men died. [lacuna?] The Emperor Romanos sent to all the monasteries and lavras, likewise to the Holy City and to Rome, and he summoned holy monks to the number of three hundred. On Maundy Thursday he put on the tunic and vestment he used to wear [as emperor] and stood in front of everybody in the church when the priest was about to elevate the divine and holy bread. And he had written all his sins in a document which he bore; now he declared them publicly before them all. The monks cried out: 'Lord, have mercy', and shed tears. Making an act of obeisance to each one of them, [Romanos] asked his forgiveness. All the monks granted him forgiveness; the communion was

> [distributed] and then they went into the refectory. A scourge was given to a youth who whipped his feet, saying: 'Come into the refectory, wicked old man [*kakogêros*]'. When all were seated, the emperor sat down, weeping and lamenting. The document in which his sins were inscribed he sealed and sent to the remaining [*sc.* at home?] monks likewise to the saintly Dermocaïtês, sending also some money [two *kentênaria*]for the monks at Olympus so that they would pray for his spiritual salvation. When Dermocaïtês received the document and the money he ordered all the monks to fast for two weeks and to pray for [Romanos'] sins. While Dermocaïtês was standing at prayer one night, a voice came to him from an invisible source: 'God's love of man has triumphed'. Having heard this voice three times, he took the document, opened it and found it clean, without even a single [letter] on it. He summoned all the monks and showed it to them, whereupon they glorified God. All the monks granted remission [*aphesimos*] and sent [the document] to the Emperor Romanos. It was buried with him.

(*Theophanes Continuatus* 4.4, *CSHB* 33: 438,20–444,14; also in *PG* 109: 456C–457C).

6/2 censure: *epitimion*.

6/14–15 *cf* Tale 4,38–39.

6/29–30 *cf* Job 5:9, 9:10.

Tale 7: *BHG* 1449nb, W707: THE PRIEST WHO FELL INTO FORNICATION.

In the *Philotheos Historia* of Theodoret (†*ca* 466) there are several instances of monks who incarcerated themselves in dark little dungeons of one kind or another and loaded themselves with heavy chains. In fact most of the men mentioned seem to have been *egkleistoi*, *i.e.* recluses, solitaries. Acepsimos (c.15) was sixty years in such an *oikiskos*, but he came out once a week to draw water. Eusebios (18.2) walled himself in, but his cell had no roof. Tombs (6.7–10, 9.3–4) were also used by these recluses, but their way of life did not go unchallenged. Eusebios was strongly reproached by a certain Ammianos for failing in his duty to his neighbour (4.4). It worked for a little while, but then he re-entered his cell, placing such heavy irons on himself that he was forced always to look down. This was to frustrate the demons, he told Acacios (4. 6–7). ('The monk's cell is the furnace of Babylon where the three children found the Son of God and it is the pillar of cloud in which God spoke to Moses', Nau 206 = Pelagius and John 7.38. Compare the introductory notes to Tale No. 21, below).

This tale is one of several about unworthy priests, most of whom have fallen into the sin of *porneia*—a notoriously difficult word to translate—meaning any forbidden sexual activity in thought, word, or deed. Tale No. 9 (*BHG* 1449e), Tale 17 (*BHG* 1277a/1449q W717), and *BHG* 1449p W067 (described in notes to Tale 17) and 1449pb W055 (mentioned below) all have a common theme: *porneia* disqualifies a cleric from exercising his ministry. Thus the bishop who had a jewish mistress (*BHG* 1442n, W008) withdraws to a monastery; the one who got his nurse with child (*BHG* 1322h, W527, Nau 032) into the desert. Each subsequently distinguished himself in piety. Agalianos of Imbros was a priest and only twenty years old when his wife died (*BHG* 1318m, W012) so he consoled himself with a girl of the parish and tried to get round the regulations by celebrating the Liturgy, but always having his disciple [*mathêtês*] receive communion in his stead. This went on until one day the sanctuary doors closed in his face at the Great Entrance, and opened only when he promised to desist from the exercise of his office. This is not, however, because the ministrations of an unworthy priest are thought to be *invalid* that he must desist; two stories make this very clear: Anastasius LVI and Nau 254 (Pelagius and John 9.11). The latter recounts the vision of a thirsty anchorite who sees a golden well, bucket, and cord. A leper comes and offers him water from the well, but he refuses until a heavenly voice commands him to drink (*cf* Acts 10:9–16). The stories make it clear *why* the ministrations of unworthy clergy are valid; it is not they who minister, but angels who stand in their stead. In *BHG* 1444v, W117 (Anastasius XLIX) a Cypriote priest accused of all manner of sacrilege (but not of *porneia* in this case) admitted everything *except* defiling the Eucharist for (he said) whenever he went to celebrate the mysteries, an angel came and bound him to a column, performing the rite himself (this *ca* 625 *AD*; there is a very similar story of a Constantinopolitan deacon, *BHG* 1444v *bis*, W117). In *BHG* 1317g, W007, a Saracen woman, a priest's mistress, sees him bound and replaced by an angel at the altar and so does the bishop's Jewish mistress in *BHG* 1442n, W008; see Tale No. 9 (below) for the replacement of an unworthy priest (bound) by an angel at a baptism.

Paul of Monembasia clearly believed that *porneia* in a priest was unforgivable and resignation of his orders was the only possible course. He would have endorsed this passage in Tale No. 17,63–65: 'Even though you raise the dead, you are not worthy to wear a stole or to celebrate the liturgy or to perform any priestly function'. This was not altogether the universal belief; in *BHG* 1322hb, W017 (very similar to Nau 31) a bishop who has fallen into *porneia* confesses publicly and resigns, but the people wish him to remain. He lies down and says he will not be bishop of anybody who fails to trample him underfoot. When all have done so, a heavenly voice signals that he has been forgiven, for his great humility. This, however, is exceptional. But see the summary of *BHG* 1449p in the notes to No. 17, below. There a priest is eventually forgiven a single and inadvertent act of adultery—after three years of rigorous penance. More typical is the story in the as yet unpublished *BHG* 1449pb, W055: *de sacerdote indigno* (very similar to an early story in the *Vita Benedicti*, Gregory, *Dialogues*, 2.16.1–2) of a priest who continued to function after he had fallen into *porneia*. The Lord allowed an evil demon to seize him, which only Benedict himself could eject. And it returned the moment he disobeyed the saint's command by eating meat or resuming his priestly function, finally to become inejectible.

The present story of an unworthy priest has two close parallels, both found in the 'systematic' collection of apophthegmata, also known as 'Pelagius and John'. The first concerns a monastic deacon who, falling into sin, crawled into the innermost hidden place (*kruptêrion esôteron*) of a cell saying 'bury me alive' (*PJ* 5.26, Nau 177). This story has a happier ending though: when the Nile refused to rise, they brought him out, and at his prayers it did rise; his forgiveness is assumed. In *PJ* 5.41 (Nau 175; *BHG* 1449y, W550) an anchorite (not a cleric) who has fallen into *porneia* seals himself up in his cell for a year and then receives a signal that he is forgiven.

7/6 2 Peter 3:9.

7/12 'trampling on my own conscience': the identical expression occurs in 9/49.

7/39 John 6:37.

Tale 8: *BHG* 1449b, W708: THE THREE MONKS TAKEN PRISONER IN AFRICA.

Of all the tales of Paul this is the most unusual. For one thing it takes the reader to distant Italy and to even more distant Africa; it is both the longest story and the only one which introduces Moslems.

8/1 Calabria, the 'heel' of Italy, was still an effective part of the Empire in the tenth century.

8/2–3 Both this tale and the next one clearly indicate that boys could still be bought and sold. By Nov. 6 of Leo VI the boy could become a monk at the age of ten, so he may still have been under that age. The text says nothing of the monk's intention of adopting the boy, but it is worth noting that in the time of Leo VI (Nov. 24) adoption became a somewhat tighter bond than ever before: adoptive and born children were forbidden to marry each other on the grounds that adoption took place by a religious ceremony which made them fully and truly the children of their adopting parent(s), hence blood brothers and sisters of their adoptive siblings.

8/21 One hundred *nomismata* is a very large sum of money, 455 gr of gold. A semi-skilled labourer would have to work eighteen days to earn one *nomisma*.

8/23 There may be a *lacuna* at the beginning of the second paragraph for, as the text stands, 'the market place' makes little sense.

8/33 The miraculous paralysing of an arm raised to strike is an old theme of the tales, e.g. *Pratum Spirituale* cc. 15, 70, 133 (CS 139:11, 53, 109). For the prototype [?] see the story of The man of God from Judah and King Jereboam in 1/3 Kings 13, 1–10. But at the prayers of a righteous person far more than limbs could be immobilised. In *Historia Monachorum in Ægypto* 6.2 robbers are immobilised (CS 134:68); in 8.24–29 an entire pagan procession; in *Historia Lausiaca* c.31 an entire enemy host (p. 74); and in *Pratum Spirituale* c.83 a ship (CS 139:66–67). See also Theodoret of Cyrrhus, *Historia religiosa* 15.2.

8/35 Prince of Believers: the Greek text has *oumurmnê[n]* (sometimes oumêrmnên). Assuming this to be an arabic word and allowing for the customary distortion, the most likely equivalent that the Arabists amongst the writer's friends have been able to suggest is [Amir-] al-Muminin, an honorific title for a leading citizen meaning 'Prince [or Emir] of Believers'. Cf ἀ ερου ν ῆς in John Scylitzes *Synopsis Historiarum*, ed. J. Thurn (Berlin 1983) 42.15; 67.13 and 20; 74.2 and 24, etc.

8/38 'the sole witnesses': *monomartyres*, apparently an advisory council to the 'Prince of Believers', both religious and secular in character—as one would expect in a Moslem context.

8/44 *Cf* Dan 4.34a.

8/52 'Good old man', *kalogêros*, could equally mean *monk*.

8/66 *monerion* appears from the context to be an arabic word, but my colleague Professor Martin Stern, an experienced *arabissant*, can think of no semitic root from which it might derive. If it were greek word, one would immediately think of *moneretês*, one who rows alone, which looks promising but clearly does not fit: this *monerion* was a large vessel (sloop?). This might be the Saracens' attempt to say *monoreme*. We know there were biremes and triremes having two and three banks of oars respectively; why not the monoremes with but one bank? Such a vessel might well have been called *monoremium* in Italy, which might easily have become *monerion* in passing (1) into another language and (2) into the writer's Greek. I am guessing. It is just possible that *Monerion* is a proper noun, i.e. the *name* of the ship, in which case the root could just suggest the Prophet's birth-place, Medina. There the trail gives out.

8/85–86 *Cf* John 2:7, 2/4 Kings 2:19–22. The story of Theodore the Eunuch in *Pratum Spirituale* c.173 is similar, but he made the sign of the cross over the sea. Then he made the sailors draw what they would, and it was fresh water (CS 139:142). A similar situation arises in c.174; Gregory the anchorite urges prayer and this provokes heavy rain (p. 143).

Tale 9: *BHG* 1449e, W709 THE CHILD WHO HAD A VISION AT HIS BAPTISM.

This is basically another unworthy priest story, but it has some interesting details, not the least of which is the precise dating (*cf* Tale 1) which is very unusual in tales.

9/1 Leo (VI) 886–912 and Alexander 886–913.

9/2 Peloponnese: The Theme of Peloponnesos was created by Nicephorus at the beginning of the ninth century with its capital at Corinth. The person in this story, however, is not *the* governor (*stratêgos*) who would have his seat at Corinth, but *a* governor (*archôn*) who could have been located at any centre in the Theme.

9/2 Slav, *skythês:* Scythian usually means Slav in middle-byzantine literature. The Slavs occupied most of the Peloponnesian hinterland (and the entire Balkan penninsula) in the sixth-seventh centuries but they were gradually assimilated by the Empire in the course of the ninth century. No doubt pockets of un-assimilated Slavs remained and it is not impossible that these were on occasion compelled to sell their children into slavery. The alternative explanation is that the child was a prisoner from the wars against Bulgaria, but these wars did not fare well in Leo VI's time. The child was only ten at the time of the story, and it is unlikely that soldiers would have troubled to bring away a small child; moreover an *archôn* would not have thought a Bulgar could be a Christian at that time. He might very well (on the other hand) have thought that all the Slavs *inside* the Empire were.

9/3–4 The *archôn* is sufficiently affluent to afford his own priest and chapel. He apprentices the child to the priest it would seem, no doubt so that he could serve his master more efficiently after having learned to read and write. *Cf* the case of Saint Andrew the Fool c.2 (*PG* 111: 629D–632B) a Slav and a slave who was taught his letters so he could (as he did) serve his master as *notarios*. His *vita* is a notorious fiction but fiction rarely reflects what was unknown.

9/8 It is curious that the child *knew* he had not been baptised for infant baptism was the norm. This he must have been told, which would suggest that 'the Slavs from whom he came' made something of the fact that they were not Christians, which might again point to Bulgaria.

9/9 Small children receive holy communion far more often than most adults in the Orthodox Church.

9/18 It would appear that the baptism took place within the context of the eucharistic liturgy.

9/29 For another case of angelic baptism, see *Pratum Spirituale* c.207 (CS 139:185–187).

9/37ff. The dialogue between the *archôn* and his chaplain is very interesting, for it is the former who assumes the role of pastor and mentor to the latter.

9/44 What the priest's fault was is not specified. By analogy with other stories one would assume *porneia* (any sexually related sin) but this is not stated nor do any of the manuscripts add it.

9/56–57 1 Peter 1:12.

Tale 10: *BHG* 1449h, W710: THE MONK IN THE CAVE.

In some ways this is the most curious story in the collection. It is wholly monastic in character but it also deals with more than one monastic theme. The monk who over-reaches himself is a well-established figure in the tales, the most striking instance being *BHG* 1450x, W629, Nau 620 (Tale No. 19, below). That is about a monk whose spiritual pride is his own undoing, blinding him to the realities of his pilgrimage. This story deals with the same theme but goes further. It also deals with the relationship between the monk and the monastic community and has some obvious but not often stated things to say. The most appealing aspect of the story is the extraordinary glimpse it afford us of the caring nature of the higoumen. As father of the community he could simply have refused the brother's request. Or, having granted it, could have left the monk to the consequences of his folly. But, like a wise father, he gives the monk the rope he asks but then, at considerable pains to himself, intervenes to stop him hanging himself. The reader is left to suppose that in this way he secured a sober, useful member for his community. It is a touching story, for the compassionate side of eremitic monachism is not often openly revealed. *Cf* Paul Euergetinos, *Synagôgê* 1.41: 'It is dangerous for inexperienced [monks] to live alone', proposition supported by eight citations, *e.g. PJ* X.110 (Nau 243), Theodore of Pherme 16, Poimên 96, Heracleios 1, and the following unrecognised apophthegm (Evergetinos 1.41.1.2):

> An elder was asked: 'How is it possible for a man to live alone?' and he answered: 'Unless an athlete compete against many he cannot learn how to win, so that he can do battle one-on-one with the adversary. And the monk, if he does not compete with the brethren and gain mastery over his dark-thoughts [*logismoi,*] he can neither live alone nor withstand the onslaught of his dark thought'.

Unlike most of the stories of Paul, No. 10 does not seem to have any obvious sources in the tales-tradition, but *cf* 14448i (= Nissen 7) which has some curiously similar traits. The notion that demons could appear as angels is not unknown, but it is rare. Only two other instances come to mind: in one, the disguised demons call a brother to the church service and show him bright light. He consults an elder who recognises the strategems of the evil ones and successfully warns him off (Nau 224 = Pelagius and John X.93; there is more to this story but it is not pertinent here). The other story is a very tragic one: demons disguised as angels completely deceive a brother living in the desert. One day his father (*i.e.* the man who begot him) comes to visit him and the demons persuade him that the father has come to kill him. The monk seizes an axe and slays his father, whereupon an unclean spirit sets on ***him*** and strangles him (Nau 480). Neither of these is exactly a remarkable tale, especially in comparison with the story of *The Monk in the Cave*. It will easily be observed that this has most of the characteristics of the *récit tardif*; it is not a simple one-act drama so to speak, but a careful working-out of a situation to a satisfactory conclusion. In this respect it contrasts sharply with *BHG* 1450x (No. 19) where a monk falls victim to his pride and is eventually destroyed by it. Monastic readers would not fail to note the difference: the monk in *this* tale is saved because he belongs to a community which has a loving father. The monk of *that* tale seems to be completely on his own, hence a helpless victim of whatever the forces of evil choose to do to him. It also seems as though in this tale, as in no other, Paul manages to bring his characters alive and to give them three-dimensional attributes which render them credible. This is something which can be said of very few tales in the entire tradition; it is achieved by the quality of the dialogue; note especially the interlocution with the angel/demon in c.2.

10/1 Gregory: the Arabic rext reads 'Sergius'.

10/17–18 John Climacus, *Scala Paradisi* Grade I, c.22 (*PG* 88:641B–644A) quoting Ecclesiastes 4:10.

10/20 Matt 18:20.

10/32 'For Satan himself is transformed into an angel of light', 2 Cor 11:14.

10/34 After the temptation of Jesus, 'angels came and ministered unto him', Matt 4:11.

10/66 2 Peter 3:9.

10/103 *Pallium,* also known as *himation,* is a dark cotton mantle worn by monks and nuns. 'Habit' would be a reasonable translation here. It is not to be confused with the broad stole of the same name wrapped around the shoulders of eastern bishops and the smaller version of it conferred on western archbishops by the pope.

10/109 Simon Magus: Acts 8:9–25.

10/115 Reference has already been made to this passage (in the Introduction) which, together with its full doxology, seems to suggest the conclusion, not merely of one tale, but of a series of tales.

10/117 Prov 4:23.

10/121 1 Peter 1:17.

Tale 11: *BHG* 873n, W711: THE MAN WHO CONFESSED TO AN ICON OF OUR LORD JESUS CHRIST.

As we noted in the Introduction, this and the three following tales may not be by Paul of Monembasia; on the other hand, it cannot be certainly alleged that they are not.

11/1 Saint John Chrysostom (*ca* 347–407), Patriarch first of Antioch, then of Constantinople, died in exile. His relics were later translated to the capital where he was buried near the sanctuary of the Apostles' Church. His tomb was held to have powerful healing properties as was the myrrh which it exuded.

11/17 There is the testimony of a poem by Constantine the Rhodian written between 931 and 944 that there was already an image of Christ on the ceiling in the middle of the Church of the Holy Apostles by his time (ed. F. Legrand, *Revue des Études grècques* 9 (1894) 32ff; see lines 626ff and 737ff, trans. Cyril Mango, *The Art of the Byzantine Empire 312–1453* [London 1972] p. 200). It may have been put there in the time of Basil I (see Henry Maguire in *DOP* 28 [1974] 121–122) but little else is known of it. A later (twelfth-century). *Pantokrator* in the same location is also said to have inspired a confession: see Maguire, p. 133, and Mango, p. 232. (This note was graciously contributed by Professor Maguire and Dr Jane Timken Matthews).

11/30 1 Tm 2:4.

11/32 Ez 18:23.

Tale 12: *BHG* 1449a, W712: THE WOMAN FOUND ON AN ISLAND WITH HER SON.

This appears so obviously to be an alternative version of Tale 1 that it seems improbable it would have appeared in the same collection. And yet in *Pratum Spirituale* c.205 (CS 139:183–184) is almost certainly a doublet of c.39 (pp. 29–30).

12/1,2 Of Mark the Monk and the monastery he is said to have founded nothing else is known. The Church of Saint Agathonicos, however, is well known: it was an important building, already old when Justinian restored it, located in the central district of Constantinople known as Kainoupolis [Janin, *Églises et monastères*, pp. 7–8.]

12/25 *Helladôn*: lit. 'I am from the country of the Hellads', presumably meaning the theme (military district) of Hellas which together with the themes of Thrace, Macedonia, and the Peloponnese accounted for what is today Greece, the southern Balkans, and European Turkey.

12/26 Larissa, the capital of Thessaly, was in the Helladic theme.

12/25–30 *Cf Didascalia Apostolorum* XVII (iv) 1, speaking of the responsibility of Christians to adopt orphans: 'Whoever has a son, let him adopt a girl; and when her time is come, let him give her to him for wife that his work may be completed in the ministry of God. But if there are any who are unwilling to do this because they would please men and by reason of their riches are ashamed of orphan members . . .' (ed. and trans. R.H. Connolly [Oxford, 1929] 152–153). This early third-century text seems here to prescribe and foresee a very similar situation to that which the lady describes, but see the note on 8/2–3 above: the marriage would not have been allowed after Leo VI's new legislation.

12/50 'I found a boat', compare the curious story of *The Drowning of Mary, Pratum Spirituale* c.76 (*PG* 87:2928–2930; CS 139:57–59). A single woman could apparently find passage on a ship without difficulty. Notice that the lady of Tale No. 1 (line 70) also made her get-away by sea.

12/56 Psalm 105:5.

12/94 'say nothing of what you have seen'; see the note on 5/58–59.

Tale 13: *BHG* 1449k, W713: THE WOMAN WHO DIED AND CAME BACK TO LIFE AGAIN.

This story should be compared with a tale of Gregory the Great (*Dialogues* 1.12.1–3) in which Severus the Priest arrives too late to attend a dying man. As he prays, the corpse revives and tells how *taetri homines* drove him hence but were stopped by *pulchrae visionis iuven* ordering him to be taken back because the priest was weeping. Thus the man gained seven days' remission for repentence; he died joyfully on the eighth day.

Another somewhat similar tale is told by John Rufus, Bishop of Maiouma, in *Plerophoriai* c.38: Ammianus the *scholasticos* had a good but dyophysite wife who fell gravely ill. In a vision angels lead her into a dark stinking place of tears, then to a place of light and glory. 'These are of your husband's (monophysite) faith; the others are of yours', they say, and offer her a one-year extension of her life if she opts for his. She does, and he joyfully welcomes her back to life—for one year exactly.

13/40 Lk 16:20.

Tale 14: *BHG* 1175, W714: BLESSED MARTHA THE ABBESS.

Title: Blycharos: could also mean 'the brackish water'.

14/60; **V** and the manuscript used by Janning (**J**) continue: 'These things were composed by the aforesaid Paul, bishop of Monembasia, a man born and raised [*gennêma kai thremma*] in the same city', but this reading is not supported by the other manuscripts. Nor is it to be found in the text of Cod. Paris. Arab. 276, the ending of this story there being rendered thus by Sauget: 'elle s'en alla vers notre Seigneur et lui demanda [*sic*] la récompense précieuse et éternelle pour son ascèse et sa patience'.

The following tales (Nos. 15–23) are anonymous. They are included to illustrate the genre of the *récit tardif*, the kind of tale Paul tried to write—and might even have pioneered.

Tale 15: *BHG*1449x, W509: THE NAKED NUN (*DE CANONICA NUDA*).

Introductory note: This story and the one following were included in the French edition of Paul's tales, not because there was the slightest likelihood that they were written by Paul, but because they are striking examples of a yet more developed form of the *récit tardif* than that which Paul used. They represent *a fortiori* two separate tendencies respectively which can be seen in Paul's work: the expansion of an existing tale (No. 15); and the combination of several tales into one narrative (No.16). As Hippolyte Delehaye pointed out ('La vie de sainte Théoctiste de Lesbos', *Byzantion* 1 [1924] 191–197) there is a simpler version of this story which can be dated with some accuracy. It is in the *Life* of Cyriacus, anchorite in Palestine, who died in 556, written by Cyril of Scythopolis, who was his contemporary [*AA SS* sept. viii: 147–158, and ed. A.B. Schwartz, *Kyrillos von Skythopolis*, in *Texte und Untersuchungen* 49.2 (Leipzig, 1939) 222–235; translation by R.M. Price, *Cyril of Scythopolis: The Lives of the Monks of Palestine*, CS 114 (Kalamazoo, 1991) pp. 245–261]. As this narrative may have connections with several tales in the present volume, it may not be inappropriate to give the relevant passage in translation.

> [c.17, continued] I think it right to recall here some spiritually beneficial tales which Abba John told me whilst we were travelling through the wilderness. He showed me a place which he said was the tomb of the blessed Mary. I was amazed at this and asked him to explain to me about her. He answered: 'Not long ago, I and my disciple, Abba Parammôn, were going to visit Abba Cyriacus. Looking from afar, we saw something which had the appearance of a man standing by a wild tamarisk and we thought it was one of the reculses in that place, for there were then many recluses in those parts. So we made haste to make an act of obeisance to him. [c.18] As we approached the place, he disappeared. Torn with fear and cowardice, we stood and prayed, thinking him to be an unclean spirit. When we had finished the *amen*, we looked around here and there and found an underground cave into which we suspected the true servant of God had slipped down and was hiding from us. When we were beside the cave we began calling to him and beseeching him, saying: 'Father, do not deprive us of your prayers and of your good company'. He finally, but only just, replied: 'What do you want of me, for I am a woman?' And she asked us, saying: 'Where are you going?' We answered: 'We are going to visit Abba Cyriacus the recluse. But tell us: what is your name? How do you live, and what brought you here?' She said, 'Go away

> and when you come back I will tell you'. When we swore that we would not leave before learning all about her, she answered saying: 'The name by which I am called is Mary. I was a female musician [*psaltria*] [at the Church] of Christ's Holy Resurrection and the devil caused many to be scandalized on my account. Afraid that I might be called to answer for such scandals and add more sins to my sins, I earnestly besought God to deliver me from the charge of those scandals. [c.19] One day when my heart was sorely pricked by fear of God I went down to the holy [Pool of] Siloam [cf. John 9:7, Neh 3:15] and filled this vessel with water. I also received this palm-leaf basket full of beans and by night I went out of the Holy City, entrusting myself to God, who led me here. And behold, I have been here eighteen years and, by the grace of God, the water has not failed nor the basket of beans diminished to this day. Nor have I seen any man, except for you today. But go', she said, 'fulfill your task and visit me on your return'. On hearing this we journeyed to Abba Cyriacus and we told him these things. He was amazed when he heard it and said: 'Glory to you, oh God, who have so many hidden saints!' [This is a form of the familiar aphorism: 'How many hidden servants God has, and they are known to him alone']. 'Go down, my children, and do as she told you'. We received some food from the holy elder and came to the cave. We knocked in the customary way for recluses' [i.e. they knocked and called out 'Bless'!, expecting the response; 'The Lord'!] and when nobody answered, we went in—and found her dead. Not having the wherewithal to prepare her for the tomb and bury her, we went up to our Lavra [monastery] of Souka. We brought back everything that was needed; we celebrated her funeral and buried her in the cave, sealing the door with stones'.

Delehaye says that this tale, which circulated in the Palestinian deserts and is reported in a slightly different form by John Moschos, is the basis of the entire story of Saint Mary the Egyptian. He thinks that Sophronius based his *Life* on this tale and on Jerome's *Life* of Paul the hermit, of which more in the notes to the next tale.

It would be remiss not to note in passing a tale which in some ways resembles the present one and yet contrives to be very different from it: *BHG* 1318w, W009: *De Syncletica in deserto Iordanis.* In this story the eighteen-year-old daughter of a distinguished Constantinopolitan avoids marriage with the son of another distinguished family by asking to fulfill her vow to visit the holy places while still a virgin. At Jerusalem she evades her retinue and, for three hundred pieces of gold (= 1.365 kg), she persuades a monastic elder to give her a habit and two books. She then spends twenty-eight years in a cave and is taken for an eunuch. (*Cf BHG* 80e, W047, described in notes to Tale 20 below). The narrator of the story found her once, but could never find her again. The editors of this story (Paramelle and Flusin) think it originates in the sixth century.

To complete the dossier, here is the version, mentioned above, from *Pratum Spirituale* c.179, 'The Life of a Lady Religious [*sanctimonialis feminae* in the translation of Fra Ambroggio] who was from the Holy City' (*BHG* 1440kj, W354):

> We visited John the anchorite, known as 'the red', and he told us that he had heard Abba John the Moabite say that there was a nun [*monastria*] in the Holy City who was very devout, progressing in the service of God. The devil resented this virgin, so he implanted a satanic desire in the heart of a certain young man. That wondrous virgin perceived the demon's subterfuge and [foresaw] the young man's destruction. So she put some [beans] soaked in water into a basket and went into the wilderness. By her withdrawal she brought peace and serenity to the young man whilst she herself attained the security which is borne of solitude. A long time afterwards, by the providence of God, so that her virtuous conduct should not remain unknown, an anchorite saw her in the wilderness of the holy Jordan and he said to her: 'Amma [mother], what are you doing in this wilderness?' Not wishing to reveal herself to the anchorite she said to him: 'Forgive me; I have lost my way. But of your charity, father, and for the sake of the Lord, show me my path'. By divine inspiration he knew all about her. He said to her: 'Believe me, amma, you have neither lost your way nor are you looking for the path. You know that lies are of the devil, so tell me the real reason why you came here'. Then the virgin said to him: 'Forgive me, abba. A young man was in danger of falling into sin on my account and for that reason I came into the wilderness. I thought it was better to die here than to be an occasion of stumbling to somebody, as the Apostle [Paul, 2 Cor 6:3] says'. The elder asked: 'How long have you been here?' 'Seventeen years, by the grace of Christ', she replied. 'What do you eat?' asked the elder. She produced the basket containing steeped [beans] and said to the anchorite: 'I brought this basket away from the city with me containing these few steeped [beans] and so great has been the providence of God to me that I have been able to eat of them all this time and they have not decreased. And this too you should know, father: that his goodness has so sheltered me that in all these seventeen years no man ever laid eyes on me until you did today. Yet for my part, I could see all of them'. When the anchorite learned this, he glorified God (CS 139:148–149).

15/6 Lions are frequently mentioned in the desert literature (at least fourteen times) and even on one occasion a leopard, so there is no doubt that they were present. For the best of lion-stories, see *Pratum Spirituale* c. 107: of Abba Gerasimos and Jordanes the Lion (CS 139:86–88). In

Philotheos Historia of Theodoret of Cyrrhus 15.2 Abba Acepsimas emerges from his cell once a week, by night, to draw water. He was so bent over by all the chains he wore that a passing shepherd mistook him for a wolf (*cf* John 10:12 to appreciate the irony) and would have stoned him, but his arm was suddenly paralysed.

15/7–9 *Cf* the elder who brought two lion-cubs to church wrapped in his cloak and said: 'If we kept the commandments of our Lord Jesus Christ these animals would fear us. But because of our sins we have become slaves and it is rather we who fear them' (*Pratum Spirituale* c.18; CS 139:13).

15.15 In the older version the woman is not seen alive by the witnesses, merely heard.

15.23 *Kanonikê*, changed from *psaltria* in the older version, a lady-cantor. *Kanonikê* means a consecrated virgin or widow, but it is less clear whether it necessarily means (as the word seems to imply) one living under a religious rule, hence the translation *nun* is less than satisfactory. See Peter Brown, *The Body and Society*, p. 264.

15.35–36 Luke 9:10.

15.36 Romans 10:13.

15.47 There are cyclic variations in the level of the Dead Sea, the nature and periodicity of which there is insufficient data to determine. Towards the end of the last century a causeway formerly linking an island to the shore was submerged. The fords south of Lisân and the path which formerly rounded the Ras Feshkah also became impassable. Thus R.A.S. Macalister, 'Dead Sea', *Encyclopaedia Britannica*, 11th edition (1911) 7:879a.

15.53 The basket of beans and the vessel of water recall the story of Elijah and the widow of Zarephath in 1/3 Kings 17, 9–16: 'The barrel of meal shall not waste, neither shall the cruse of oil fail . . .' (v.14). *cf* Maësymas, the very poor but most hospitable parish priest in Theodoret's *Philotheos Historia* 14.2 who had two inexhaustible jars, one of grain, the other of oil.

15.60 The request for *new* clothes does not altogether agree with the image projected thus far of one who has completely abandoned the things of this world. It is a touching indicator that there remains in her something of the woman; but it is also an excellent indication of the ways in which old stories were 'touched up' to produce *récits tardifs*. The appeal of the story has certainly been strengethened, but possibly at the expense of its capacity to edify.

15.70 The report of the anchorites resembles the story relayed by Cyril of Scythopolis much more closely than that which goes before, but naturally with the omission of certain features which have already been related.

Tale 16: *BHG* 1449i, W716: SERGIUS, THE *DÊMOTÊS* OF ALEXANDRIA ('THE *SERGIUS*').

For a fuller discussion of this text and its implications see John Wortley, "The spirit of rivalry in early Christian monachism," *Greek, Roman and Byzantine Studies* 33/4 (1993) 1–22.

It is abundantly clear that Paul of Monembasia and writers like him did not hesitate to combine two or more themes of the old tales-tradition into new patterns. The distinction of the *Sergius* lies largely both in the skill with which its writer has done this and also in the lengths to which he carried the practice. But the story has other curious features too. Not the least is its extraordinarily long 'line of transmission'. The anonymous writer (1) says that a monk named Abbakoum / Habakkuk (2) claimed to have read 'in an old book' (3) of one Elpidius (4) who met Pyrrhus (5) in the desert, who told him of Sergius (6) from whom he heard the two stories which lie at the heart of the tale: 'the woman released' and 'the virgins protected'. Nearly all tales, like the *apophthegmata* before them, begin with some authenticating formula, such as 'Abba NN said . . .' Later—in some of the later stories in the early seventh-century *Pratum Spirituale*, for example—one sometimes finds a formula such as 'Abba NN said that Abba MM told him . . . ,' and even occasionally (but very rarely) a *third*-hand story comes to light. But it is very much to be doubted whether there is anywhere else in the entire tales-tradition anything which purports to depend on a *sixth*-hand report. It should also be noted that the dependence on an alleged written source ('an ancient book'), whilst it is a familiar literary device elsewhere, never again occurs in the tales tradition, so far as one can tell.

Given these two considerations alone, it would appear that the *Sergius*, far from being a simple piece of *reportage* (which is all the earlier tales were, for the most part) is a literary contrivance which is only a very little, if at all, dependent on an oral source. For the last three persons in the 'line of transmission' are also important characters, indeed the main characters, in the action as a whole.

It is by examining that 'action as a whole' that the real complexity of the *Sergius* is thrown into relief. The action consists of four independent narratives: the tale of Elpidius and Pyrrhus (**A**); Pyrrhus' and Sergius' story (**B**); and the two narratives which Sergius relates (**C** and **D**). The remarkable thing is that these tales are not related consecutively; they are set inside each other, like Chinese boxes, so to speak. Using the letters assigned above, the plan of the work can be expressed thus:

$$\mathbf{A^1\ B^1\ C\ D\ B^2\ A^2}$$

The climax of the 'action as a whole' is placed with unerring judgement right at the centre, between **C** and **D** (Pyrrhus' acknowledgement that Sergius is at least his spiritual equal). The author seems to have a passion for symmetry. Witness the nice balance of the characters in opposing sections and the way questions raised in one half of a story are answered at the corresponding point in the remaining half. For example, Sergius' growing suspicions of Pyrrhus' motives in $\mathbf{B^1}$ are balanced by his request to become the older man's monastic companion in $\mathbf{B^2}$.

Yet if the form of the *Sergius* points away from the tales- tradition, the content certainly does not. This can be seen most clearly in Pyrrhus' prayer in **B**[1]: 'With whom have I my portion?'—that is, 'who is my spiritual equal?' There are several tales of a desert father who, being informed (often at his own request) that there is someone (usually 'in the world') equal or superior to him in piety, sets out to search for that person, and is humbled on meeting the person. The best-known of these is probably the tale of Saint Antony being sent to the leather-worker of Alexandria (Nau 490; *cf* Nau 67). In a closely related and similar story, Macarius is sent to two married ladies of the same city (*BHG* 999yb, W637, Nau 489, Pelagius and John 20.17). For other 'comparison' stories of various kinds, see E.A. Wallis Budge, *The Paradise of the Holy Fathers* (London, 1907) 1.104; *Historia Lausiaca* c.34, W206; *BHG* 2125, W035, in *PG* 65:168–169; and *BHG* 1438i, W538, Nau 067; very similar to Nau 490 and 631. Usually the father is sent to a city.

Older however than all these tales, and possibly the inspiration of them, is a slightly different one. It is to be found in Jerome's *Life of Saint Paul of Thebes* (ed. K.T. Corey in Oldfather and Corey, *Studies in the Text-Tradition of Saint Jerome's* Vitae Patrum, [Urbana, 1943] pp. 158–172), a sort of appendix to Athanasius' *Life of Saint Antony*. The passage in question tells how, being already ninety years old, Antony was in the desert when 'the idea came into his mind that there was no monk living in the desert more perfect than himself' [*haec in mentem eius cogitatio incidit nulum ultra se perfectum monachum in eremo consedisse*, c.7]. Therefore he prayed that he might know whether this was true. That, at least, is what the text which was translated into Greek said. The critical edition of the Latin text shows that the word *perfectum* is an interpolation and that, far from falling victim to any invidious pride, all Antony was wanting to know was whether any monk was living any *further into* the desert than was he, *i.e.* in yet remoter zones. By the time the Greek translation was made, the change of meaning brought about by the insertion of the word *perfectum* had already taken root, and thus it was disseminated throughout the hellenophone world, where it gave rise to a number of imitations.

As with Elpidius and Pyrrhus in the *Sergius*, Paul of Thebes (one hundred and sixteen years old) is a monk who lives in a yet more remote part of the desert and to him Antony goes. At first Paul resists all contact with the visitor (a familiar *topos*). Then, announcing his own approaching death, he sends Antony away on a mission. But when the latter returns, he finds the older man already dead—and buries him. Obviously, **A**[2] of the *Sergius* almost exactly corresponds to the second part of this story, even to death having overtaken the elder somewhat earlier than he seems to have expected. Similar, though less striking, parallels with the earlier part of Paul's *Life* are to be found in both **A**[1] and **B**[1] of the *Sergius*. There is nothing surprising about this for there are many, many tales which owe something to this one small work of Jerome of *ca* 364 (*e.g.* the Story of the Naked Nun, No.15, above). The influence need by no means have been direct.

Another 'comparison' story, much less influential than Paul's *Life* to be sure, may nevertheless have had a more direct influence on our author. It is 'The Tale of Paphnutius' in *The History of the Monks in Egypt*, or rather, the first section of this three-part tale (*HME* 14.2–15; *cf Historia Lausiaca* 98.16ff). It is just possible that when, at the beginning of the *Sergius*, Abbakoum claims to have found what follows 'in an old book', he might have been stating the literal truth, and 'The Tale of Paphnutius' might have been the passage to which he was referring. The story has undergone radical transformation, to be sure, but not to the extent that it is unrecognisable.

Paphnutius' tale tells how he was in the desert where monks ought to be when he posed a similar question to that which is asked in most comparison stories: 'To whom am I like?' In his case, an angel appears and says: 'You are like the flute-player [*aulêtês*] living in this city [Heracleopolis].' Paphnutius goes to the city and finds the flute-player, who admits to being a sinner, a drunkard, a lecher and, until recently, a brigand. However, in response to the elder's persuasion he admits to two good deeds. Once he saved a 'virgin of God' from being ravished by his fellow brigands (whose captive she was) and restored her to her village. And another time he found a handsome woman wandering about alone in the desert; her story was this. For two years her husband had been in prison (subject to frequent floggings) for three hundred pieces of gold owing in taxes. Her three dear children had been sold into slavery and she herself was frequently apprehended and flogged by the governor's agents. 'Take me where you will as your slave [*therapainis*], for in three days I have not eaten,' she said. Bringing her to the robbers' cave, the brigand gave her three hundred pieces of gold and led her to the town where she liberated husband and children. When the flute-player had finished his story he threw his pipes to the ground and followed Paphnutius into the desert, where he died three years later (CS 34:95ff). The similarities with **B**[1], **C** and even part of **B**[2] are too obvious to be spelled out.

There are other stories which may have lent something to the *Sergius*; for instance *The Life of Saint Theodoulos the Stylite* (*Acta Sanctorum* maii 6 [1688] 756–765, [3rd edn.] 748–755; see cc. 12–18, and Delehaye's comments in *Les Saints stylites, Subsidia Hagiographica* 14 [Brussels, 1923] cxviii-cxx: 'Il serait aisé d'en trouver les éléments à travers la littérature du Moyen âge'). Taken at its face value (which is almost certainly misleading,) this document would be dated to the late fourth century. Perched on his column at Damascus, Theodoulos asks in prayer: 'With whom shall I inherit the kingdom?' A voice replies: 'With Cornelius the actor [*pandouros*] from the city of Damascus'. The saint bitterly laments being classed with this 'flute player of the demons', which might suggest some connection with the story just mentioned above. He descends from his column, goes into the city and asks to be directed to Cornelius the actor. A citizen takes him to the hippodrome and there is Cornelius, a musical instrument in one hand and a prostitute in the other. Theodoulos presses him for details of his virtue, which reduces him to laughter; but finally, he tells his tale. One night he was returning to his house after a late-night show, and there was a pretty woman standing in the shadows. He pressed her into his embrace and at first she seemed willing enough. But then she started aside like a broken bow and burst into tears. It appears that she is the child of parents of standing, but an orphan. She has been married to a less-than-satisfactory man who quickly ran through the dowry she had brought him. He had now been in prison for eight months, for debt, and he was dying of hunger. She has tried begging, but in vain, and thus she is reduced (much against her will) to prostituting her charms. When Cornelius heard this, he ran to his house, gathered up all the money he could find or borrow, all articles of value and even his theatrical costumes. He wrapped all this in a cloth and gave it to the woman to pay her husband's debts, which amounted to four hundred gold pieces. In addition to general similarities there are also some striking verbal resemblances between this story and the *Sergius* (mainly in **B^1** and **C**).

One last story which should be noted (though here the similarities are less striking) occurs in *Pratum spirituale* (c.186, *PG* 86:3061D–3064D; CS 139:158–159) where it is said to have been told to the author by his own brother, Moschus the Merchant. One day this man was going to the baths in Tyre when he saw a woman sitting in the shadows who agreed to follow him. Failing to persuade her to share his supper he proceeded to take her to bed, where she burst into tears. She told him that her husband, a merchant, had lost everything in a shipwreck and was now languishing in gaol. She had taken to prostitution to feed herself. She needed five pounds of gold to redeem her husband. Moschus gave her the money and let her go unharmed. That is not the end of the story, but the rest is of no concern here.

In the light of the foregoing remarks, not very much is left of the *Sergius* which has not been accounted for in one way or another. In fact, all that remains is Sergius' second story (**D**), but it is too important a remainder to be overlooked, for it might be the heart of the whole matter. So far as composition is concerned, it does somewhat resemble the flute-player's claim (in *The Tale of Paphnutius*, part one) to have delivered one 'virgin of God' from being raped by his fellow brigands. If this *is* the germ from which the story sprang, then the author is deserving of almost as much credit for his prodigious imagination as if he had invented it *ex nihilo*. In either case, in the Tale of the Nuns Preserved he would seem to have produced what must be the most outrageous, if not the least credible, story in the entire tales-tradition, and that is rather unlikely. He was, in all probability, a monk writing for monks, to emphasise some element of monastic teaching. 'Cette histoirette,' wrote

Halkin of the *Sergius*, 'évidement légendaire, a une portée très elevée: toutes les pénitences et les austerités d'une longue vie d'ascèse ont à peine autant de valeur et de mérite aux yeux de Dieu que de deux actes de charité vraiment désintéressée.' [Whilst this tale is obviously fictitious, it has a very high meaning. Even a lifetime of penitential and ascetic exercises is of less value in God's eyes than two truly altruistic charitable deeds; Halkin, *Recherches et documents*, p. 266]. It is perhaps stretching credulity a little too far to suggest that someone sufficiently advanced in religion to appreciate so high a doctrine as that could have (or would have) deliberately devised such a story. Might it not rather be that, although we cannot trace any similar story elsewhere in the tales-tradition, **D** had nevertheless an independent and previous exsitence? Even as told by Sergius it has the sound of a tale that was laughed over in taverns, for it will readily be noted that there is nothing inherently christian about it. Christians are by no means the only people who have maintained institutions for unmarried ladies, nor do they have a monopoly of the common decency which would be offended by the violation of those ladies. In other words, this could be a story of almost any age and any place. The author of the *Sergius* may have rescued it from the tavern (so to speak) and used it to convey a high doctrine, much in the way in which the Wesleys in the eighteenth century 'rescued' tunes from the theatre and set their hymns to them.

DATE AND ORIGIN OF THE *SERGIUS*

There is a georgian translation of this tale in a manuscript clearly dated 977 AD, and as this is believed to be dependent on a pre-existent Arabic translation, a *terminus ante quem* of at least the middle of the tenth century would seem to be indicated (See J.-M. Sauget, 'Le *Paterikon* du manuscript Arab 276 de la Bibliothèque Nationale de Paris', and especially its appendix, 'Les *Histoires utiles à l'âme* de Paul de Monembasie', *Le Muséon* 82 [1969] 363–404). Thus arises the question of whether it could be the work of Paul of Monembasia, as some late manuscripts (and *BHG*) claim. The style suggests that it is not. Although Paul wrote very simply, he was clearly capable of more sophisticated Greek if he chose to write it (*cf* the concluding passage of Tale No. 10), whereas the writer of the *Sergius* seems to be working at the full extent of a rather limited acquaintance with the language, perhaps even in a language not originally his own into which he is translating (as was true of the Gospel according to Mark). Also Paul is a very consistent writer; he would never allow one of his characters to say: 'I have not seen the face of a man in seventy years and more' and then go on to tell how the same character had been in Alexandria four years earlier and had enjoyed the company of Sergius ever since. Nor would Paul allow his narrative to swing back and forth between the first and third persons singular. We may add that all Paul's tales are set in a more or less contemporary (tenth-century) context, not in some vague, distant past. But the most telling point is that in Paul's stories certain 'set phrases" (*e.g.* 'God the good, the lover of men') and a very few biblical quotations recur with surprising frequency: Not a one of either is to be found anywhere in the *Sergius*. It can be added that some of Paul's stories (the ones with women in them) are to be found in the thirteenth-century Cod. Athen. B.N. 513 (**A** of the new edition; see the general introduction) in a form which agrees very closely with the consensus of other early manuscripts. This codex also contains a text of the *Sergius*, but in a form so revised that it bears little resemblance to any other early manuscript of the Greek text. Thus, the *Sergius* would appear to belong to a different codicological tradition from that of Paul's work.

The *Sergios* was edited by Gerôn Basileios Karakallinos on the basis of Cod. London. addit. 28270 in *Hagioritikê Bibliothêkê* 20 (1956) 383 and 21 (1956) 33–35. There is Latin translation of the Armenian version in *CSCO* 361, subsidia 43 (Louvain, 1975).

NOTES ON THE TEXT

dêmotês: this word has been left untranslated because its general meaning is unclear. Obviously it does not have its usual meaning, a member of a circus-faction (see G. Schirò, 'Un significato sconosciuto de *dêmotês*', *Rivista di cultura classica e medievale* 7 [1965] 1006–1016). An obviously respectable *dêmotês* of Constantinople is referred to in a tale found amongst the appendices to the *Plerophoriai* of John Rufus, Bishop of Maïouma (*PO* 8:174 [575] ll. 29, 34 etc). but this is not the same as the one found here. Its specific meaning is unmistakable; Sergius says: 'I am in charge of [the whores] and without my consent nobody can lay a finger on them. [A client] must speak to me, and then I provide him with whichever whore he wants' [73–75]. In other words, he is the commissioner for prostitutes. It is perhaps not irrelevant to point out that *only* Sergius' second story (**D**) requires that he exercise that office, further evidence perhaps that **D** is the original kernel of the whole complex. Perhaps one can go even a little further: if **D** were an element newly imported to the tales-tradition by the author of the *Sergius*, might it not have been known to him in a tongue other than Greek? And might not that foreign-language version have used a term for the commisioner of prostitutes which our author mistakenly took to be the Greek word *dêmotês*?

16/2 Tamiathaïs = Coptic Tamiati, now Damietta, on the eastern branch of the Nile about 18 km from the mouth.

16/46 etc., a tavern [*kapêleion*]. The tavern is the very antithesis of 'the desert', because it is in a sense the epitomy of all that is evil not only in 'the world', but in the world's worst aspect: the city. *Cf Pratum Spirituale* c.194, in which an older monk warns a younger whom he has seen entering a tavern: 'Do you not know that monks who live in cities are wounded through their eyes, their hearing and by their clothes? You went into a tavern of your own free will. You hear things you do not want to hear and you see things you would rather not see, dishonourably mingling with both men and women. Please do not do this, but rather fly to the wilderness where you will find the salvation you desire' (CS 139:169).

16/67 'what good have you done?': *cf Pratum Spirituale* c.207. This is a splendid tale of a rich orphan woman who saves a man from hanging himself by giving him all her wealth to pay his debts. She sinks deeply into prostitution in her poverty but at the end requests baptism. It is however angels, not men, who baptise her, and when this is revealed, the bishop asks her: 'Tell me, daughter, what good have you done?' She finally confesses the generous act which brought her to penury (CS 139:185–187).

16/89 The possibility of a debtor's children being sold into slavery was a very real one; *cf* Macarios 7 in the *Alphabetikon*.

Tale 17: *BHG* 1277a/1449q, W717: THE DRUNKEN PRIEST.

According to *BHG* this text was published by Stephane Binon in *Documents grecs inédits relatifs à Saint Mercure de Césarée* (Louvain, 1937), but in fact that volume contains only short extracts from the tale, and that from a 'vulgarised' manuscript. Binon lists five manuscripts, all of them sixteenth or seventeenth century, and all (it would appear) vulgarised to a certain extent. The *Novum Auctarium* of *BHG* lists two editions of the tale, but according to Binon (p. 174, note 2) one of these is a mere paraphrase; the other has proved unobtainable. The Greek text from which the present translation has been made is from Codex Lesbos Monê Leimônos 148, ff. 361–365. [The translator finally obtained and used the edition of this text in *Hagioreitikê Bibliothêkê* 18 (1953) 34–36, 85–87 which is based on a manuscript superior to Leimônos 148].

The introductory notes to Tales Nos. 6 and 7 are relevant here too.

17/1 The article of Binon, mentioned above, gives a complete dossier on the legendary Saint Mercury.

17/15 There is a very similar story of 'an unworthy priest' (so far as the earlier part of it is concerned): *BHG* 1449p, W067 ed. J. Wortley, 'An unpublished anecdote of an unworthy priest and Saint Basil', *Analecta Bollandiana* 97 (1979) 363–371: In the time and in the diocese of Saint Basil the Great there was a parish priest, lawfully married; but there was also a woman who burned with sinful lust for him—and had her way with him in a curious manner. Returning home in the dead of night from a Christmas dinner at which he had partaken a little too freely of the wine-jar, the priest fell fast asleep on the doorstep when he failed to rouse his sleeping wife within. The wicked woman came by and led him into adultery by making him think he was a-bed with his wife. The wife soon realised that something was wrong, for her husband no longer shone like the sun at the altar but looked like a black-faced one [*aethiops*] *i.e.*, a demon. The indiscretion of the adulteress revealed all and the priest admitted it to Saint Basil. The saint prescribed a year's vigorous penance, then a second and even a third. When the priest and his wife came back a third time, the saint was occupied with the obsequies of a local magnate, so he invited the priest to put on his stole and join the clergy. When he, last of all, intoned the prayer over the corpse, it sat up and announced that the three-year repentance of the priest had found favour in the sight of God. His restoration to the exercise of his priestly functions seems to have followed.

In that story, as in the one under review, the point (which is carefully spelled out) is that priests ought not to get drunk. Both agree that the great danger of drunkeness is that it leads to *porneia*, but No. 17 adds another danger: it might lead to a priest having licit sexual relations when he ought to be abstaining, *i.e.* when he is about to celebrate the Divine Liturgy. The ruling on this is to be found in the thirteenth canon of the Quinisext Council of 692, the Council 'in Trullo' or *Penthectos*, as it is sometimes known. The main thrust of the canon is to condemn the Roman church for disallowing married clergy. It insists that no clergyman up to and including the rank of priest is to be required to separate from his legal wife, nor (say the fathers) are they

> depriving them of their mutual intercourse at a convenient time (*tên pros allêlous kata kairon ton prosêkonta omilias*). But we know, as they who assembled at Carthage said (with a care for the honest life of the clergy) that subdeacons who handle the holy mysteries and deacons and presbyters should abstain from their consorts according to their own course [of ministration] (*kata tous idious orous ek tôn symbiôn egkrateuesthai*). For it is meet that they who assist at the divine altar should be absolutely continent (*egkrateis einai en pasin*) when they are handling holy things,

trans. H.R. Percival (*SLNPNF* series II, 14:371–372), who adds the following notes:

> Van Espen (*Tractatus Historicus*) observes that Clement VIII ruled that a Greek presbyter should abstain from his wife for a week or three days before offering the Eucharist. But Fleury and others think that the Greeks misunderstood. The Canons of Carthage of 419 generally require total abstinence of all the major orders, *e.g.* Canons 3 and 4. But it is Canon 25 to which Quinisext 13 refers: '*Bishops*, deacons, priests and subdeacons should abstain from their wives according to the former statutes, *secundum priora statuta*'. The text is clearly defective, as there is an alternative reading, *secundum propria statuta*. Presumably the East Romans

> knew this or yet another reading when they translated it *kata tous idious orous*, which is quite a different thing (pp. 444–445).

Yet, however they came by it, the Greeks obviously took Quinisext 13 seriously (Van Espen observes that it is, in fact, also to be found in *Corpus Iuris Canonici* and in Gratian's *Decretum*: pars I dist. XXXI c. xiii). Or at least there were bishops and/or monks (who were required to be single) who wanted it to be taken seriously; hence this story. No other like it, however, is known to the present writer, nor has he been able to discover how seriously the prohibition of Quinisext 13 was usually taken. It is clearly incompatible with *Didascalia Apostolorum* VI (xxi) 1–8 (ed. and trans. Connolly [Oxford, 1929] pp. 240–250) which states explicitly that no licit sexual activity ever excludes from the sacraments. Peter Brown (*The Body and Society*, p. 256) cites *The Answers of Apa Cyril* (ed. and trans. W.E. Crum [Strasbourg, 1915] p. 199 Coptic, p. 103 trans). to suggest that both clergy and the faithful laity were expected to avoid intercourse on Saturday, Sunday, Wednesday and Friday, throughout the forty days of Lent, 'and before the other feasts at which they might take the eucharist'. Brown's comments on this are, as always, most illuminating.

17/50 That priests were believed to have the power to loose and bind angels as well as men is illustrated in *BHG* 1444x, W121 (referred to with approval in *BHG* 1318z, W058) where a priest obliges the angel to restore the soul of a baby who died at its baptism between the water and the oil of chrismation.

17/185 Lk 13:47.

Tale 18: *BHG* 1450kb, W861: THE TALE OF THE CONVERTED ROBBER.

The Tale of the Converted Robber (which appears not previously to have been published in any language) has some very unusual features. But it is not by any means a story which stands outside the tradition of 'spiritually beneficial tales', nor even one which presents a succession of unusual features, as does (for instance) The Tale of the Proud Monk. It is a tale of lawless, violent men, of bandits and brigands; these are not uncommon in the literature of eremitic monachism. One would greatly err in supposing that the life the desert fathers led was one of uninterrupted silence and tranquillity. For those men (and women) who had withdrawn from the world had also removed themselves from the protection of such forces of law and order as there were in the *oikoumenê*. This meant that they were particularly vulnerable to the attacks of lawless persons roaming the desert places and no doubt seeking to escape from another kind of worldly snare. For the desert provided refuge not only from 'the world', but also from its legal processes and was thus the retreat both of holy men and of extremely unholy outlaws living on what they could purloin. Not a few stories have survived which speak of the exploits of these brigands and, hardly surprisingly, in many instances, of their conversion to the monastic way of life.

The oldest example is perhaps the story of Abba Patermouthios, already a legend when Abba Coprès told it to the compiler of *Historia monachorum in Ægypto* at the end of the fourth century. The first monk ever to establish himself in that particular part of the desert, Abba Patermouthios had previously been a notorious bandit with a bad reputation for robbing (pagan) tombs. That clearly was not his only source of revenue, for one night he attacked 'the hermitage of a virgin', intending to make off with all he could find within. He got up onto the roof but could then find neither a way into the cell nor the means of regaining the ground. Sleep overtook him and (as though in a dream) he saw a king who reproved him for his misdeeds. This king also offered him the command of a monastic community if he would abandon his evil ways. When he awoke, the virgin was beside him, speaking to him as to a friend. Following her directions, he went to the church and embraced Christianity. In a remarkably short time he became an illustrious monk and the spiritual father of monks. He was particularly distinguished by the care with which he attended the dying brethren and prepared their corpses for interrment. He is one of the very few fathers ever credited with raising the dead (albeit temporarily) and the only one said to have delayed the setting of the sun on one occasion—until he arrived at the village for which he was bound (*HME* 10 *passim*, and especially 12–14; CS 34:82–87). In short, he became a truly distinguished abba.

One of the most curious of bandit-stories (from the same collection) may be almost as old (*HME* 9.5–7; CS 34:80–81). Abba Amoun, a luminary of the desert in the generation before the compilers of *HME* arrived, was no bandit, but was frequently troubled by bandits. They were always relieving him of bread and his other meagre supplies. So one day he summoned two great serpents from the desert to guard his door. When the bandits saw them, they fell to the ground, half dead. Amoun reproved them for being more savage than the beasts, which, at least, respected Christians. Then he entertained them kindly and they mended their ways. Later (says the story) they too performed similar miracles, which seems to imply that they had joined the monastic ranks, but this is not certain.

Another story in the same collection concerns a monk whom the Jerusalem enquirers actually saw: Abba Theon (*HME* 6.1–3; CS 34:68). He was an erudite father who lived in silence for thirty years in a desert cell near Oxyrrhynchos and was famed for his miracles. Every day he would stretch out his hands through the window of his cell to touch the sick and disturbed persons who flocked to him for healing. Then one night, when he was alone, bandits attacked, hoping to find gold. Presumably they imagined—quite incorrectly—that people paid, or made thank-offerings, for the cures they obtained at the hands of the monk. Theon gave himself to prayer and the bandits were immobilised before his door. They were still there when the people in search of cures arrived next morning. These realised what had happened and they were all for delivering the bandits 'to the fire', presumably because they too had suffered at the outlaws' hands from time to time. To be burnt alive (which seems to be what is implied) might seem a somewhat draconian punishment for banditry, but it has to be borne in mind that banditry often included murder and many other atrocities; also that it was an age of draconian punishments so far as the world was concerned. The monks themselves seem to have been somewhat less severe; we read of a whip reserved for the punishment of bandits at Nitria (*Hist. Laus.* p. 25, 17). Abba Theon, however, was moved to be even more merciful than the monks of Nitria. For once, he opened his mouth and spoke: 'Let them go, safe and sound—or the gift of miracles will desert me'. The bandits regained control of their limbs, but they did not then disappear over the horizon. They entered monasteries in the vicinity where they duly repented of their sins.

Writing perhaps a quarter of a century later than the anonymous author of *HME*, Palladios has left us the most striking example of a bandit-turned-monk: the celebrated Moses the Black (or 'the robber', *HL* c.19 and note 33). Presumably of Coptic origin, Moses had formerly served a person of distinction in domestic matters. But his conduct became so disorderly that, slave though he was, his master discharged him. He then took to the life of banditry with a vengeance, becoming the acknowledged chieftain of a band. One of his exploits is recorded: he crossed the Nile and killed an unfortunate shepherd who tried to hide himself in the sand. Four of the best sheep were brought back to the other side and eaten; the fleeces were sold for wine, of which they drank a very great deal and then returned to their band. Exactly what happened to bring about Moses' conversion is not clear; the next we hear of him he is well and truly established in a monastery. But then he in turn is attacked by four bandits (who do not realise who he is). Moses, however, has lost none of his former capability for he adroitly binds them and brings them back to the brethren. 'It is forbidden for me to harm anybody; what do you want to become of these fellows?" he asks. When the four realised who he was and what was happening to them, they decided (perhaps not entirely for reasons of piety) that they too would embrace the monastic life. So much for Moses, whom Butler described as 'one of the most striking and spiritual figures of the desert'.

Neither of the two great sixth-century collections of apophthegmata (*alphabetikon, systematikon*) contain stories of bandits who became monks, but there are two in the early-seventh century *Pratum Spirituale*, cc. 143 and 166; CS 139:115–116 and 136–137. The first tells of David who was the chief of a band of about thirty robbers in the district of Antinoë. He was responsible for practically every conceivable form of mischief. Then one day, for unspecified reasons, David simply walked away from his band and came knocking at the monastery door. 'I want to become a monk', he told the porter, but the higoumen would have refused him. 'The brothers here work very hard', he said, noticing that the aspirant was advanced in years [*oti gerôn hupêrchen*]; 'you could not keep up with the rule of the monastery', and so forth. Finally, the other lost patience. 'Look here, I am David, the bandit-chief and I have come here to weep for my sins. Either you admit me, or I will go back to being a bandit, bring my comrades, kill you all and overthrow your monastery'. The higoumen opted for the lesser of two evils. David was tonsured and, despite the superior's reservations, soon surpassed all his new brothers in monastic virtues. So much so that one day he received an angelic message telling him that his sins were now forgiven. Deeply aware of how heinous these had been, David was reluctant to believe the message. The angel threatened him with the same punishment which Zacharias received for his unbelief. David's response shows that he had lost nothing of the forthright manner of speaking one might well associate with men who feared no authority. In effect, he says to the angel: 'It would have made more sense to have deprived me of my powers of speech back in the days when I was performing evil deeds in the world, rather than now when I am here, singing the praises of God.' Like the higoumen, the angel found the logic of the argument convincing. David was permitted to retain his powers of speech, but only for the singing of psalms; never at any other time or for any other purpose. It should be added that John Moschos' informant claimed to have seen David, which would indicate that all this took place in the middle or later-middle sixth century.

The other story from the *Pratum* is much more sombre. It concerns a bandit who became a monk in a Palestinian lavra and then was hidden by the monks in a monastery near Gaza. After nine years of honest perseverance there he returned to the abba who had tonsured him and asked to be 'secularised'—'give me back my lay clothes'. (This, incidentally, is the only case of a monk asking to be 'secularised' in the whole of the tales-tradition which has yet come to my notice). It must be the abba who tonsured him who secularises him, on the basis of the axiom that only he who bound can loose—which as we have seen is taken *very* seriously in the tales (*cf BHG* 1322d,e / W001; 1322u,v / W040; 1449g / W706, 1449s / W039; 1277a/1449q / W717, *Hist. Laus.* c. 70 / W220 *etc*). The monk explained to the reluctant father that, in spite of his diligence in penitence, he was ever haunted by the vision of a child he had murdered, reproving him for his crime. He put on his lay-clothes and went to Diospolis (Lydda). He was arrested and, the next day, beheaded.

Not by any means do all the tales of bandits end up with the malefactors being converted to the monastic way of life. We might consider the story of Spyridon, for instance, in the *alphabêtikon*, a man who was a *pastor* in both senses of the word: both a bishop (at Trimithuntes) and a shepherd. Bandits came by night to steal from the sheepfold—but found themselves bound tightly to its fence by invisible powers. Next morning the episcopal shepherd came, admonished them, released them, and gave them a ram for good measure. This might have been to encourage them to breed sheep rather than to steal them.

There is a story which recurs in the tradition of bandits who repent when, as they withdraw from a monastery which they have thoroughly looted, an elder presents them with something which they have overlooked: *e.g.* in Pelagius and John (the *systematikon*) 16, 13; Zosimus 12; Nau 337. They are so impressed that they restore all and go their way in wonder at the holiness of the elder. But it does not always work out like that. We hear of one father, following the example in the *apophthegmata*, who offers to some bandits who are robbing the place three pieces of gold which they had overlooked, and they take them! (*Pratum Spirituale* c.212; CS 139:190–191). On the other hand, when Abba Euprepios offered bandits his staff (which was the only thing they had not taken from him), they refused it. So he sent it along with others who were going in the same direction (Euprepios 2 in the *alphabêtikon*).

Bandits were evil men to be sure, but they were not utterly devoid of goodness, as some tales tell. For instance: it was a well known fact that Abba Paphnoutios drank no wine. One day he came across some bandits sitting drinking. Their chief knew him and knew he drank no wine; yet, seeing the father wearied by his journey (*i.e.*, intending no harm), he came to him with a cup in one hand and a sword in the other. 'Drink this wine,' he said, 'or I will kill you'. Paphnoutios did as he was bidden—and then the chief was ashamed of what he had done. But the abba's gentle retort won him over: 'I believe that for the sake of this cup (*cf* Mt 10:42) God will have mercy on you in this world and in the next'. The chief said: 'I believe in God, for from this time on I will harm no one any more', and the elder acquired the entire band because he renounced his own will for the sake of the Lord' (Paphnoutios 2 in the *alphabêtikon*).

John Moschos tells a sad story of a palestinian bandit, Cyriacos the Wolf, who afflicted the region of Emmaus (Nicopolis). He and his band (which included Christians, Jews, and Samaritans) terrorised the local population with their inhuman cruelty. One day, when the chief was not there, the band fell on a company returning from Jerusalem with infants who had just been baptised there. The men fled while the band made off with and raped the women, leaving the newly-baptised infants lying on the ground. The bandit-chief met the fleeing men and, on learning what had happened, hastened to remedy the situation. He beheaded the members of his band who had perpetrated the atrocity and restored the babies to their fathers (the mothers being reluctant to receive them in their soiled condition). Then he saw the whole company safely home. Some time later he was arrested and gaoled, but after ten years, he was released. He always believed that it was because he had saved the newly-baptised infants that he escaped execution (*Pratum Spirituale* c.165; CS 139:135–136).

A yet later tale, from the time when the disciples of the Prophet Mohammed were beginning to trouble the desert (*i.e.* well into the seventh century) tells of an elder who lived seventy years in the desert in great asceticism without receiving any sign or vision from God. He prayed about this and was rewarded by a heavenly voice which told him to go into the inner desert. When he got there he was seized by a bandit who could scarcely conceal his delight. For (said he) the monk would be his one-hundredth kill and would thus ensure him of the joys of paradise. The elder asked for a last drink of water before he died and the bandit not only agreed to this request but went himself to get the water. As he stooped down to the river, however, he seems to have had a heart attack, for he fell down dead. The heavenly voice came again to the monk, this time telling him to give the dead man a decent burial: he had earned it by his obedience, that is, by his willingness to fulfill the monk's request (*BHG* 1450q, W843).

Against this background the Tale of the Converted Robber is to be seen. It will quickly be noted that in some ways it fits very easily into the general picture. There is a band of robbers with an outstanding chieftain. Some deed of particular gravity is planned and partially executed, but takes an unexpected turn, as a result of which all the robbers end up monks. Not all the stories mentioned above follow that outline all the way, but almost every one of them represents some segment of it. The underlying message is nearly always perceptible: brigands might be the dregs of society and the most feared members of it, but they are still men, formed in the image of God. And when the conditions are right, even these most depraved beings, guilty of the worst crimes imaginable, can cast off their evil ways (by the grace of God) and embrace the angelic profession. In this, too, the present tale is no exception; it runs true to form.

Yet it does have some remarkable features. In the first place, it has to do with a ladies' monastery or convent. Nunneries do not figure very often in the tales, nor for that matter in early christian literature generally. Gregory of Nazianzen makes a reference to what is undoubtedly a ladies' monastery (*PG* 36:577A, *parthenôn*). The two references to a *parthenôn* in *Historia Lausiaca* (cc.203, 205) leave it open to doubt whether these were really religious communities or merely retreats for single ladies (but see Peter Brown, *The Body and Society*, pp. 264–266). Theodoret of Cyrrhus († *ca* 466), however, has a story which makes it clear that there were several monasteries of women in the Antioch-region in his time: There was a *debauché*, a former *stratêgos* who had in his service an unmarried girl whom he desired (she was of marriageable age). She left her family and fled to a women's residence where there was a community of ascetics.

The master was so angry that he seized the mother of the girl, beat her and hung her up until she revealed in *which* monastery the girl was hiding. Blindness intervened to prevent him searching further, but the message is clear: there were too many convents in the area for him to search them one at a time (*Philotheos Historia* 9.12).

The monastery in the present story was in one of the suburbs of Antioch and, from the fact that the brigands could contemplate an attack on it, we might conclude that it was on the very edge of the inhabited area; even perhaps a little way out into the country, since it was obviously very securely fortified against attack. There were sixty sisters living there and it was (presumably) sufficiently wealthy to make it an attractive prize for the robbers.

Now a second remarkable feature of this tale becomes apparent. The arch-brigand asks his twelve-member gang how entrance is to be effected; one of them comes up with a rather pedestrian suggestion, which is turned down. Then the chief shows how intelligence might succeed where violence will fail: he will disguise himself in the cowl of a mesopotamian [monk], clearly a reference to some distinctive feature of a monk of Mesopotamia (possibly a monophysite) as opposed to one of Egypt or of Syria-Palestine. No other brigand-story credits the lawless men with intelligence of this order.

The ruse works and in he goes. The sixty sisters mistake him for a holy man and receive him with great honour according to custom. We may compare Gregory of Nyssa, *Life of Macrina* c.16: (when the brotherhood heard of Gregory's approach) 'the entire group of men came out of the monastery to meet me; it is their custom so to honour whom they are pleased to receive by going out to meet them. For *their* part, the choir of virgins, arranged in good order by the church, awaited our entry' (see notes 3 and 4 *ad loc.*, ed. Pierre Marvel, *Sources Chrétiennes* 178 [Paris, 1971]). They likewise proceed to wash his feet and to receive a blessing from the water. Then one sister who has been paralysed for many years is restored to health on contact with that water. This is the point at which the story takes a most unusual turn. Few in the Byzantine world would have disputed that miraculous cures did occur from time to time, often in connection with holy objects such as relics. There was general agreement about how these miracles came about. The relics of the saints were regarded as an extension of their presences beyond death in a way analogous to the continuous presence of Jesus in the sacramental species. So the relics themselves were in some sense 'divinised', *i.e.* possessed of divine life, since it was by divinisation that saints became saints. Thus the relics were important means of grace: 'breaches in the dyke between heaven and earth' (as Peter Brown once described icons) through which prayers could be hastened on their way and blessings be received.

One would have thought that so important an idea, especially if (as seems to be the case) it was one easily discerned in the earliest strata of christian belief, would have been treated at some length by at least one of the fathers, but this apparently was not so. Perhaps this was because nobody ever thought it necessary to explain these things, any more than it was necessary to teach people to breathe. But it means that to reconstruct the living tradition concerning the relics, one has to glean material from secondary clauses and subsidiary statements in a small number of writings on other subjects which accidentally mention relics. Even when it is done, the gleanings hardly amounts to a systematic theology of relics. Little, in fact, can be added to what Cyril of Jerusalem wrote about the Prophet Elisha . . . .

> who twice raised the dead: once in his lifetime and once after he died. Whilst he was alive, he brought about a resurrection by his own *psychê*, but we are not only to honour the *souls* of the righteous; we are also to believe that power [*dynamis*] reposes in their corpses, for when the dead man was cast into the grave of Elisha, that man was revitalised on contact with the prophet and the body of the prophet provided the dead man with a soul. The dead and buried gave life to the dead. Yet that which provided life, *itself* remained dead. Why was this? Since Elisha did not revive, it was so that the deed should not be imputed to his soul alone; and to demonstrate that, even when the soul has departed, there remains a certain *dynamis* in the bodies of the saints, because they have been inhabited for so many years by righteous souls whose ministers they were. And let us not be lacking in belief that this is so, little children. For if handkerchieves and *smêkynthia* (which are external things) raised up the sick on contact with their bodies, how much more likely is it that the body of the prophet itself raised the dead man?

(Cyril of Jerusalem, *Catacheses* 18.16, *PG* 33:1036B–1037A [my translation], referring to 2/4 Kings 13:20–21. There is a similar exegesis of the same passage in *Constitutiones Apostolicae* 6.30, *PG* 5:988–989). At the end of this passage Cyril is referring to a passage in *Acts* which had considerable influence on the theory and practice of relic-devotion:

> God worked extraordinary miracles [*dynameis*] by the hands of Paul to the extent that it sufficed merely to apply handkerchieves or linens [*soudaria ê simikinthia*] which had been in contact with his body to the sick; then they were cured of their diseases and the evil spirits went out of them (Ac 19:12).

This is clearly a reference to *indirect* healing by an intermediary substance, not too different from the case of the woman in the gospel who had haemorraged for twelve years. She was cured merely by touching the hem of Jesus' garment, at which point he is said to have been aware that power had gone out of him (Mk 5:26–34 [Mt 9:20–22; Lk 8:43–48]). Peter and John appear to have healed the lame man at the Gate Beautiful merely by looking into his eyes (Ac 3:1–12), and elsewhere the mere shadow of Peter is said to have worked cures (Ac 15:5). In the process of time the idea that healing *dynamis* could be communicated indirectly by material objects was developed to considerable lengths: the very dust, for instance, from a martyr's shrine or a liquid poured over his bones could mediate *dynamis*. Or, to cite an extreme example, the fruit of a tree which had grown from the staff of a martyr was considered to be wonder-working (see *The Passion of Saint Themistocles*, c. 24, ed. John Wortley, *Anal. Boll.* 94 [1976] 32.

Whatever the process of communication might be, however, that which was communicated was from God, in accordance with the text 'Every good gift and every perfect endowment is from above, coming down from the Father of lights' (James 1:17). Moreover, what made this comunication possible was the outstanding holiness of the person of the first party. Had the Byzantine world been asked whether that role could possibly be served by a person who was an arch-robber and a perpetrator of evil deeds, the unanimous response would have been that it could not. And yet here we have a tale in which the healing grace of God is alleged to have been communicated by means of a wicked imposter's foot-water. It says something which is very rarely said elsewhere: that in this case, the healing of the paralysed sister took place within the subjective processes of her own mind, not by the intervention of the healing *dynamis* of the Almighty, or at least not so by the usual channels. (Note that in the longer version she is made to attribute her cure to the *prayers* of the holy man. If this was an attempt to save the situation, it only results in rendering the irony of it the more acute.) That a subjective element is necessary for a healing to take place is perfectly clear: 'Thy faith hath made thee whole' is axiomatic. But in the vast majority of recorded cases, the faith of the individual cooperates with a means of *dynamis* to produce the required results. It is easy enough for us to think that many of the relics in circulation probably were not what they purported to be, but it is almost unknown for a hagiographical source to admit that they might ever not have been, or that healing ocurred other than in the supposed manner.

BHG 1440kb, W871 is not unique in this respect. In the twenty-fourth miracle of SS. Cosmas and Damian, two people, a lame man and a dumb woman, are cured, ostensibly by the intervention of the saints, but in fact (and very obviously) by shock (see *Kosmas und Damien, Texte und Einleitung*; ed. Ludwig Deubner [Leipzig and Berlin, 1907] Wunder 24, pp. 162–164). There is a similar case in the west, in an anecdote told by Jacques de Vitry:

> I heard that many lame and deformed persons assembled at the tomb of a certain saint to be cured. But when they had been there

> two days and had still not been healed, they wanted to leave . . . . The priest addressed them: 'Do you want to be healed, so that you can go and run of your own accord?' They replied: 'We do want that, sir'. Then said the priest: 'Throw away all your canes', and when they were thrown away: 'Wait a little until fire is brought. For he who is the most disabled amongst us must be burnt. Then I will cast the ashes of his body over the others and they will be healed'. Each and every one of them now became very afraid that he would be judged to the most disabled, and thus be burned. Each began to force himself to such an extent that they all at once began to run away. Not one of them remained who did not leave the place without a cane: fear adds wings to feet!

(*The Exempla or illustrative stories from the sermones vulgares of Jacques de Vitry* [Jacobus Vitriacensis], ed. Thomas Frederick Crane; *Publications of the Folk-Lore Society*, No.26 [London, 1890] No 254.)

Doubtless there are other tales, both in east and west, which betray a somewhat irregular attitude to miraculous healings. But they are exceedingly rare, and the distinction of the Tale of the Converted Robber is enhanced by being one of them.

The text of the Tale of the Converted Robber has survived in two forms (shortly to be published in *Byzantion*), conveniently identified by reference to the Greek manuscripts as *APQ* and *LE*. The second of these is almost twice as long as the former and it is the longer version (*LE*) which is translated here. There is little doubt that the former is the older, possibly dating back to the end of the period in which the apophthegmatic tales flourished, *i.e.*, to the first half of the seventh century. Even the shorter version has detail and narrative of an order which set it apart from the succinct, laconic tales of the sixth century. There are ironic twists and hidden implications in it which are not to be discerned even in the more elaborate stories of John Moschos.

This shorter version, however, may not be an altogether original story. It might well have been inspired by a yet older story: one of the tales of the sixth-century Daniel of Scêtê which his disciple carefully preserved (English translation forthcoming, Cistercian Publications). Unlike (for instance) the tales of Anastasios the Sinaïte or Paul of Monembasia, these are not stories which the eponymous hero told, but mostly stories *about* him. The collection is in fact entitled *Ta kata ton Abban Daniêl* / Τὰ κατὰ τὸν ἀββᾶν Δανιήλ, 'The File on Daniel' (see *BHG* 2099z-2102d *etc*); many of its items were edited by Léon Clugnet in *Révue de l'Orient Chrétien* 5 (1900) 49–73 & 370–391.

The story in question is No. 7 in Clugnet's collection, No. 3, *pace* Halkin and W461 in the *Répertoire* of beneficial tales, *BHG* 2101, W461: The tale of the virgin who used to pretend to be drunk [*de virgine quae ebrietatem simulabat*—a very determined eye might even detect a similarity to *de latrone converso* in that '*simulabat*']. Here is the relevant passage from the centre of the story (Clugnet pp. 68–69) in translation—with the passages which suggest similarity with the other story expressed in italics:

> When [Daniel of Scêtê] came to Hermopolis, he said to his disciple: 'Go and *knock at that women's monastery* known as Abba Jeremiah's; *there are about three hundred nuns living there*'. The disciple *went and knocked; the portress said* to him in a small voice: 'Welcome, true believer; what can I do for you?' He said to her: '*Call the mother*-archimandrite for I wish to speak with her'. The other replied: 'She never meets with anybody; but tell me what it is you want and I will speak to her'. He said: 'Tell her *a certain monk* wishes to speak with her'. She went and told her; then the higoumenê came and said to the brother in a small voice: 'The amma sent me to ask you what you want', to which the brother retorted: '*That you would do us the favour of letting us sleep here, I and the elder, so that we not be devoured by wild beasts, for it is evening*'. The amma said to him: 'No man ever came in here; it is better for you to be devoured by wild beasts outside than to be inside'. The brother said: 'It is Abba Daniel of Scêtê [who seeks shelter]'. When she heard this, *she opened both doors and went out at a run and so did all the community and they made a carpet of their shawls stretching from the door down to where the elder was, grovelling at his feet and licking his soles.*
>
> When he came into the monastery, the lady [-abbess] *brought the great basin and filled it with warm water and herbs. She drew up the sisters in two choirs and they washed the elder's feet,* also the disciple's. Then, taking another vessel, she brought the sisters [close] and taking water from the basin, *she poured it on their heads. Then she poured some on her own breast and head*. The sisters all looked like stone, motionless and silent. Their entire concern was the divine office and in that they were as the angels. Then the elder said to the higoumenê: 'Are they honouring us or are the sisters always like this?' She said: 'Your servants are always like this, lord-and-master [δέσποτα,] but pray for them'. The elder said: 'Tell my disciple . . . [lacuna?] . . . *one [of the sisters] lay sleeping in the forecourt dressed in tattered rags*'. The elder asked: 'Who is this, sleeping here?' [The higoumenê] said: 'It is one of the sisters; she is a drunkard and we do not know what to do with her. We fear we will stand accused if we throw her out of the monastery, and if we leave her here, she degrades the sisters'. The elder said to his disciple: '*Get the basin and throw it on her*'. When he had done this, *she revived* as though from a drunken stupor. The amma said: 'She is always like this, lord-and-master'.

The rest of the story tells how it was revealed to Daniel that the sister was in fact a very holy person and it ends with the aphorism familiar to readers of the *Lives* of holy fools: 'How many hidden servants He has, [and they are known to Him alone.] (πόσους κρυπτοὺς ἔχει δούλους [καὶ μόνῳ αὐτῷ γνώρι μοί εἰσιν]).

The structural similarities are even more striking than the particulars: Someone thought to be a monk gains unusual access to a large ladies' monastery where he is welcomed and honoured as a great holy man by the entire community. He has his feet washed by all. The water is then used as an ἐυλογία for the sisters as a whole and for one in particular in whom it produces (or allows to be revealed) extraordinary effects. It seems at least not impossible that the two stories are linked in some way.

Whatever the origins of the story of the Converted Robber might be, it is the longer version which is of the greater interest from a literary point of view, for the characteristics of the *récit tardif* are clearly discernible here. It attempts to reproduce the characteristics of an earlier tale (which may itself be founded on a yet older one), and it expands on and enhances the appeal of the original(s). What makes this case so particularly interesting is that it is a rare case of a tale's antecedants having survived in recognisable form; hence we are able to trace the development of the tale to a certain extent.

This can be done (for instance) by posing the question: How has the later redactor treated his material? In general, being aware of the main irony of the story (the brigand's mounting confusion as he confronts first the entire assembled company of sisters and then their unaccountable devotion to him), he has exploited this to the full. He has given the arch-brigand two speeches (instead of one) in which he attempts to protest his unworthiness. The irony is intensified by the sisters' response to his first protest, which they take to be a demonstration of his great humility. But there are many other, lesser, ways in which the appeal of the story has been heightened: for instance, there is the manifestly irritated response of the robbers after their chief has derided all their suggestions for getting into the monastery. The action is now protracted by the chieftain first telling the band what he is going to do and say, then going ahead and doing it—the description being modified at each telling. (The reference to a Mesopotamian [monk] is presumably ommitted because nobody would know what it meant after the loss of the eastern provinces). Once the robber-chief is in the monastery, details are given of how the sisters were assembled (two hundred and sixty of them, not the mere sixty of the older version). A mere hint in the older version has been seized upon to locate the sick sister *in an upper room*, and to say that she was a *paralytic*—details with overtones recalling the Gospel stories of the ministry of Christ. As in the case of the chieftain's entry, we have two accounts of the sister's healing: first of what actually happened; then her own words describing it before the community. The first of these is given a quasi-evagelical termination: 'This was done that the scripture might be fulfilled', followed by a citation of a very rarely quoted text (Mt 10:41) which nevertheless is not impertinent here. It is, however, the last scene, in which one has to imagine the dialogue between the chieftain and his band shouted through a still-closed gate, which achieves the rare quality (almost completely unknown in spiritually beneficial tales) of being at once hilarious and deadly serious.

The longer version is a *relique de byzance* rather than of eremitic monachism. It is a fine piece of re-writing, obviously from the pen of someone who knew what he was doing most of the time. One can only repeat of him what was said of Paul of Monembasia: 'Il eût fallu qu'il préparât le chemin pour un Boccace byzantin', [he should have paved the way for a byzantine Boccaccio.] Unfortunately, there is not the slightest indication that one came after him.

Tale 18: NOTES ON THE TEXT

18/3 Theodoret says that in his time (early fifth century) there were many women who had embraced the monastic life, living in the hinterland of Antioch either as recluses or in communities, to the number of about two hundred and fifty, all sleeping on the same lowly mats, using their hands to process wool and their tongues to sing hymns (*Philotheos Historia* 30.4).

Presumably the robber would have to hide his hair to carry off the disguise, because a monk, having been tonsured, would have no hair, or very little of it.

'I am ashamed to stay in the city': the meaning of this is unclear.

Sêmantron: monks and nuns in the east are rarely summoned to prayer, not by bells, as in the West, but by the striking of a wooden sounding-board (occasionally a metal plate) which is suspended horizontally and struck with a mallet. There are also portable *sêmantra* about two metres long which can be struck as they are carried around the monastery-precincts.

Tale 19: *BHG* 1450x, W629: THE PROUD MONK.

This tale of the monk who became a torturer is surely both one of the most remarkable and one of the most enigmatic of all the tales. It manifests all the characteristics which distinguish the *récit tardif* from the *apophthegmata* and earlier tales which preceded it, and from the *exempla* which came later (and in the west). And yet those very characteristics are so pronounced that the tale is scarcely typical of its genre. There are other considerations which set it apart. For instance, there is the anonymity of it. Apart from the reference to Scêtê at the beginning (in the Armenian text only, see below) not a person or a place is mentioned by name, which is most unusual. Then again, it is a very complex story. In the *Sergius* the complexity arises from the weaving together of different tales. Here there is a single story, but it goes through five stages of development, closely dependent on an initial situation which is somewhat vaguely defined. It is a study in miniature of the progressive collapse of a man with a tragic flaw in his character and there is nothing else like it among the tales. There is also an unusually large 'cast', and it is a very, very violent story. Add to this the complete absence of familiar tales-motifs (even of the repentance-reconciliation motif) and the unusual nature of this tale is obvious. Yet in spite of its rare qualities (for it is, by any standards, a very good story), the Greek text (of which over a score of manuscripts are known to exist) was only recently published; see John Wortley, 'A *narratio* of rare distinction: *de monacho superbo, BHG* 1450x', *Analecta Bollandiana* 100 (1982) 351–363. There is a French translation of the text of Cod. Paris. Coislin 126 ff. 339v–341v (the C of the above edition) in *Les sentences des pères du désert*, nouveau recueil, édité par Dom L. Regnault et les moines de Solesmes, 2e édition (Solesmes, 1977) 144–146, while the Armenian version has been available for many years (*Apophthegmes des pères, collection systématique arménienne, Vies des saints pères*, 2 vols [Venice, 1855] item 5.20. A Latin translation is now available: L. Leloir, *Paterica armeniaca a PP. Mechitaristes edita [1855] nunc latine redita*: *CSCO* vol. 361, *Subsidia* vol.43 (Louvain, 1975) items 5.20 A,B, pp. 22–26. see also J. Wortley, 'De Monacho superbo: BHG 1450x, a mediaeval Greek anecdote', *Florilegium* 1 (1979) 126–139.

As with most tales, the age of this one is almost impossible to state with any accuracy, for although the manuscripts of the renaissance era attributed it to Paul of Monembasia, it is clearly the work of a man whose Greek style was quite different from Paul's. Moreover, its inclusion in the venerable Cod. Paris. Coislin 126 rather suggests that it had already gained a place in an accepted tradition even before Paul's work was properly in circulation. But is it just a little older, or a lot older than Paul's work? The lone monk, the fleeing officer, the hereditary office, the provincial administration as here portrayed—these all tend at first to suggest a situation remote both in time and space from tenth-century Constantinople (or Monembasia). But on closer examination, perhaps they are not so improbable as they seem. It would be idle to pretend that torture, repression, and violence were absent from the Byzantine world of the Macedonian era, and we know from Paul's stories that proud monks certainly were not. So whilst this story might to a certain extent be the imaginings of a late ninth- tenth-century *romancier*, he too, like Paul, might be presenting us with a mirror of his times.

As we have already indicated, the story has come down in two forms, Greek (*Gr*) and Armenian (*Arm.B*)., of which the Armenian is the longer version, though not by a great deal. One would normally assume that the longer version is an expansion of the shorter (hence older) version, but in this case, the opposite may be true. The Greek version picks up all the sensationalism of the story, but little of its meaning and has not much understanding of what is going on. For instance *Gr* seems unaware of the tradition (going back to the reforms of Diocletian and Constantine) of hereditary offices, fully explained by *Arm.B*. It might therefore possibly be the case that the Armenian version is the older, and for that reason, where it differes from *Gr* or adds anything of substance, *Arm. B* has been followed in the present translation.

Tale 19: NOTES ON THE TEXT

19/2 The monk's choice of Isaac as a role-model might be intended to indicate his ignorance of scripture, for Isaac is nowhere portrayed as a person of exceptional patience, unless perhaps (having been the victim in Abraham's abhortive sacrifice [Gen 22]) as an example of the great monastic virtue of *hypomonê*, patience. Isaac is, however, portrayed in Gal 3.16 and 4.21–23 as a type of Christ and of the church.

19/15 officer, *stratiôtês*: as *miles* in the west, this word went from denoting any soldier to designating one of rank and, ultimately, an officer.

19/17 king, *basileus*, or 'emperor' (*Arm B* omits *my*).

19/18 the girl and child (*korê, pais*) are slaves, since they are later referred to as property ('handmaid and house-boy,?'); see lines 103–104, 'my child-slave and virgin handmaid'.

19/¶2 Mr Constantine Zuckerman has kindly pointed out that the failure of the populace to come to the aid of the officer might indicate that he is meant to be a deserter, and that the entire action is supposed to take place within the Empire.

Tale 20: *BHG* 2027, W042: ANNA, WHO WAS RENAMED EUPHÊMIANOS.

The Greek text of this story is published in *Synaxarium Ecclesiae Constantinoplitanae*, 173.16–177.46; the line references of the translation refer to the Greek text, a= p.173/174, b= p.175/176, c= p.177/178, edited in the apparatus of the *Synaxarium* as it is only found in the *M** codices (see *Synax.CP* pp. xxxviii ff).

This tale well illustrates the difficulty of clearly designating a genre of tales. Whilst on the one hand it contains many elements frequently associated with the tales-tradition, on the other, it comes very near to being a *vita* (or a part of one).

20/a18 Blachernae: the palace complex (including a famous church of the Theotokos) where the main land-wall joined the Golden Horn.

20/a21 Leo IV, the Khazar, 775–780. This charge is somewhat difficult to believe, for, far from being the savage persecuter of the icons and of monks that his father, Constantine V Copronymus (741–775), had been, he seems to have pursued a program of non-violent iconoclasm and actually to have befriended the monks (Theophanes, 449). The worst that can be said of him seems to be that he whipped those who secretly introduced icons into the palace (Theophanes 453).

20/b15 Of the female disguised as a monk taken to be a eunuch there are at least two other known examples. In *BHG* 80a Anastasia the patrician, having fallen foul of the empress Theodora, takes ship and flees to Abba

Daniel the Scetiote. He clothes her, pretending she is an eunuch. At his command she remains in a cave twenty-eight years, summoning him only at the moment of death. He gives her Communion, prays with her and then buries her, cautioning his disciple (who has noted that this was no eunuch) to be silent on the matter. Another example is *BHG* 1318w, W009 (see notes to tale No. 15, above).

Tale 21: *BHG* 1322n, W486: THE BOY CAST INTO THE FURNACE AND SAVED.

This title is not found in the manuscripts; it is the one supplied by Halkin in *BHG*. The text was edited by Th. Nissen in *Byzantinische Zeitschrift* 38 (1938) 361–365 (No. 8).

This story has been included because it may be a very early example of a *récit tardif*. It is not a very good one, or a very attractive one with its blatantly anti-jewish bias. But it is interesting as an attempt to forge together certain well-established tale-themes into a single, longer narrative. It is also interesting that, unlike most of the tales included in this book, here we have one which has no apparent Constantinopolitan connection or indeed a connection with any city. It is rural and almost totally unmonastic.

The themes used here are:

1. The children who played at celebrating the eucharist. *Pratum Spirituale* c. 196 (*BHG* 1318x, W364; CS 139:172–174) is a long and more detailed account of the incident. Whether this story was germane to the *Pratum* or not, there is little doubt that it was used by the writer of the present story.

2. The jewish glass-blower at Constantinople who thrust his son into the glass-furnace for partaking (inadvertently) of the christian eucharist: *cf BHG* 1076k, W488 (= Mioni 12,) also in Evagrius, *HE* 4.36, *PG* 86/2:2769, but this story comes in several versions. It is usually set in Justinian's time (527–565) and usually the child claims to have been comforted by a woman in purple.

3. The purple-clad woman is still there in what might be an earlier version of the present story, found in Cod. Paris Graec. 1596, pp. 60–61. There the tale is attributed to John of Melitene and is set in Armenia (by Ararat). The story goes much as here except that it is simpler. The Jewish father (neither a glass-blower nor a rabbi) throws the boy into the furnace himself, once only. And it is the bishop who comes (once only) and finds the child when he goes to investigate why there is no heat in the bath.

4. Clearly underlying all these furnace stories is the story of the three children in the burning fiery furnace of Babylon, to which most of them refer (Dan 3:19–30). That story is particularly beloved of eastern Christians who annually celebrate the Feast of the Three Children (formerly with dramatic representation)

on 17 December: see *Synax. CP.* 317, 15–320, 8. The furnace was of course taken to pre-figure the holy sepulchre, the three children the persons of the Trinity and so forth. There is a tale in the *Plêrophoriai* of John Rufus, bishop of Maïouma (c. 14 in *PO* 8:1–161), of an Egyptian prophet, Abba Andrew (an anti-Chalcedonian) who had a vision of many bishops heating up a hot furnace in which they tightly enclosed *a child*, splendid like gold, for three days. After that the child emerged safe and sound; it was Jesus. 'The bishops have crucified me again' he said, 'which was true, for the Nestorians were sick with the sickness of the Jews in that they said it was a man and not God that they had crucified'. (The *Plêrophoriai*—'informations', were written in Greek shortly after 512 and contain many useful memories of the 'Chalcedonian crisis' following the Council of 451, but only the syriac translation has survived). It would appear that considerably greater religious significance would have been seen in this complex of stories by our ancestors than springs immediately to our eyes.

Notes on c. 1:

New Lavra: the New Lavra was founded in 507 by a group of malcontents from Saint Sabas' monastery further north in the hills of Judaea. The story is thus given a background very similar to those of *Pratum Spirituale* (to which Nissen suggested it belonged).

his son or his boy: *i.e.* his son or his slave/hired youth.

c. 2:

eucharist: *synaxis*, lit. 'a service', but nearly always the Eucharist.

chief rabbi: *archirembê.* It appears that *rabbi* was pronounced *rebbi* in certain dialects.

'one is holy': in the eastern rite, the celebrant invites the faithful to communion by raising the Holy Bread and exclaiming: 'Holy [gifts] to the holy [people]' and the response is: 'One is holy, one is lord: Jesus Christ, to the glory of God the Father'. Then the people receive (see F.E. Brightman, *Liturgies Eastern and Western*, vol. 1 [Oxford, 1896] p. 341).

c. 4:

magistrate: *kathedrarios*, a very rare word, trans. *Dorfschulze* (village mayor) by Nissen, but obviously something more important.

emir: *amêra*, a common designation of a Moslem authority.

c. 5:

pieces of gold, *nomismata, i.e.* 10 x 4.55 gr.

close up the furnace: *anachriein*, lit., 'anoint' it. It would appear that once the fire was burning well, a slab [*plax*] was placed over the mouth of the furnace. In all likelihood this would then be 'sealed' (another possible meaning of the word) with wet clay to prevent more than a very little air getting in. The fire would burn slowly and for a long time, even a whole week (see below).

c. 6:

Master: *Adonaï*, a nice bit of *local colour*.

c. 9:

counsellor: *symboulos*.

It is difficult to grasp the role of 'the counsellor'. Obviously an authority superior to the emir, he is at first angered by the boy's adhesion to Christianity (which suggests he is a Jew), but then he adumbrates not only the chief rabbi but also his religion in ways which make this very unlikely. Nothing can be drawn from the last passage where he commits the boys to monasteries; this is a feature of earlier stories which have survived. It is not impossible that both emir and 'counsellor' are Muslims whose tolerant rule (in pre-Turkish times) the Christians had cause to appreciate. As the last section of the tale clearly indicates, the author is primarily concerned to villify the Jews with whom the Christians were forced to cohabit as equals under Moslem rule.

seal and guards: an oblique reference to Matt 27:62–66.

c. 11:

evil deeds: John 5:43, 8:24.

Tale 22: *BHG* 1318y, W051: THE TWO BROTHERS.

The text was edited by Hippolyte Delehaye in his *Mélanges d'hagiographie grècque et latine, Subsidia Hagiographica* No. 42 (Brussels, 1966) item 29, 'Un group de récits "utiles à l'âme'" pp. 389–393, from Cod. Paris. suppl. graec. 28, ff.343–344 (defective). The tale is also found in Codd. Ann Arbor 41, Oxon. Holkham 43, and Marciano II.101.

This is in some ways the most puzzling of all the tales contained in the present collection. The paradox is this: it is written in a Greek style significantly more sophisticated than that of Paul of Monembasia. Therefore, unless he was capable of deliberately elevating his style on occasion, or unless we are looking at a quasi-'Metaphrastic' version of an earlier text (neither of which is beyond the bounds of possibility), this is not one of his compositions. Yet it contains many elements that are also encountered in the first ten stories of this volume, in those which there is good reason to believe are the work of Paul. If that were all there was to it, the explanation would be that Paul had an imitator, as indeed Tale No. 12 (The Woman Discovered on an Island with her Son) suggests he might have had. But this tale also contains elements reminiscent, sometimes directly reminiscent, of other stories (some of them included here) which are most unlikely to have any connection with Paul whatsoever. In some ways, The Tale of the Two Brothers is a crossroads where many of the elements of the tales-tradition intersect.

This has led to the conclusion that there was indeed a tradition of tales-writing in the tenth century to which Paul clearly belonged, but of which he was by no means the only, or even the best, practitioner.

It was a tradition which drew on more or less the same legacy of commonplaces and which sometimes did little more than rearrange them in different patterns in order to illuminate some one religious doctrine rather than another. As Delehaye observed, the teaching of the present story is less elevated than usual, demonstrating (as it does) that monks have no monopoly on sanctity. 'Mais l'auteur exagère à ce point les privilèges de son laïc que la parabole en prend je ne sais quelle teinte anticléricale, si ce néologisme est de mise ici,' commented the learned Bollandist [the author so exaggerated the privileges of his layman that the parable takes on a decidedly anticlerical flavour, if it is not too much of an anachronism to use that word in this context]. It may not have escaped the reader's notice that there are 'anticlerical' elements in some of the other stories too, especially in *The Proud Monk* [No. 19].

22/4 *mnêsikakia*: lit., 'remembering evils'.

'the one had no wish to set eyes on the other'; *cf* Tale No. 15,55–56, 'I did not wish to see them nor they me'.

22/9–15 Compare this speech with Tale No 11,11–13.

22/16 This favourite formula of Paul (*ho eusplagchnos kai philanthropos Theos*) occurs a number of times here. This and the following four lines bear a most striking similarity to Tale No. 7,6–8. The quotation is 1 Tim 2:4; in the equivalent position Tale No. 7 quotes 2 Pet 3:9 which is almost identical. Tale No. 3 also has to do with confessing to an elder on Mount Olympus.

22/25 'have you not heard . . .'. *cf* Tale No. 10,17.

Ephraem: Saint Ephraem the Syrian (*ca* 306–373) whose voluminous works are mainly in verse and in Syriac, but which circulated in Greek from a very early date. Ephraem is cited more frequently than any other single author by Paul Euergetinos, *ca* 1050. See (most recently) the article in *DACL* 15:590–597; also *DS* 4:800–815.

22/30 In Tale No. 7 also the elder on Olympus tells the penitent there is no remedy for his sin, but suggests no alternative path.

22/33 Jn 13:34; Mt 18:22.

22/81 *cf* Tale No. 12, 99–100: 'then, together with her son, she withdrew to the innermost part of the island'.

22/92 There is a lacuna in the manuscript here.

22/100 *cf* the speech of Sergius the *dêmotês* of Alexandria, Tale No. 16,69–74.

22/105–6 Mt 5:7.

22/109 From this point the story begins to resemble Tale No. 5 in a number of ways.

22/111 'The Lord will arrange *etc.*': This expression, or something very similar to it, occurs three times in Paul's Tales, Nos. 2 (26–27) 4 (38–39) and 6 (14–15) (also *cf* No. 9, 41 and 51). It also recurs in this story, lines 133–4 below.

22/125 The re-appearance of the dead brother greatly resembles the re-appearance of the dead bishop in Tale No. 6.

22/140–1 *cf* Tale No. 5,58–59.

22/151 There are sixteen more lines of text which contain an extended and highly theological ascription of praise.

Tale 23: *BHG* 1442mb, W491: THE JUDGEMENTS OF GOD, ed. Mioni (6), Nissen (2).

This story bears a remarkable likeness to the well-known episode of The Hermit (*L'Hermite*) almost at the end of Voltaire's *conte philosophique, Zadig ou la destinée.* As comentators on Voltaire point out, the origins of this episode are to be sought in the Talmud and so, presumably, are those of the present tale. This makes it of particular interest for, whilst Talmudic origins might well be suspected for several of the tales, in only two cases have these been definitely established; the other one is *BHG* 1322zk/1438p, W600, Nau 450: *de Hebraeo divite / de lapide pretiosa in veste Aaron, Systematikon* 5.48: A man at Jerusalem who had acquired great riches by unjust means, prompted by Prov 19:17, sold all and gave to the poor, thereby lending to God. But nobody helped him in *his* poverty, until one day he had the good fortune to buy, very cheaply, a stone which a jeweller recognised as the much sought-after gem which had fallen from Aaron's ephod. In return for it, the high priest generously rewarded the man—and made him rich again. [George the Monk, *Chronicon*, ed. C. de Boor p. 216, 24–218, 8; *PG* 110:268–269].

Thy judgements . . . . Ps 35:6.

SELECT BIBLIOGRAPHY

Apophthegmata Patrum, Collectio alphabetica: *PG* 65:71–440, supplemented by J.-C. Guy in *Recherches sur la Tradition grecque des apophthegmata patrum*, Brussels 1962, trans. Jean-Claude Guy, *Les Apophtegmes des Pères du Désert*, Bellefontaine 1966 and trans. Benedicta Ward, *The Sayings of the Desert Fathers*. Oxford and Kalamazoo 1975.

Apophthegmata Patrum, Collectio systematica: critical edition: *Les Apophtegmes des Pères: collection systématique chapitres I-IX, introduction, texte critique, traduction et notes* by Jean-Claude Guy, Sources Chrétiennes 387, Paris 1993 (two more volumes to follow); early Latin translation of Pelagius and John, *PL* 73: 851–1052; complete French translation by J. Dion and G. Oury, *Les Sentences des Pères du Désert: Recueil de Pélage et Jean*, Solesmes 1966, and L. Régnault, *Les sentences des pères du désert: nouveau recueil*, Solesmes 1970. No english translation as yet.

Barlaam and Joasaph: trans G. R. Woodward and H. Mattingly, London: Loeb 1914.

Brown, Peter: *The Body and Society: Men, Women and Sexual Renunciation in Early Christianity*. New York 1988.

Butler, C. See Palladius, *Historia Lausiaca*.

Chitty, J. Derwas: *The Desert a City; An Introduction to the Study of Egyptian and Palestinian Monasticism under the Christian Empire*, Oxford 1966; rpt. Crestwood, New York.

Climacus. See John Climacus.

Davidson, Gladys R. *The Minor Objects, Corinth XII*, Princeton 1952.

de Boor, Charles. See George the Monk.

Delehaye, Hippolyte: 'Vita Sancti Nicephori episcopi Milesii saeculo x', *Anal. Boll.* 14 (1895) 130–166.

———. 'La vie de sainte Théoctiste de Lesbos', *Byzantion* 1 (1924) 191–200.

———. See *Synax. CP.*

———. 'Un group de récits "utiles à l'âme'", *Mélanges d'hagiographie grècque et latine, Subsidia Hagiographica* No. 42. Brussels 1966: Pp. 384–393 (item 29).

Didascalia Apostolorum, ed. and trans. R. F. Connolly. Oxford 1929.

Evagrius. *Historia Ecclesiastica*: *PG* 86:2415–22906; also ed. Bidez and Parmentier. London 1898; english translation with Theodoret, *HE* (*q.v.*), in Bohn's Ecclesiastical Library (1854) pp. 251–467. French translation by André-Jean Festugière OP, 'Evagre, *Histoire Ecclésiastique*', *Byzantion* 45 (1975) 187–488.

Euergetinos. See Paul Euergetinos.

George the Monk, *Chronicon*: ed. Charles de Boor, 2 vols. Stuttgart, 1904.

Gouillard, Jean: 'Le Synodicon de l'Orthodoxie', *Travaux et Mémoires* 2 (1967).

Gregory the Great, *Dialogues:* ed. Adalbert de Vogüé, trans. Paul Antin. Sources Chrétiennes 260, 265. Paris 1979, 1980.

Gregory of Nyssa, *La vie de sainte Macrine*. ed. and trans. Pierre Marval. Sources Chrétiennes 178. Paris 1971; translated by W. K. L. Clarke, *The Life of Saint Macrina* (London 1916); by Kevin Corrigan (Toronto: Peregrina, 1987); by Joan M. Petersen, in *Handmaids of the Lord* (Kalamazoo, 1996).

Halkin, François. See also *BHG*.

———. *Recherches et Documents d'hagiographie byzantine*. Subsidia Hagiographica 51. Brussels, 1971.

Janin, Raymond. *La Géographie ecclésiastique de l'empire byzantin*, première partie: *Le siège de Constantinople et le patriarcat oecuménique*, tome trois: *Les églises et les monastères*, deuxième édition. Paris 1969.

Jerome (Hieronymus). See *Vita Sancti Paul Thebaei*.

John Climacus, *Klimax tou paradeisou* [*Scala Paradisi*, The Ladder of Paradise]. *PG* 88:585–1248; English translation by Lazarus Moore. London 1959.

John Rufus, Bishop of Maïouma, *Plerophoriai*: ed. and trans. F. Nau, *Patrologia Orientalis* 8:1–161.

John Moschos: *Pratum Spirituale*; ed. J.P. Migne (after Fronto Ducaeus and J.-B. Cotelier), with the latin translation of Florentine humanist Ambrose Traversari ('Fra Ambrogio') 1346–1439, PG 87:2851–3112; french translation by M.-J. Rouët de Journel, *Le Pré Spirituel*, Sources Chrétiennes 12, Paris 1946; italian translation by Riccardo Maisano, *Giovanni Mosco, Il Prato*, Naples 1982; english translation by John Wortley, *The Spiritual Meadow of John Moschus*, CS 139, Kalamazoo 1993; a new edition of the greek text and french translation are in preparation by Philip Pattenden.

Kalliga, Haris. *Byzantine Monemvasia*, (as yet) unpublished Ph.D. Dissertation. London 1987.

Kominis, Athanasio. 'Paolo di Monembasia', *Byzantion* 29/30 (1959–60) 231–248.

Laurent, Vincent. 'La liste épiscopale du synedicon de Monembasie', *Echos d'Orient* 32 (1933).

———. *Le Corpus des Sceaux de l'Empire byzantin* V/1. Paris 1963.

Lausiac History: See Palladius

Liddell and Scott. *A Greek-English Lexicon*, compiled by H. G. Liddell and R. Scott. Oxford 1883, 1940.

Mioni, Elpidio. 'Il Pratum Spirituale di Giovanni Mosco', *Orientalia Christiana Periodica* 17 (1951) 61–94.

Moschos or Moschus. See John Moschos; see also Mioni and Nissen.

Nau, F. 'Histoires des solitaires égyptiens', *Revue de l'Orient chrétien* 12 (1907) through 18 (1913) *passim*. Greek text of the first four hundred tales found in Cod. Paris. Coislin 126, and a French translation of tales 1–215.

Nissen, Th. 'Unbekannte Erzählungen aus dem Pratum Spirituale', *Byzantinische Zeitschrift* 38 (1938) 351–376.

Palladius, *Historia Lausiaca:* ed. C. Butler, Texts and Studies 6, Cambridge 1898–1904; trans. W. K.Lowther Clarke, London 1918; and Robert T. Meyer, Ancient Christian Writers 36, Westminster, Maryland 1965.

Paramelle, Joseph and Bernard Flusin. 'De syncletica in deserto Iordanis, *BHG* 1318w', *Anal. Boll.* 100 (1982) 305–317.

Patlagean, Evelyn. 'L'histoire de la femme déguisée en moine et l'évolution de la sainteté feminine à Byzance', *Studi Medievali* s. III 17 (1976) 597–623.

Paul Euergetinos. *Euergetinon: A Collection [synagôgê] of the inspired sayings of the godly and holy fathers gathered together from the entirety of divinely inspired literature*, sixth edition, four volumes. Athens 1980.

Peeters, Paul, ed. 'Arab xiii', 'Histoire de l'invention des corps des saints Valère l'évêque, Vincent le diacre et

Eulalie (ou Anastasie) la vièrge dans le Péloponnèse', *Anal. Boll.* 30 (1911) 301–304.

———. ed. 'Arab xiv', 'Narratio miraculi quod contingit in imagine sancti Cyri thaumaturgi [apud Monembasiam]', *Anal. Boll.* 25 (1906) 236–240.

Pratum Spirituale: See Moschos, John.

Rufinus, *Historia Monachorum:* PL 21:467–540.

Sauget, J. M. 'Le Paterikon du MS Arabe 276 de la Bibliothèque Nationale de Paris', *Le Muséon* 82 (1969) 363–403; and its appendix: 'Les *Histoires utiles à l'âme* de Paul de Monembasie', *ibid.*, pp. 395–404.

Sophronios, Patriarch of Jerusalem. See Moschos, John, and *Vita Sanctae Mariae Aegyptianae.*

SPD: Recueil de Pélage et Jean. Jean Dion and Guy Oury, edd. Solesmes 1966, 1976.

SPD: Nouveau Recueil. Lucien Regnault, ed. Solesmes 1970, 1977.

SPD: Troisième recueil et Tables. Lucien Regnault, ed. Solesmes 1976.

SPD: Collection alphabétique. Lucien Regnault, ed. Solesmes 1981.

SPD: Série des anonymes [Systematikon]. Lucien Regnault, ed. Solesmes-Bellefontaine 1985.

Systematikon: See *Apophthegmata Patrum, Collectio systematica.*

Theodoret of Cyrrhus, *Philotheos Historia* ['Religious History']: ed. and trans. Paul Canivet and Alice Leroy-Molinghen, *Histoire des moines de Syrie*, Sources Chrétiennes 234, 257. Paris 1977, 1979; translated by R. M. Price, *A History of the Monks of Syria*, CS 88, Kalamazoo 1985.

Theophanes, Chronographia: ed. Charles de Boor, 2 volumes. Leipzig 1883, 1885.

Vita Sanctae Macrinae. See Gregory of Nyssa.

Vita Sanctae Mariae Aegyptianae: *PG* 87:3697–3726.

Vita Sanctae Theoctistae Lesbiae: Acta Sanctorum Nov. vol. 4: 224–233.

Vita sancti Andreae sali: *PG* 111:625–888.

Vita sancti Basilii junioris, *BHG* 246z–260.

Vita Sancti Pauli junioris, *BHG* 1474: ed. H. Delehaye, *Anal. Boll.* 11 (1892) 19–74, 136–181.

Vita Sancti Pauli Thebaei (Jerome's *Life of Saint Paul of Thebes*): ed. K.T. Corey in Oldfather and Corey, *Studies in the Text-tradition of Saint Jerome's* Vitae Patrum. Urbana 1943: pp. 158–172.

Wortley, John: 'BHG 1450x: a narratio of rare distinction', First edition of Greek text with introduction and notes, *Anal. Boll.* 100 (1982), Festschrift Halkin, 351–363.

———.'De Monacho superbo: BHG 1450x, a mediaeval Greek anecdote', *Florilegium* 1 (1979) 126–139.

———.'An unpublished anecdote of an unworthy priest and Saint Basil', *Anal. Boll.* 97 (1979) 363–371.

———. *Les récits édifiants de Paul, évêque de Monembasie et d'autres auteurs*. Paris 1987.

———. 'Three not-so-miraculous miracles' in *Health, disease and healing in medieval culture*, the selected proceedings of a recent conference held at the Centre for Medieval Studies, University of Toronto. New York: St Martin's Press 1992

———. '*De Eustathii somnio (BHG* 1317d,) the tale of an Alexandrine banker', *Byzantion* 62 (1992) 424–432

———. 'The spirit of rivalry in early Christian monachism', *Greek, Roman and Byzantine Studies* 33/4 (1993) 1–22.

———. 'The genre and sources of the *Synagogê*' [of Paul Euergetinos] in *The Theotokos Evergetis and eleventh-century monasticism*. Belfast, 1994, pp. 306–324

———. 'Military elements in psychophelitic tales and sayings', in *Peace and War in Byzantium; Essays in honor of George T. Dennis* SJ. Washington 1995, pp. 89–105.

———. '*De latrone converso (BHG* 1450kb,) the tale of a converted robber', *Byzantion* 66 (1996).

CISTERCIAN PUBLICATIONS, INC.

TITLES LISTING

CISTERCIAN TEXTS

THE WORKS OF BERNARD OF CLAIRVAUX

Apologia to Abbot William
Five Books on Consideration: Advice to a Pope
Grace and Free Choice
Homilies in Praise of the Blessed Virgin Mary
The Life and Death of Saint Malachy the Irishman
Love without Measure. Extracts from the Writings of St Bernard (Paul Dimier)
On Loving God
The Parables of Saint Bernard (Michael Casey)
Sermons for the Summer Season
Sermons on the Song of Songs I - IV
The Steps of Humility and Pride

THE WORKS OF WILLIAM OF SAINT THIERRY

The Enigma of Faith
Exposition on the Epistle to the Romans
Exposition on the Song of Songs
The Golden Epistle
The Nature of Dignity of Love

THE WORKS OF AELRED OF RIEVAULX

Dialogue on the Soul
The Mirror of Charity
Spiritual Friendship
Treatises I: On Jesus at the Age of Twelve, Rule for a Recluse, The Pastoral Prayer
Walter Daniel: The Life of Aelred of Rievaulx

THE WORKS OF JOHN OF FORD

Sermons on the Final Verses of the Songs of Songs I - VII

THE WORKS OF GILBERT OF HOYLAND

Sermons on the Songs of Songs I-III
Treatises, Sermons and Epistles

OTHER EARLY CISTERCIAN WRITERS

The Letters of Adam of Perseigne I
Baldwin of Ford: Spiritual Tractates I - II
Gertrud the Great of Helfta: Spiritual Exercises
Gertrud the Great of Helfta: The Herald of God's Loving-Kindness
Guerric of Igny: Liturgical Sermons I - II
Idung of Prüfening: Cistercians and Cluniacs: The Case of Cîteaux
Isaac of Stella: Sermons on the Christian Year
The Life of Beatrice of Nazareth
Serlo of Wilton & Serlo of Savigny
Stephen of Lexington: Letters from Ireland
Stephen of Sawley: Treatises

MONASTIC TEXTS

EASTERN CHRISTIAN TRADITION

Besa: The Life of Shenoute
Cyril of Scythopolis: Lives of the Monks of Palestine
Dorotheos of Gaza: Discourses
Evagrius Ponticus:Praktikos and Chapters on Prayer
The Harlots of the Desert (Benedicta Ward)
John Moschos: The Spiritual Meadow
The Lives of the Desert Fathers
The Lives of Simeon Stylites (Robert Doran)
The Luminous Eye (Sebastian Brock)
Mena of Nikiou: Isaac of Alexandra & St Macrobius
Pachomian Koinonia I - III
Paphnutius: A Histories of the Monks of Upper Egypt
The Sayings of the Desert Fathers
Spiritual Direction in the Early Christian East (Irénée Hausherr)
Spiritually Beneficial Tales of Paul of Monembasia
Symeon the New Theologian: The Theological and Practical Treatises & The Three Theological Discourses
The Syriac Fathers on Prayer and the Spiritual Life (Sebastian Brock)

WESTERN CHRISTIAN TRADITION

Anselm of Canterbury: Letters I - III
Bede: Commentary on the Seven Catholic Epistles
Bede: Commentary on the Acts of the Apostles
Bede: Homilies on the Gospels I - II
Gregory the Great: Forty Gospel Homilies
The Meditations of Guigo I, Prior of the Charterhouse (A. Gordon Mursell)
Guigo II the Carthusian: Ladder of Monks and Twelve Meditations
Handmaids of the Lord: The Lives of Holy Women in Late Antiquity and the Early Middle Ages (Joan Petersen)
Peter of Celle: Selected Works
The Letters of Armand-Jean de Rancé I - II
The Rule of the Master
The Wound of Love: A Carthusian Miscellany

CHRISTIAN SPIRITUALITY

Abba: Guides to Wholeness & Holiness East & West
A Cloud of Witnesses: The Development of Christian Doctrine (D.N. Bell)
Athirst for God: Spiritual Desire in Bernard of Clairvaux's Sermons on the Song of Songs (M. Casey)
Cistercian Way (André Louf)
Drinking From the Hidden Fountain (Spidlék)
Eros and Allegory: Medieval Exegesis of the Song of Songs (Denys Turner)
Fathers Talking (Aelred Squire)
Friendship and Community (B. McGuire)
From Cloister to Classroom
Herald of Unity: The Life of Maria Gabrielle Sagheddu (M. Driscoll)
Life of St Mary Magdalene and of Her Sister St Martha (D. Mycoff)
The Name of Jesus (Irénée Hausherr)
No Moment Too Small (Norvene Vest)
Penthos: The Doctrine of Compunction in the Christian East (Irénée Hausherr)
Rancé and the Trappist Legacy (A.J. Krailsheimer)
The Roots of the Modern Christian Tradition
Russian Mystics (S. Bolshakoff)
The Spirituality of the Christian East (Tomas Spidlík)
Spirituality of the Medieval West (André Vauchez)
Tuning In To Grace (André Louf)
Wholly Animals: A Book of Beastly Tales (D.N. Bell)

TITLES LISTING

MONASTIC STUDIES

Community & Abbot in the Rule of St Benedict I - II (Adalbert De Vogüé)
Beatrice of Nazareth in Her Context (Roger De Ganck)
The Call of Silent Love, Carthusian Novice Conference
The Finances of the Cistercian Order in the Fourteenth Century (Peter King)
Fountains Abbey & Its Benefactors (Joan Wardrop)
A Gathering of Friends: Learning & Spirituality in John of Forde
The Hermit Monks of Grandmont (Carole A. Hutchison)
In the Unity of the Holy Spirit (Sighard Kleiner)
The Joy of Learning & the Love of God: Essays in Honor of Jean Leclercq
Monastic Practices (Charles Cummings)
The Occupation of Celtic Sites in Ireland by the Canons Regular of St Augustine and the Cistercians (Geraldine Carville)
Reading Saint Benedict (Adalbert de Vogüé)
The Rule of St Benedict: A Doctrinal and Spiritual Commentary (Adalbert de Vogüé)
The Rule of St Benedict (Br. Pinocchio)
Towards Unification with God (Beatrice of Nazareth in Her Context, II)
St Hugh of Lincoln (D.H. Farmer)
Serving God First (Sighard Kleiner)
The Way of Silent Love
With Greater Liberty: A Short History of Christian Monasticism and Religious Orders
The Wound of Love: A Carthusian Miscellany

CISTERCIAN STUDIES

A Difficult Saint (B. McGuire)
A Second Look at Saint Bernard (J. Leclercq)
Bernard of Clairvaux and the Cistercian Spirit (Jean Leclercq)
Bernard of Clairvaux: Man, Monk, Mystic (M. Casey) Tapes and readings
Bernard of Clairvaux: Studies Presented to Dom Jean Leclercq
Bernardus Magister
Christ the Way: The Christology of Guerric of Igny (John Morson)
Cistercian Sign Language
The Cistercian Spirit
The Cistercians in Denmark (Brian McGuire)
The Cistercians in Scandinavia (James France)
The Eleventh-century Background of Cîteaux (Bede K. Lackner)
Image and Likeness: The Augustinian Spirituality of William of St Thierry (D.N. Bell)
An Index of Authors & Works in Cistercian Libraries in Great Britain I (D.N. Bell)
An Index of Cistercian Authors and Works in Medieval Library Catalogues in Great Britain (D.N. Bell)
The Mystical Theology of St Bernard (Etiénne Gilson)
Nicolas Cotheret's Annals of Cîteaux (Louis J. Lekai)
The Spiritual Teachings of St Bernard of Clairvaux (J.R. Sommerfeldt)
Studiosorum Speculum
William, Abbot of St Thierry
Women and St Bernard of Clairvaux (Jean Leclercq)

MEDIEVAL RELIGIOUS WOMEN

Lillian Thomas Shank and John A. Nichols, editors

Distant Echoes
Peace Weavers
Hidden Springs: Cistercian Monastic Women, 2 Vol.
What Nuns Read: Books & Libraries in Medieval English Nunneries (D.N. Bell)

STUDIES IN CISTERCIAN ART AND ARCHITECTURE

Meredith Parsons Lillich, editor

Volumes II, III, IV now available

THOMAS MERTON

The Climate of Monastic Prayer (T. Merton)
The Legacy of Thomas Merton (P. Hart)
The Message of Thomas Merton (P. Hart)
Thomas Merton: The Monastic Journey
Thomas Merton Monk (P.Hart)
Thomas Merton Monk & Artist (Victor Kramer)
Thomas Merton on St Bernard
Toward an Integrated Humanity (M. Basil Pennington et al.)

CISTERCIAN LITURGICAL DOCUMENTS SERIES

Chrysogonus Waddell, ocso, editor

Hymn Collection of the Abbey of the Paraclete
Institutiones nostrae: The Paraclete Statutes
Molesme Summer-Season Breviary (4 volumes)
Old French Ordinary and Breviary of the Abbey of the Paraclete: Text & Commentary (2 vol.)
The Cadouin Breviary (two volumes)
The Twelfth-century Cistercian Psalter
The Twelfth-century Usages of the Cistercian Lay-brothers
Two Early *Libelli Missarum*

Cistercian Publications is a non-profit corporation. Its publishing program is restricted to monastic texts in translation and books on the monastic tradition.

North American customers may order these books through booksellers or directly from the warehouse:

Cistercian Publications (Distributor)
St Joseph's Abbey
Spencer, Massachusetts 01562
tel: (508) 885-8730 ❖ fax: (508)-885-4687

Editorial queries and advance book information should be directed to the Editorial Offices:

Cistercian Publications
Institute of Cistercian Studies
Western Michigan University
Kalamazoo, Michigan 49008
tel: (616) 387-8920 ❖ fax: (616)-387-8921

A complete catalogue of texts in translation and studies on early, medieval, and modern monasticism is available at no cost from Cistercian Publications.